SUSPENSE

The Radio Program, Television Program, Comics and Mystery Magazines

by Darryl Shelton

Suspense: The Radio Program, Television Program, Comics and Mystery Magazines
by Darryl Shelton

© 2007 Darryl Shelton

All rights reserved.
No part of this book may be reproduced in any form or by any means, electronic, mechanical, digital, photocopying or recording, except for the inclusion in a review, without permission in writing from the the publisher.

www.Bearmanormedia.com
1-800-566-1251 (Order line only)

ISBN13: 978-1-59393-088-2
ISBN10: 1-59393-088-7

Printed in the United States

Book Design and Typesetting by Sun Editing & Book Design, suneditwrite.com
Cover Design by SUN Editing & Book Design

Published in the USA by Bear Manor Media
PO Box 71426
Albany, GA 31708

Contents

Introduction	i
Acknowledgments	iii
Ten Things about Suspense You Probably Didn't Know	1
Episode Guide: the Radio Series	3
History: the Television Series	175
TV Guide Reprint	177
Episode Guide: the Television Series	179
Kraft Suspense Theatre: an Episode Guide	207
The Best of Suspense	215
The Mystery Magazine	219
The Comic Books	223
Fury and Sound	231
Radio Script for the "Lost" Episode of "The Keenest Edge"	251
About The Author	273

Introduction

Resting in your hands is a thick tome of information related to the radio and television series *Suspense*. It has taken me five years to amass the dates, titles, casts, trivia and other materials that make up the majority of this book. With so many episodes available on audio cassettes and compact discs, the need for a book such as this would be welcome to every fan of *Suspense*. Or so I thought. That's when I discovered that there were already three broadcast logs available to purchase, each authored by a different historian, and most impressively, a thick tome amounting to 450-plus pages authored by Martin Grams Jr.

Since I had already begun my task of arranging the material I worked so hard on, my instincts took over and I finished this project. I was forced to be selective because a program what lasted more than 20 years of broadcasting really needs an encyclopedia and no publisher would accept such a large piece. What you will find within these pages is an episode guide for each and every radio episode, a television guide for both series, the contents of the mystery magazines and comic books, one radio script and one short story. The short story is an adaptation from an original *Suspense* radio broadcast that has been "officially" listed as "lost" in the realm of radio recordings. The script is of the same.

It is my hope and fondest wish that you, the reader, appreciate the work and effort that went into this book and make a great reference guide for your collection. After having been turned down by two publishing companies and, with great assurance from Ben Ohmart of Bear-Manor Media, this book is now complete.

Enjoy the book,

Darryl Shelton

Acknowledgments

A question that was asked by a few friends was "How do you get information about a radio program that went off the air more than 40 years ago?" The answer is "a lot of help." I am listing their names below.

Terry Salomonson of Audio Classics©, for allowing me to reprint the ratings listing in the beginning of the episode guide. He also sent me a number of recordings without financial compensation. His website, www.audio-classics.com, is a wealth of information.

Ben Ohmart of BearManor Media for helping make my dreams come true.

Tim Brooks and Earle Marsh, authors of *The Complete Directory to Prime Time Network and Cable TV Shows, 1946-Present*.

Roy Bright and Alice Lucia for sending me many copies of the radio shows to listen to.

Paul Coulier for pointing me in the direction of many websites and books that makes reference to *Suspense*.

Arleen Canfield, Vinnie Sawyer, Sonny Malone, Roy Bright, Terry Salomonson and Colin Jarrett for proofing over my manuscript.

Last but not least, Martin Grams Jr. and his secretary Michelle Vinje. Mr. Grams wrote a thick volume entitled *Suspense: 20 Years of Thrills and Chills* and he opened his door and heart to help assist me with my project. He sent me a thick packet of newspaper articles, magazine clippings, radio scripts and other material related to *Suspense* for aid in my research. We talked at great length over the phone (twice) about *Suspense*. He gave me permission to reprint whatever I needed for my book, from his now out-of-print book without asking for any financial compensation. His generosity helped make this book happen.

Angela Shelton, my wife, for her support.

Darryl Shelton, September 2006

Dedication

To my wife Angela
my daughter Jesse
and *Suspense* fans national and international.

Suspense or tension

IS THE FEELING OF UNCERTAINTY and interest about the outcome of certain actions an audience perceives in a dramatic work. According to Aristotle's *Poetics*, suspense is an important building block of drama. In very broad terms, it consists of having some real danger looming and a ray of hope. The two common outcomes can be

The danger hits, whereby the audience will feel sorrowful

The hope comes true, whereby the audience will first feel joy, then satisfaction.

If there is no hope, the audience will feel despair.

TEN THINGS ABOUT SUSPENSE YOU PROBABLY DIDN'T KNOW

SCRIPTS AND STORIES DRAMATIZED ON the *Suspense* program were written by a variety of writers, including submissions submitted to the producers and sponsors from faithful listeners. Among a few surprises were a deaf mute in Brooklyn, a night watchman in Chicago, a cowhand in Wyoming, and former prison inmates.

The television series *Alfred Hitchcock Presents* and *The Alfred Hitchcock Hour* ran ten years on various networks and featured adaptations of stories also dramatized on *Suspense*. Part of this was because the same writers were reusing their own stories for the Hitchcock program. Another reason was because Hitchcock himself was an avid fan and faithful listener of the series.

When Auto-Lite began sponsorship, they allowed a wide variety of stories to be dramatized but after one television episode in late 1949 prompted a large number of letters and phone calls protesting a scene in which a woman drank a glass of blood, the sponsors decided to steer toward more true crime dramas rather than fiction to avoid such protests.

The "Sorry, Wrong Number" script was spoofed on the October 17, 1948 broadcast of *The Jack Benny Program* with Barbara Stanwyck, the star of the big-screen movie.

In 1948, *Suspense* became a stage play scripted by William Spier and featured a brief number of performances on the stage near Santa Barbara.

Robert Montgomery was not only the host and occasional performer for the hour-long broadcasts of *Suspense*, but for a number of broadcasts he was also the producer!

William Spier's girlfriend at the time was performing brief supporting roles and cameos, unbilled, in a number of *Suspense* broadcasts from 1946 to 1947.

When Agnes Moorehead first received the "Sorry, Wrong Number" script, when it was titled "She Overheard Death Speaking," she thought it was so morbid that she never even finished reading the script.

When a severe and unknown illness kept William Spier in bed for a while, he passed the hours by quizzing his nurse on medical methods of committing murder.

A newspaper article, dated September 1953, quoted Elliott Lewis of saying that *Suspense* would have another decade. He was close enough in his prediction since the radio show went off in 1962.

AUDIENCE RATINGS:

(First Season) C.E. Hooper — (1942 to 1943)
(Second Season) C.E. Hooper 8.5 (1943 to 1944)
(Third Season) C.E. Hooper 13.2 (1944 to 1945)
(Fourth Season) C.E. Hooper 14.7 (1945 to 1946)
(Fifth Season) C.E. Hooper 18.2 (1946 to 1947)
(Sixth Season) C.E. Hooper — (1947 to 1948)
(Seventh Season) C.E. Hooper 16.4 (1948 to 1949)
(Eighth Season) A.C. Nielsen 15.6 (1949 to 1950)
(Ninth Season) A.C. Nielsen 10.3 (1950 to 1951)
(Tenth Season) A.C. Nielsen 11.3 (1951 to 1952)
(Eleventh Season) A.C. Nielsen 8.1 (1952 to 1953)
(Twelfth Season) A.C. Nielsen 6.0 (1953 to 1954)
(Thirteenth Season) A.C. Nielsen — (1954 to 1955)
(Fourteenth Season) A.C. Nielsen – (1955 to 1956)

Ratings supplied by Terry Salomonson.

Episode Guide: The Radio Series

Wednesday — 9:30 p.m. to 10:00 p.m. (E.S.T.)

June 17, 1942
#1 "The Burning Court"
   With Charles Ruggles and Julie Haydon. A murderer's identity is revealed during a fancy dinner party, and the guilty party may be a 17th-Century poisoner. The first episode of the series and the first of six produced and directed by Charles Vanda.

June 24, 1942
#2 "Wet Saturday"
   Clarence Derwent plays Mr. Princey, who discovers his daughter was involved with a murder. He attempts to cover the fact by framing an innocent neighbor.

July 1, 1942
#3 "The Life of Nellie James"
   Stars Jeanne Cagney, sister of actor James Cagney. Script written by Harold Medford.

July 8, 1942
#4 "Rope"
   With Richard Widmark in the cast. Two boys commit a murder and then attempt to toss clues out toward the victim's father, as a tease, to see if he discovers his son's death.

July 15, 1942
#5 "The Third Eye"

(Cast Unknown) Plot based on the short story of the same name by R.W. Chambers. This episode is not known to exist in recorded form.

July 22, 1942
#6 "Witness on the Westbound Limited"

(Cast Unknown) After surviving a train wreck, a victim is taken in as a border with the family that rescued him, only to discover one of their own was responsible for the wreck. This was the final of six consecutive episodes produced and directed by Charles Vanda. This episode is not known to exist in recorded form.

July 29, 1942
#7 "Philomel Cottage"

Based on the Agatha Christie story, Alice Frost and Eric Dressler are two newlyweds who moved into Philomel Cottage, and before settling down, Frost begins to suspect her husband of planning her murder. Beginning with this episode, William Spier began producing the series and John Dietz began directing. Dietz would direct a total number of 17 episodes before leaving *Suspense*.

August 5, 1942
#8 "Finishing School"

Actress Margo stars as a school teacher who discovers her students practice an unusual late-night séance to revive the spirits of the dead. Their practice has already resulted in the death of one student. Can Margo stop them before another murder occurs? This episode features an all-female cast.

August 12, 1942
#9 "Suspicion"

Pedro Decordoba stars as a suspicious husband who discovers the root of his chest pains when he reads in the papers about a cook who poisons her employers. After having his coffee analyzed, his suspicions are cleared. But when the police come to arrest his house cook, Pedro is shocked to learn that his wife, played by Helen Lewis, may have had a hand in the deed. Based on the short story by Dorothy L. Sayers.

August 19, 1942
#10 "The Cave of Ali Baba"
This was the second of two consecutive episodes based on the short story *The Adventurous Exploit of the Cave of Ali Baba* by Dorothy L. Sayers. Lord Peter Whimsey is an undercover detective who has been unmasked among a crime society. If he plays his cards right, they won't dispose of him so quickly. Who knows what evidence about their existence he left behind? Stars Romney Brent and Ian Martin. Robert Lewis Shayon replaces director John Dietz for this one episode. He would return to the director's helm for three episodes in July and August of 1943.

August 26, 1942
Pre-empted due to a Hollywood special for the war cause.

September 2, 1942
#11 "The Hitch-Hiker"
One of the best episodes of the series. Orson Welles stars as Ronald Adams, a cross-country driver being haunted by the mysterious figure of a hitch-hiker. He continues to appear along the side of the road, ahead of Ronald's automobile, no matter how fast he drives. Could the mysterious figure be Mr. Death beckoning for a fare?

Lucille Fletcher wrote this script with Orson Welles in mind. Fletcher's husband was Bernard Herrmann, a staff musician for CBS, who also composed and conducted the music score for much of Welles' radio work, including this *Suspense* broadcast. Welles liked "The Hitch-Hiker" radio play and he performed the spooky drama a total of four times during his radio career. The first time was on *The Orson Welles Show* on November 10, 1941. *Suspense* was the second time. Third was on *The Philip Morris Playhouse* on October 15, 1942. The final time it was performed was on *The Mercury Summer Theater on the Air* on June 21, 1946. The screen rights to this radio drama were purchased and dramatized for the CBS-TV series *The Twilight Zone* in 1959, switching the sex of the lead from a male to a female.

The same script was recreated in 1964 with David Goldin in the lead, and Eli Segal supplying the sound effects. Goldin would later found Radio Yesteryear® and for more than two decades make radio programs such as *Suspense* available for collectors.

September 9, 1942
Pre-empted due to a speech by Averill Harriman, U.S. Land Administrator.

September 16, 1942
#12 "The Kettler Method"
Gloria Stuart makes her only appearance on *Suspense* in this episode, as a young lady who returns home to visit a family relative, only to discover that the inmates of a mental hospital have escaped bondage and want to cure people's headaches with sharp surgical instruments. John Gibson and Guy Repp have large roles in this episode. Guy Repp was a supporting actor for thousands of radio broadcasts originating from New York, and he would play numerous roles on *Suspense*, especially during the program's final two seasons.

September 23, 1942
#13 "A Passage to Benares"
Based on the short story by T.S. Stribling. An American and English detective joins forces to solve a crime in which all of the witnesses were drugged. As the investigation continues, one of the detectives suspects his partner of being involved with the crime. With Paul Stewart and Alan Hewitt in the cast.

September 30, 1942
#14 "One Hundred in the Dark"
With Eric Dressler and Alice Frost. When an expensive piece of jewelry is stolen during a society party, the hostess locks the doors and turns out the lights. Informing the guests that she will slowly count to 100, the hostess gives the guilty party ample amount of time to return the ring to the coffee table before the lights go on.

This was an effective episode for the *Suspense* series. As the count nears 100, tension is built as the radio audience listens for the sound of the jewelry to be dropped on the coffee table. This was the final episode of the summer series. This was the final episode to feature Berry Kroeger as the announcer for *Suspense*.

Tuesday — 9:30 p.m. to 10:00 p.m. (E.S.T.)

October 27, 1942
#15 "The Lord of the Witch Doctors"
   A German disguises himself as a local witch doctor to control part of Africa, a necessity the German Army needs for the war. A British commander, played by Nicholas Joy, tries to foil the witch doctor's plan. This was the first of nine episodes in which Joseph Kearns was the *Suspense* announcer. Beginning with episode 24, the host of the series would be known as "the Man in Black."

   John Dickson Carr became a staff writer for *Suspense*, and this episode marked his first of 22 contributions to *Suspense*. Many of his scripts were originally written for another radio series while he was in England shortly before his arrival to America.

Tuesday — 10:00 p.m. to 10:30 p.m. (E.S.T.)

November 3, 1942
#16 "The Devil in the Summer House"
   With Martin Gabel and Leslie Woods. Mr. Parker receives a letter revealing the solution to an unsolved mystery from 25 years ago, implicating him in the villainous plot.

Tuesday — 9:30 p.m. to 10:00 p.m. (E.S.T.)

November 10, 1942
#17 "Will You Make a Bet With Death?"
   With Michael Fitzmaurice and Ted de Corsia. An eccentric and wealthy uncle places a bet with his young nephew, offering his inheritance if the boy can survive the next six months. As the weeks and months pass, no attempt is made on the young man's life. Has the uncle lost the courage to keep up with his end of the bargain? This radio script would be recycled ten years later into the mystery novel, *The Nine Wrong Answers*.

November 17, 1942
#18 "Menace in Wax"
   With Joseph Julian. Two newspaper reporters find a hidden code among the playing cards held by wax figures in a wax museum. Suspecting foul play, they attempt to help the war cause by solving the mystery.

November 24, 1942
#19 "The Body Snatchers"
   The true crimes of Burke and Hare are revisited with this episode about medical students who dig up fresh corpses for medical examination. When the bodies appear to be too fresh, Scotland Yard investigates.

December 1, 1942
#20 "The Bride Vanishes"
   Hanley Stafford and Leslie Woods play a honeymooning couple, who pay a visit to a small coastal island where, legend has it, a bride walked out on the veranda and vanished.
   From 1948 to 1949, John Dickson Carr's scripts were performed again for an American radio program called *Cabin B-13*. This script was performed on that show on December 12, 1948.

December 8, 1942
   Pre-empted due to a speech entitled "The Petroleum Problem," presented by Senator Harold Ickes, Secretary of the Interior.

December 15, 1942
#21 "'Til Death Do Us Part"
   Peter Lorre plays Erwin, a jealous husband who poisons his wife and ties up her lover, with the intentions of burning the house down and implicating her in the crime. Mercedes McCambridge plays the wife. This script was performed again on the radio program *Cabin B-13* for the broadcast of December 19, 1948.

December 22, 1942
#22 "Two Sharp Knives"
   Based on the short story by Dashiell Hammett. With Stuart Erwin in the cast. An innocent man is accused of a murder he didn't commit,

and after he is jailed, his body is found hanging by the neck with his own belt.

December 29, 1942
Pre-empted due to a special CBS presentation entitled "Twelve Crowded Months," a review of the best broadcasts of 1942.

January 5, 1943
#23 "Nothing Up My Sleeve"
With Elisa Landi and George Coulouris. A locked room murder mystery has an ingenious solution when it involves a lawyer with a love for the game of pool.

January 12, 1943
#24 "The Pit and the Pendulum"
With Henry Hull. Scripted by John Dickson Carr, from the short story by Edgar Allen Poe. A man is accused of a crime and finds himself subjected to a torture worse than hot coals. Strapped to a surgical table, he watches as a huge, sharp pendulum swings back and forth, lowering a little with each swing, destined to cut him in half.

The copyright for Edgar Allen Poe's stories expired decades ago so many mystery and horror radio programs have used Poe's stories frequently including *The Columbia Workshop*, *The CBS Radio Mystery Theatre*, *The Greatest Story Ever Told*, *Molle Mystery Theater*, *Radio Guild* and *The Weird Circle*.

This is the first *Suspense* broadcast to bill the series' host as "the Man in Black." Joseph Kearns, who was the announcer for the previous episodes, is assigned the duty of host. The "Man in Black" would remain billed until March of 1945.

January 19, 1943
#25 "The Devil's Saint"
Peter Lorre is a father, who protects his daughter from young men wanting her hand in marriage. He claims the daughter is not of sound mind. Can he prove this before a young man takes her away to be married? This was the final episode to be directed by John Dietz. This was the final episode to originate from New York. The program moved to

Hollywood, where movie stars were more easily accessible. Bernard Herrmann ceased supplying the music with this episode, since the show moved to the West Coast.

January 26, 1943
#26 "Death Went Along for the Ride"
Ralph Bellamy plays George, who picks up a female hitch-hiker and soon finds himself the intended murder victim of a gang of criminals. William Spier is still the producer, and this episode marks the first of many for director Ted Bliss. This was the first episode broadcast from Hollywood. Lucien Morewek and Lud Gluskin would supply much of the music scores for this series beginning with this episode, but Bernard Herrmann's opening signature music would remain the theme for a while.

February 2, 1943
#27 "The Doctor Prescribed Death"
With Bela Lugosi and Geraldine Fitzgerald. Lugosi plays a psychiatrist who theorizes that a man who wants to commit suicide can be driven to murder. When his publisher laughs at his notion, Lugosi decides to prove his theory. This episode was one of two scripted by J. Donald Wilson, who was also responsible for creating and writing another CBS anthology, *The Whistler*. This script would later be dramatized on *The Whistler* on June 11, 1944.

February 9, 1943
#28 "The Hangman Won't Wait"
An innocent woman wakes from a case of amnesia to find herself in prison, framed for a murder she did not commit. With the case open and shut, it takes one man, played by actor Sydney Greenstreet, to help save her from hanging only hours away. Only half of this broadcast is known to exist in recorded form.

February 16, 1943
#29 "In Fear and Trembling"
With Mary Astor and Verna Felton. A wife discovers her husband and lover plan to kill her and make it look like an accident. This

episode was one of two scripted by J. Donald Wilson, who was also responsible for creating and writing another CBS anthology, *The Whistler*. This script was also dramatized on *The Whistler* under a different title.

February 23, 1943
#30 "Will You Walk Into My Parlor?"
With Geraldine Fitzgerald and Sir Cedric Hardwicke. A Scotland Yard inspector poses as a fortune teller to solve a crime, and tells young lovers that their destiny is death. Only half of this broadcast is known to exist in recorded form.

March 2, 1943
#31 "The Night Reveals"
Fredric March plays a fire inspector in search of a pyromaniac. The clues lead to the identity of his wife, which he will not accept until it is too late. March reprised the same role for the May 26, 1949 broadcast of *Suspense*.

March 9, 1943
#32 "The Phantom Archer"
With Ralph Bellamy and Walter Hampden. A rich aunt was found dead with an arrow in her chest, and two men seek out the truth regarding her murder, dismissing the notion that a "Phantom Archer" was responsible. Scripted by John Dickson Carr. A recording of this radio broadcast does not exist.

March 16, 1943
#33 "Cabin B-13"
Scripted by John Dickson Carr. Newlywed Anne discovers her husband is missing soon after they board a luxury liner. The other passengers claim she came on board alone, but she knows they are all fibbing. It's up to her to solve the mystery. Ralph Bellamy guests.

March 23, 1943
#34 "The Customers Like Murder"
With Roland Young and Peggy Conklin. Almost a rip-off of *Mr. and Mrs. North*, a mystery writer and his secretary are mistaken for a doctor

and nurse, and find themselves treating two real-life crooks. Scripted by John Dickson Carr.

March 30, 1943
#35 "The Dead Sleep Lightly"
With Walter Hampden, Lee Bowman and Susan Hayward. Mr. Templeton receives a death threat over the phone from his late wife, and before he can do something about it, his corpse is found. Did the dead wife come back to avenge herself? Scripted by John Dickson Carr, this script was performed again on the radio program *Cabin B-13* for the broadcast of December 19, 1948. Ted Osborne subs for Joseph Kearns as "The Man in Black" for two consecutive episodes.

April 6, 1943
#36 "Fire Burn and Cauldron Bubble"
With Paul Lukas. Scripted by John Dickson Carr. A woman is found dead from a knife wound in her eye, during a stage performance of Shakespeare's *Macbeth*. Ted Osborne subs for Joseph Kearns as "The Man in Black" for two consecutive episodes.

April 13, 1943
#37 "Fear Paints a Picture"
With Nancy Coleman and Bea Benaderet. A young lady is willed a fortune provided she does not go mentally insane before her 21st birthday, like her mother before. Joseph Kearns returns as "The Man in Black."

April 20, 1943
#38 "The Moment of Darkness"
With Peter Lorre, Wendy Barrie and George Zucco. Scripted by John Dickson Carr. A murder takes place during a séance and all suspicion turns on the spirits since everyone in the room was holding each other's hands.

April 27, 1943
#39 "The Diary of Saphronia Winters"
Scripted by Lucille Fletcher. Agnes Moorehead plays the title character, who, after marrying Ray Collins, finds herself living in a deserted

hotel with 125 empty rooms. Her husband is demented and she discovers she is his prisoner within the mansion. Berne Surrey, the sound effects artist for this episode, accidentally stabbed his hand by accident during the climax of the drama.

May 4, 1943
#40 "Death Flies Blind"
With Richard Dix, Gale Page and Montagu Love. A plane full of passengers discovers their pilots are missing and try to land the craft without any knowledge of how to fly a plane. Where was the plane's destination? Scripted by John Dickson Carr.

May 11, 1943
#41 "Mr. Markham, Antique Dealer"
With Paul Lukas and Heather Angel. An antique dealer has been blackmailing a nice couple and finds himself the victim of his own misdeeds, till another man catches the couple in the act of murder. Scripted by John Dickson Carr.

May 18, 1943
#42 "The A.B.C. Murders"
Real-life husband and wife, Charles Laughton and Elsa Lanchester, guest in this thriller based on the Agatha Christie novel. A killer leaves a clue at the scene of a crime, a case with the engraved letters a, b and c.

May 25, 1943
#43 "Sorry, Wrong Number"
Agnes Moorehead portrays an invalid who overhears a murder plot courtesy of a wrong connection over the phone. When she phones the operator and police, she is forced to accept her fate when they are powerless to prevent the murder due to a lack of information.

When this episode was performed on the East Coast, Hans Conried, a cast member playing the role of a killer, delivers the important line cue too soon, confusing the radio audience. The week after, the *Suspense* announcer apologizes to the radio audience for the confusion, and reveals the producer's intention of redoing the same script in the near future. This fact has been questioned by numerous fans on the internet, even when the East Coast and West Coast broadcasts exist in recorded form. Proof of this incident was verified in Martin Grams Jr.'s 1998 book on *Suspense* when he reprinted the very words the announcer gave during the broadcast of June 1.

"The producer of *Suspense* felt that it was incumbent to reply herewith to the many inquiries to the solution to last week's story of the woman on the telephone titled 'Sorry, Wrong Number.' Due to a momentary confusion in the studio, an important line cue was delivered at the wrong time and some of our faithful listeners were uncertain to the outcome of the story. For them they knew that the woman, so remarkably played by Miss Agnes Moorehead, was murdered by a man whom her husband had hired to do the job. We should also like to announce that in response to many hundreds of requests, this *Suspense* play will be repeated within a few weeks."

June 1, 1943
#44 "Banquo's Chair"

With Donald Crisp and John Loder. Blackheath, near London, October 23, 1903. A recipe for confession heats up when a murder suspect goes to a dinner party, unaware that a visit by the victim's ghost is on the menu. But as the evening progresses and the tension rises, the players in this little game discover that the trick may be on them. Based on the short story of the same name by Robert Croft Cook. There were intentions to title this drama "The Extra Guest," but a decision was made days before the broadcast to keep the title the same as the story.

June 8, 1943
#45 "Five Canaries in the Room"

With Ona Munson and Lee Bowman. A young man wakes to find himself in the same room as a corpse. When the police get involved, his alibi is thrown away when he cannot prove the building has a fifth floor. Chanting canaries is the clue. This was the final episode of the series to be scripted by John Dickson Carr. The original title of this drama was "Five Canaries."

Suspense

Tuesday — 10:00 p.m. to 10:30 p.m. (E.S.T.)

June 15, 1943
#46 "Last Night"
With Kent Smith and Margo. Based on the short story *The Red Tide* by Cornell Woolrich. A weekend party is not forgotten when guest Margo suspects her husband of doing away with one of the guests. But not just any guest, but an elderly man who recently acquired $25,000.

June 22, 1943
#47 "The Man Without a Body"
With George Zucco and Wendy Barrie. A great role for George Zucco. A murder is committed and the townsfolk suspect an invisible man of committing the deed. The prime suspect is George Zucco, who plays a recluse professor who hides a few shady secrets from the public. It was suggested in this radio play that the villain was German, a decision made by CBS when they learned that the villain was Italian, going against the studio's policy to make villains American, British, German or Japanese for obvious reasons.

June 29, 1943
#48 "Uncle Henry's Rosebush"
With Agnes Moorehead, in a story that pre-dates Hitchcock's *Rear Window*. Aunt Julie is suspected of killing Uncle Henry and burying the body under the newly-planted rose bush in the backyard. Her niece returns to discover the truth about the uncle's disappearance.

July 6, 1943
#49 "The White Rose Murders"
Maureen O'Hara proves her love to a detective by offering herself as bait to help catch a psycho killer on the loose. Based on the short story *The Death Rose* by Cornell Woolrich. This was the final episode to be directed by Ted Bliss before he left for a three-week vacation. Bliss would return four episodes from now.

July 13, 1943
Pre-empted because of the All-Star Baseball Game.

July 20, 1943
#50 "Murder Goes for A Swim"

Warren William and Eric Blore reprise their film roles from the *Lone Wolf* Columbia movies, presently seen in movie theaters. A woman was found murdered, her body floating in a swimming pool. The Lone Wolf and his valet Jamison recall the events of the case through use of a flashback. This broadcast was a pilot proposal for a radio series based on the *Lone Wolf* character. This was the first of three consecutive episodes to be directed by Robert Lewis Shayon. Ted Bliss went on vacation for three weeks.

Jim Bannon replaced Joseph Kearns as "the Man in Black" beginning with this episode, the first of five consecutive broadcasts. Bannon recalled, "For about six weeks I did the announcing on one of the thriller shows called 'Suspense' but that was strictly a short-term fill-in job. Joe Kearns, who usually does it, was sitting in the Derby bar one night, minding his own business, when a GI next to him came on with what has almost become a standard question to civilians, 'How come you're not in uniform?' The fact that Kearns couldn't whip a pint of cream in a Waring Blender didn't matter. Joe swears he didn't make any sort of a smart answer but the guy clobbered him anyway and broke his jaw. While his face was wired together, I did his show."

July 27, 1943
#51 "The Last Letter of Dr. Bronson"

With Laird Cregar and George Coulouris. Dr. Bronson establishes a hypothesis that man cannot kill another man for five reasons. To prove his point, he makes himself set up as a possible murder victim for five different scenarios, giving each person a chance to pull the trigger.

August 3, 1943
#52 "A Friend to Alexander"

Robert Young is a man who keeps dreaming of the Aaron Burr/Alexander Hamilton duel and starts to enact the scene with real loaded pistols. His wife, played by Geraldine Fitzgerald, tries to talk him out of it. Based on the short story by James Thurber.

August 10, 1943
#53 "The Fountain Plays"

With Edmund Gwenn, Wendy Barrie and Dennis Hoey. Another murder plot but this one involves a water fountain. Based on the Dorothy Sayers short story. Hoey would later reprise the same role for episode 119.

Saturday — 7:30 p.m. to 8:00 p.m. (E.S.T.)

August 21, 1943
#54 "Sorry, Wrong Number"

Agnes Moorehead and Hans Conried reprise their roles from the May 25 broadcast, because of their initial on-air goof from months before. It is this broadcast that brings the radio play the notoriety the *Suspense* program deserved. The original title of this radio play was "She Overheard Death Speaking."

August 28, 1943
#55 "The King's Birthday"

With Dolores Costello, George Zucco and Martin Kosleck. Victor has been receiving notes telling of his attempted suicide on the midnight of the king's birthday. At first he thought they were a hoax, but when the clock strikes eleven, his fears grow. Berry Kroeger replaced Ted Osborne as "the Man in Black" for this episode, the first of three consecutive broadcasts.

Thursday — 10:30 p.m. to 11:00 p.m. (E.S.T.)

September 2, 1943
#56 "The Singing Walls"

With Preston Foster and Dane Clark. Based on the short story *C-Jag* by Cornell Woolrich. A man wakes to find himself a suspect in a murder case. His only chance to clear his good name is to find a man who talks like he has a frog in his throat.

September 9, 1943
#57 "Marry for Murder"

With Lillian Gish, Ray Collins and Otto Kruger. A man suspects his neighbor of murder.

September 16, 1943
#58 "The Cross-Eyed Bear"

Virginia Bruce plays a woman who answers an advertisement and finds herself involved in a police case. John Loder also stars. Based on the novel by Dorothy Belle Hughes. Ted Osborne returns as "the Man in Black," replacing Berry Kroeger. This would also mark Osborne's last appearance as the host. This was the final episode for director Ted Bliss.

September 23, 1943
#59 "The Most Dangerous Game"

Orson Welles and Keenan Wynn star in a thrilling game of cat and mouse when a professional hunter gets tired of hunting animals, and wants to hunt a man for sport on his private island. Based on the short story by Richard Connell. Joseph Kearns is the permanent "Man in Black" beginning with this episode. William Spier, who produced most of the *Suspense* broadcasts, began as director with this episode. This same script would be dramatized on October 1, 1947 on *Escape*.

September 30, 1943
#60 "The Lost Special"

With Orson Welles. Based on the short story by Sir Arthur Conan Doyle, this mystery involves the disappearance of a train and no evidence that it was removed from the tracks. This same script would be dramatized on February 12, 1949 on *Escape*.

October 7, 1943
#61 "Philomel Cottage"

With Orson Welles and Geraldine Fitzgerald. Same script performed back on July 29, 1942. The first of a two-part story entitled "Donovan's Brain" was originally planned to be dramatized on this date.

Tuesday — 10:00 p.m. to 10:30 p.m. (E.S.T.)

October 19, 1943
#62 "Lazarus Walks"

With Orson Welles and Hans Conried. A man returns to life after being clinically pronounced dead for four minutes. He soon discovers he has the ability to read other people's minds, and a curse of never being

Suspense

able to tell a lie.

October 26, 1943
#63 "The After Dinner Story"

Otto Kruger stars as an eccentric old man who invites four guests, all suspects in the unsolved murder of his son, to a private dinner party. After informing them they have all been poisoned, he offers the antidote in exchange for a confession.

November 2, 1943
#64 "Statement of Employee Henry Wilson"

Gene Lockhart stars as Henry Wilson, jealous that another employee won a promotion over him. After murdering the employee, Henry hears the dead man's voice haunting him. Gene Lockhart commented about his appearance on the show: "An actor always gets a real starring part on *Suspense*, and beyond that, he has a role with real 'meat' to it. Something he can get his teeth into and do a real job if he's any good at all. *Suspense*, to me, is radio's top show." Lockhart would return to *Suspense* to reprise the same role for the broadcast of September 26, 1946.

November 9, 1943
#65 "Cabin B-13"

With Philip Dorn, Dennis Hoey and Margo. Same plot and script from March 16, 1943.

November 16, 1943
#66 "Thieves Fall Out"

Gene Kelly stars as Arthur Kramer, who gets over his head with gambling debts and murder.

November 23, 1943
#67 "The Strange Death of Charles Umberstein"

Vincent Price is an Allied spy who needs to remain undercover with a false identity. His mission is jeopardized when his true identity is discovered. This was the final episode sustained by the network. Beginning next week, the program would be sponsored.

Thursday — 8:00 p.m. to 8:30 p.m. (E.S.T.)

December 2, 1943
#68 "The Black Curtain"
Cary Grant stars as Peter Townsend, who attempts to find out his true identity, and whether or not he committed a murder, when he finds himself an amnesia victim. Roma Wines became the first sponsor for *Suspense* beginning with this episode. Frank Martin has been hired as the commercial spokesman. Maxine Anderson, a representative of Roma Wines, commented publicly that "when Cary Grant comes to the *Suspense* microphone, he acts all over the place."

Based on the 1942 novel by Cornell Woolrich. This short story was adapted into a movie released under the title *Streets of Chance*, and released through Paramount weeks before this radio broadcast.

December 9, 1943
#69 "The Night Reveals"
With Robert Young and Margo. Same story and script from March 2, 1943.

December 16, 1943
#70 "Wet Saturday"
With Charles Laughton. Same story and script from June 24, 1942.

December 23, 1943
#71 "Back for Christmas"
With Peter Lorre. An English professor named Hubert murders his wife and buries her body in the basement. Marrying a younger woman and taking leave for England by passenger boat, he is surprised when a telegram reveals his wife will be "back for Christmas." This same script was previously dramatized on December 24, 1947 on *Escape*.

December 30, 1943
#72 "Finishing School"
With Elsa Lanchester, Janet Beecher and Margo. Same story and script from August 5, 1942.

January 6, 1944
#73 "The One-Way Ride to Nowhere"

With Alan Ladd. A rollercoaster comes to a full stop leaving a dead passenger in one of the seats. How could a fresh corpse be found on a moving rollercoaster?

January 13, 1944
#74 "A Dime a Dance"
With Lucille Ball and Hans Conried. Lucille Ball plays a dime-a-dance girl named Ginger who finds herself the next intended victim of a madman. William Spier wrote the script from the short story by Cornell Woolrich, and rewrote the last few pages moments before being performed during the East Coast broadcast! During this broadcast, Lucille Ball dances to *Limehouse Blues*.

January 20, 1944
#75 "A World of Darkness"
Paul Lukas plays Anton, a blind man who witnessed a murder. The police dismiss the blind man as a witness to the crime but he soon proves he heard and saw enough to solve the case.

January 27, 1944
#76 "The Locked Room"
With Virginia Bruce, Allyn Joslyn and George Zucco. Another locked room murder mystery. This time the owner of the world's largest diamond is found dead and the method by which the murder was committed remains a mystery.

February 3, 1944
#77 "The Sisters"
With Agnes Moorehead and Ida Lupino. Lydia purchases a coffin and asks the seller to hold on to the merchandise for a few weeks. Suspicious, the seller phones the police. Lupino's birthday was celebrated during the rehearsals for this broadcast.

February 10, 1944
#78 "Suspicion"
With Charles Ruggles. Same story and script from August 12, 1942.

February 17, 1944

#79 "Life Ends at Midnight"

With Fay Bainter, Dane Clark and Ralph Morgan. In need of money, Walter attempts to murder a lodger in his mother's house, whose life is ending by illness anyway, and a life insurance policy due to cash in shortly.

February 24, 1944
#80 "Sorry, Wrong Number"

With Agnes Moorehead. Same story and script from August 21, 1943. This was the third of eight performances for this script. Agnes Moorehead recreated this thriller for a Decca record album two years after this broadcast.

March 2, 1944
#81 "Portrait Without a Face"

With Michele Morgan, Philip Dorn and George Coulouris. An artist offers an art exhibit to set a trap for a murderer.

March 9, 1944
#82 "The Defense Rests"

With Alan Ladd. An ex-con is given a second chance when he is set free. Days later he returns to his defense attorney in need of help from a murder charge.

March 16, 1944
#83 "Narrative About Clarence"

With Laird Cregar in a perfect role, mimicking the characters he portrayed on screen. As Uncle Clarence, Cregar makes himself at home with the William family, having returned from India, learning the trade of hypnosis. After taking over the will of his wife and daughter, and with Clarence's ability to read other people's minds, William finds himself powerless against the force of evil.

March 23, 1944
#84 "Sneak Preview"

With Joseph Cotten and Dennis Hoey. A Hollywood film director wants to direct an espionage spy picture so to get all the realism he can, but he finds himself involved with a real spy adventure. Producer and director William Spier enjoyed slipping in-jokes in his radio productions. During this broadcast, Joseph Cotten asks "Well, if you know so much, what are you doing up here acting like a *Suspense* radio character?"

March 30, 1944
#85 "Cat and Mouse"

With Sonny Tufts and Lurene Tuttle. A radio engineer investigates the murder of a friend, and finds himself framed for another, the murder of a police detective.

April 6, 1944
#86 "The Woman in Red"

Katina Paxinou is a secretary who is hired to duplicate a former secretary that was murdered, in order for her employers to cover up the murder they committed.

April 13, 1944
#87 "The Marvelous Barastro"

"The second greatest magician" tells his strange story to *Suspense* producer William Spier who is sitting in his office going over scripts for future programs. The master magician informs the director of *Suspense* that he intends to murder a rival magician who has stolen his identity and the woman he loves. Orson Welles plays a dual role as the woman's husband *and* the man who seduces her. Director William Spier selected "The Marvelous Barastro" for Orson Welles. "I wanted a drama that would appeal to Welles' personal taste as well as being in keeping with his special talents," Spier explained. "Knowing that Orson is a magic enthusiast, I decided that a part in which he could play to this hobby would be ideal for him. The Barastro show was one of the most successful ever broadcast." The radio play was based on a story by Ben Hecht, co-author of *The Front Page*, and allowed Spier to make his first appearance on the program in front of the microphone.

April 20, 1944
#88 "The Palmer Method"

Ed Gardner leaves *Duffy's Tavern* for a spell to star in a straight drama as Joe Palmer, a professional forger who evades the police by signing up to assist troops in the Mexican revolution. He then applies his trade to escape out of his situation.

April 27, 1944
#89 "Death Went Along for the Ride"
With Gene Kelly and Walter Tetley. Same story and script from January 26, 1943.

Thursday — 7:00 p.m. to 7:30 p.m. (E.S.T.)

May 4, 1944
#90 "The Dark Tower"
With Orson Welles and Jeanette Nolan. To help publicize the Warner Bros. British movie of the same name, *Suspense* featured an adaptation of the George S. Kaufman and Alexander Woollcott stage play. An actor applies his trade to commit a murder.

May 11, 1944
#91 "The Visitor"
Eddie Bracken plays Bud Owens, who returns to his hometown, thought to be dead for the past three years. The only person not happy to see him is the young man who was suspected and blamed for Bud's death. He plans to make sure Bud hasn't forgotten.

May 18, 1944
#92 "Donovan's Brain" Part One
Orson Welles plays two roles for this presentation as Dr. Patrick Cory and William Henry Donovan. When a small private plane crashes outside his mountain resort, Dr. Cory attempts the scientific impossible by placing the brain of the dying victim into a jar and keeping it alive.

May 25, 1944
#93 "Donovan's Brain" Part Two
While the brain of William Donovan is kept alive, it starts taking command of Dr. Cory's will and the doctor soon discovers that his body is being taken over. Can he destroy his creation before his will and life is taken over completely? This two-part episode was released commercially on an LP and in 1981; the same LP won a Grammy Award for best non-

musical recording of the year.

June 1, 1944
#94 "Fugue in C-Minor"
   With Vincent Price and Ida Lupino. Eccentric Theodore Evans had a huge pipe organ built within the walls of his house. His new bride discovers he has a fascination for Johann Sebastian Bach's *Fugue in C-Minor*, and his children claim the first wife isn't dead, but hidden within the walls of the house.

June 8, 1944
#95 "Case History of Edgar Lowndes"
   With Donald Crisp and Thomas Mitchell. Edgar Lowndes makes return visits to his psychiatrist to find the cure for his headaches and a train trip may be the cure.

June 15, 1944
#96 "A Friend to Alexander"
   With Geraldine Fitzgerald and Richard Whorf. Same story and script from August 3, 1943. The first few minutes of this broadcast was postponed due to news broadcasts regarding the present Normandy invasion. This episode was based on the short story by American humorist James Thurber.

June 22, 1944
#97 "The Ten Grand"
   Lucille Ball plays a victim of a purse snatcher. Hours later her purse is recovered and she finds $10,000 in cash inside.

June 29, 1944
#98 "The Walls Came Tumbling Down"
   Keenan Wynn plays a newspaper columnist investigating the murder of a priest, and discovers the motive involves a painting worth thousands of dollars. This episode was based on the story by Jo Eisinger, and later adapted into a big-screen movie. Robert Tallman adapted the story into this radio script, which was later revamped as the audition script for *The Adventures of Sam Spade*.

July 6, 1944
#99 "The Search for Henry LeFevre"
　　Paul Muni portrays a musician, who composes the greatest piece in his life and, moments afterwards, hears the same piece over the radio. He begins a search for this mystery composer, named Henri LeRevre.

July 13, 1944
#100 "The Beast Must Die"
　　With Herbert Marshall and Dennis Hoey. After losing his son to a hit-and-run driver, a vengeful father makes deadly plans for revenge.

July 20, 1944
#101 "Of Maestro and Man"
　　Peter Lorre plays a boxing manager who is forced to sell his client to cover his gambling debts. When the boxer, played by Richard Conte, dislikes being sold like meat in a market, the manager plans to murder him to save face. According to author Martin Grams Jr., this episode was revamped for an episode of *The Adventures of Sam Spade* told through flashbacks, in which Sam, the detective, played the part of the boxer.

July 27, 1944
#102 "The Black Shawl"
　　Maureen O'Sullivan plays a young lady hired by an old spinster, played by Dame May Whitty, as a paid companion. Soon after she discovers she's a captive in the house, she meets up with the old woman's disfigured son, also a captive.

August 3, 1944
#103 "Banquo's Chair"
　　With Donald Crisp and John Loder. Same story and script from June 1, 1943.

August 10, 1944
#104 "The Man Who Knew How"
　　With Charles Laughton. Mr. Pender meets an Englishman who claims to have developed a poison that will kill the victim only when they submerge themselves in a bathtub. After reading the newspaper

account of the recent "bathtub deaths," he seeks out this Englishman at the risk of his own life.

August 17, 1944
#105 "The Diary of Saphronia Winters"
With Agnes Moorehead and Ray Collins. Same story and script from April 27, 1943.

August 24, 1944
#106 "Actor's Blood"
Writer Ben Hecht stars as himself in this tale based on his short story and adaptation for this radio script. Fredric March stars as one of a handful of men who visit Hecht's house to help establish this little mystery.

August 31, 1944
#107 "The Black Path of Fear"
Brian Donlevy plays Bill Scott, who runs off to Havana with a gangster's wife, only to discover that her husband is tailing them all the way.

September 7, 1944
#108 "Voyage Through Darkness"
Olivia de Havilland plays Judith Webster, traveling by luxury liner from England to America to help with a friend's burial. On board she meets Reginald Gardner, who may or may not be the "Blackout" killer wanted in England.

September 14, 1944
#109 "You'll Never See Me Again"
Joseph Cotten plays Ed Bliss, whose wife runs out on him after an argument. She vanishes shortly afterwards and the manhunt for his wife begins.

September 21, 1944
#110 "The Bluebeard of Bellac"
With Merle Oberon and Ludwig Donath. A modern-day "Bluebeard" has been claiming female victims and one woman suspects she may be next. In order for the police to come to her rescue, she must first gather

evidence at the risk of her life. This episode was based on an actual newspaper headline.

September 28, 1944
#111 "The Man Who Couldn't Lose"
Gene Kelly plays an insurance salesman who murders his wife to gain access to the money needed to pay off his gambling debts. Afterwards he finds himself the lucky winner of a sweepstake's ticket.

Thursday — 8:00 p.m. to 8:30 p.m. (E.S.T.)

October 5, 1944
#112 "Dateline: Lisbon"
John Hodiak plays a traitor to the United States by assisting a woman develop some pictures of Nazi spies in a neutral port. This episode was written by Harold Medford, originally for *The Whistler* under the title "Lisbon Adventure," broadcast on March 12, 1944.

October 12, 1944
#113 "The Merry Widower"
Guest Reginald Gardner murders his wife so he can run off and lead a life of royalty. He succeeds only temporarily until he is haunted by a music box. Based on Roy Vickers' short story *The Rubber Trumpet*. Franz Lehar's *The Merry Widow Waltz* was featured in the background music.

October 19, 1944
#114 "Eve"
Nancy Kelly plays the role of Eve Jeremy who, after learning that her husband has been picked up and booked for murder, races against time to clear his name. Lucille Ball was originally going to star in the role of Eve, but fell ill days before the broadcast.

October 26, 1944
#115 "Night Man"
Virginia Bruce plays an apartment resident with a guilty conscience. Believing the elevator operator is Tom Nixon, a man she testified against years ago, she alerts the police who tell her he couldn't be because Tom Nixon died a few years ago behind prison walls.

November 2, 1944
#116 "The Singing Walls"
 With Van Johnson. Same story and script from September 2, 1943. Sound engineer Robert Anderson had to create special "fog music" for this episode.

November 9, 1944
#117 "You Were Wonderful"
 Singer Lena Horne guests as a nightclub singer who finds the nightclub she is employed under new management. When asked to sing a certain song at a certain time with a radio hook-up, she suspects she's been asked to sing a code to the Germans and attempts to foil their plan. This episode was a patriotic effort to support the war cause, with Lena Horne singing "America" during the broadcast.

November 16, 1944
#118 "Dead of Night"
 Robert Cummings plays Jimmy, the concerned brother who helps move the body of his sister's late husband. Cleaning up the evidence proves difficult when his landlord won't stop following him.

November 23, 1944
#119 "The Fountain Plays"
 With Charles Laughton and Dennis Hoey. Same story and script from August 10, 1943.

November 30, 1944
#120 "The Black Curtain"
 Cary Grant reprises his role as Peter Townsend, the same role he played for the broadcast of December 2, 1943.

December 7, 1944
 Pre-empted by the Sixth War Loan Bond Drive entitled "Finish the Job."

December 14, 1944
#121 "The Lodger"
 With Robert Montgomery. A pair of landlords suspect one of their

lodgers of being the man responsible for the Whitechappel murders. Based on the novelette by Marie Belloc Lowndes.

December 21, 1944
#122 "The Brighton Strangler"
　　With John Loder and June Duprez. An actor portraying "The Brighton Strangler" on the English stage is knocked on the head during an air raid and with a severe case of amnesia, takes up the identity of his stage portrayal. Both stars starred in the movie, also called *The Brighton Strangler*, in 1945.

December 28, 1944
#123 "A Thing of Beauty"
　　June Duprez is an actress framed for the murder of a playwright. Fearing for her life, she marries the only man who can create an alibi. Originally, Ida Lupino was to play the lead, but she took ill days before the broadcast, so Duprez, who was a guest the week before, filled in for Lupino.

January 4, 1945
#124 "I Had an Alibi"
　　Keenan Wynn is intent on killing his wealthy wife so he can claim an inheritance. The original title of this episode was "Murder is Simple."

January 11, 1945
#125 "Drive-In"
　　Nancy Kelly portrays a car hop employee, who agrees to hitch a ride with a customer in order to make it to the bus stop in time. She discovers her mistake when the employee will not allow her to leave.

January 18, 1945
#126 "To Find Help"
　　Agnes Moorehead is held hostage by Frank Sinatra, who plays the role of a wanted psychopath who tears the phone cords out of the wall.

January 25, 1945
#127 "Drury's Bones"
　　Boris Karloff plays the role of a Scotland Yard Inspector whose most

recent case may involve his past. A past he does not remember because he suffered amnesia. This script would later be dramatized on May 11, 1952 on *Hollywood Star Playhouse* with Herbert Marshall.

February 1, 1945
#128 "The Most Dangerous Game"
Joseph Cotten and J. Carrol Naish star in the same drama from September 23, 1943. RKO began filming a motion picture based on this story on the same day this drama was broadcast. The movie version was entitled *A Game of Death*.

February 8, 1945
#129 "Tale of Two Sisters"
With Nancy Kelly and Claire Trevor. In a similar tradition of *What Ever Happened to Baby Jane?*, two sisters, one sane and one mentally unstable, cannot live in the same house without conflict. One of them ties the other to a chair, kills a brother-in-law, and pours kerosene on the bodies.

February 15, 1945
#130 "Sell Me Your Life"
Lee Bowman plays Joe Bland, who finds himself hired as a bodyguard, and soon finds himself framed for the murder of his employer's husband.

February 22, 1945
#131 "John Barbie and Son"
Thomas Mitchell plays John Barbie, who doesn't care what the State says; he wants to stay with his son regardless of the law. In an attempt to make a run across the border, the police might catch up to him.

March 1, 1945
#132 "My Wife Geraldine"
The police are waiting to arrest Mr. Graham, played by Edward G. Robinson, for the murder of his wife. His landlady, however, learns of his terrible secret. Mrs. Graham never existed and he's about to take a fall for a crime he never committed.

March 8, 1945
#133 "Love's Lovely Counterfeit"
   Based on the novel by James M. Cain. Humphrey Bogart guests as Ben Grace, a man who helps a crooked candidate win an election and as a reward, is placed in charge of the race tracks and gambling joints in town. When his girlfriend is charged with murder, Ben is forced to make a decision. This was the final episode to feature the series' host, "The Man in Black," played by Joseph Kearns.

March 15, 1945
#134 "Cricket"
   Child actress Margaret O'Brien plays the role of Little Florence, whose parents are dead, and her grandmother, played by actress Dame May Whitty, believes Florence needs new surroundings when the little girl suspects the house is haunted.

March 22, 1945
#135 "Heart's Desire"
   Lloyd Nolan plays a devoted bank employee who is on trial for robbery, for a crime he didn't commit.

March 29, 1945
#136 "The Taming of the Beast"
   Helmut Dantine plays a doctor who learns that his wife is dying of a brain tumor. She has a few months to live, and since he longs for the day she dies, he attempts to speed the process.

April 5, 1945
#137 "A Guy Gets Lonely"
   With Dane Clark and Howard Duff. A beautiful lady in a penny arcade is the only clue to an illegal racket in town.

April 12, 1945
   Pre-empted due to news coverage of President Roosevelt's death. A repeat performance of Dashiell Hammett's "Two Sharp Knives" was originally scheduled for this date, and was later broadcast June 7.

Suspense

April 19, 1945
#138 "Pearls are a Nuisance"
Based on the famous short story by Raymond Chandler. William Bendix plays a private eye who accepts a case for a client regarding stolen jewels.

April 26, 1945
Pre-empted due to speeches from San Francisco.

Thursday — 7:00 p.m. to 7:30 p.m. (E.S.T.)

May 3, 1945
#139 "Fear Paints a Picture"
Lana Turner plays a 20-year-old who will lose the family inheritance if she goes mentally insane by her 21st birthday. Lately she's been rambling on about the figures in the paintings moving toward her.

May 10, 1945
#140 "Reprieve"
John Garfield plays Steve, a convicted murderer who, thanks to the assistance and dedication of a female detective, is set free for the crime he did not commit. When she gets him an honest job, his decisions about legal and illegal are tempting.

May 17, 1945
#141 "Two Birds With One Stone"
Guest Dana Andrews is a mystery writer who murders his wife by pushing her body off the top of a bridge, and the police rule it a suicide. The only witness was her dog who can't be fooled as easily as the police.

May 24, 1945
#142 "My Own Murderer"
With Herbert Marshall and Norman Lloyd. A convicted murderer blackmails an attorney in exchange for shelter from the law. The attorney reluctantly agrees, and spends the remainder of the episode trying to find a way to rid his problem.

May 31, 1945
#143 "August Heat"

With Ronald Colman and Dennis Hoey. In the hot, summer August heat, two premonitions suggest Mr. Withencroft's demise. The dead giveaway is a tombstone with his name and today's date of death. The same radio script was later dramatized on the September 29, 1949 broadcast of *The Hallmark Playhouse.*

June 7, 1945
#144 "Two Sharp Knives"

With John Payne. Same story and script from December 22, 1942.

June 14, 1945
#145 "The Burning Court"

With Clifton Webb and Dennis Hoey. Same story and script from June 17, 1942.

June 21, 1945
#146 "The Story of Ivy"

Ann Richards portrays a young lady who is forced to choose between a poor husband and a rich lover. Using a little arsenic, she allows fate to make her decision.

June 28, 1945
#147 "The Dealings of Mr. Markham"

With Henry Daniell, Joan Lorring and Gavin Gordon. Same story and script from May 11, 1943.

July 5, 1945
#148 "The Last Detail"

With George Coulouris. A professor accepts an invitation to a scientific discovery that may turn the scientific world upside down. During his stay, he suspects the motive for his visit is a farce, and that he may have been kidnapped without being told. This script would later be dramatized on October 3, 1949 on *Murder by Experts.*

July 12, 1945
#149 "Footfalls"
 J. Carrol Naish plays a blind father who denies his son is involved with the murder of their wealthy boarder.

July 19, 1945
#150 "Bank Holiday"
 Bonita Granville plays a bank teller who is kidnapped during a daring robbery. She soon discovers that her kidnappers are nothing more than amateurs who want to reproduce what they saw in the movies.

July 26, 1945
#151 "Fury and Sound"
 Norman Lloyd plays the radio studio's least-liked radio director who is being driven insane, courtesy of a few tricks up a sound technician's sleeve. (See the short story at the end of the book.)

August 2, 1945
#152 "A Man in the House"
 With Joan Lorring. Emily and her mother have a peaceful existence until a killer holds Emily's mother hostage. If Emily makes a misstep, her mother's life is non-existent.

August 9, 1945
#153 "Murder for Myra"
 With Lloyd Nolan. A loving wife wishes her husband dead, so she arranges for her lover to hide in the closet with a hammer till her husband returns home.

August 16, 1945
#154 "Short Order"
 With Conrad Binyon and Gerald Mohr. Every day for the past week a horribly-disfigured man enters the diner and eats his meals. Customers leave in disgust so the owner of the diner decides to take action resulting in an exciting climax.

August 23, 1945

#155 "This Will Kill You"

With Dane Clark. A factory worker assisting the war cause falls in love with another employee. When his boss learns of the possible relationship, he begins to interfere.

August 30, 1945
#156 "Nobody Loves Me"

Peter Lorre is an emotionally distraught man, who holds a police station hostage with a loaded gun, as he recounts the worst moments of his life when nobody loved him. Lorre loved this script so much that two years later he requested to do it again for the July 31, 1947 broadcast of *Mystery in the Air*.

September 6, 1945
#157 "Sorry, Wrong Number"

With Agnes Moorehead. Same story and script from May 25, 1943.

September 13, 1945
#158 "Furnished Floor"

Don DeFore plays a widower who recently marries and keeps his new bride in seclusion in their apartment. Mildred Natwick plays the landlady who wants nothing more than to see the bride no one has ever caught a glimpse of. This radio script, written by Lucille Fletcher, was adapted for the March 10, 1952 broadcast of a television episode of NBC's *Lights Out* series.

September 20, 1945
#159 "The Library Book"

Actress Myrna Loy plays a librarian who pieces together one clue too many and suspects that a torn page from a book was used to make a ransom note.

September 27, 1945
#160 "The Earth is Made of Glass"

Joseph Cotten commits the perfect crime without lifting a finger. Leaving no clues, and no witnesses, he proves his case on paper and the police can do nothing about it.

Suspense

Thursday — 8:00 p.m. to 8:30 p.m. (E.S.T.)

October 4, 1945
#161 "Death on Highway 99"
   George Murphy plays Morton Blake, who wants a divorce from his wife. She won't grant him one, and uses a recent hit-and-run murder as the means of blackmail to keep him from bringing up the subject.

October 11, 1945
#162 "Beyond Good and Evil"
   Joseph Cotten plays a con, who escapes from prison, disguises himself as a Man of God, steals the money from the church, and plans to run away with the daughter of the paralyzed man he confesses his crime to. Jane Morgan is in the supporting cast.

October 18, 1945
#163 "Summer Storm"
   In a script written especially for *Suspense* by William Spier, Henry Fonda plays Eddie, who tries to skip out without paying his landlord. Getting caught in the act, he pushes the old man down the stairs. When the other tenants hear the commotion, Eddie hides in the attic. This episode was produced and directed by Charles Vanda, instead of William Spier.

October 25, 1945
#164 "A Shroud for Sarah"
   Lucille Ball plays Sarah who is found dead from suffering a severe beating, strangulation and stabbing. Considering she stole money from a candidate, injures her husband and turned her boyfriend in to the police, the police are not surprised.

November 1, 1945
#165 "The Dunwich Horror"
   Based on a short story by H.P. Lovecraft. With Ronald Colman. A desolate town in New England is ripe for the opportunity to welcome the birth of a newborn with tentacles. The bowels of hell open, and the disease spreads faster than the story allows. A superb horror story for

Halloween and one of the very few radio dramas ever adapted from an H.P. Lovecraft story.

November 8, 1945
#166 "The Bet"
With Lee J. Cobb. A scientist makes a bet of $50,000 that the artist visiting him couldn't keep records of his laboratory work for two years. The scientist's wife warns the artist to kill her husband for $500,000. Is this a test on the part of the scientist? This broadcast marked Lee J. Cobb's first radio appearance since he was recently released from active duty.

November 15, 1945
#167 "Murder Off Key"
A fat woman and her prize poodle were killed and the motive is not too clear to guest Zachary Scott.

November 22, 1945
#168 "Nineteen Deacon Street"
With Lloyd Nolan. A salesman rents a room that may be haunted. The room was once owned by a young girl who mysteriously disappeared, and the salesman keeps hearing her voice calling out to him.

November 29, 1945
#169 "A Week Ago Wednesday"
With Nancy Kelly and Jane Morgan. A woman dreams of her husband stabbing her to death, and wakes to find him more loving than usual. Does he have an ulterior motive?

December 6, 1945
#170 "I Won't Take a Minute"
Actor Lee Bowman drops off his girlfriend outside a store to do an errand and when he returns, he finds her missing and no one has any memory of her inside the store.

December 13, 1945
#171 "The Argyle Album"
Robert Taylor is forced to solve a mystery when a reporter is found

dead, having found the "Argyle Album," worth a fortune to anyone still alive to possess it.

December 20, 1945
#172 "Double Entry"
With Keenan Wynn and Hume Cronyn. A charming Christmas episode, in the tradition of a Damon Runyon story. Two con artists correct a shortage in the books by horse betting, and later get arrested for illegal betting.

December 27, 1945
#173 "Pink Camelias"
With Marsha Hunt. A vile employer is poisoned by her servants with arsenic-laced strawberries.

January 3, 1946
#174 "The Angel of Death"
With Paul Henried. John is accused of murdering his wife and her lover. After being found guilty of the crime, the police have still been unable to find the bodies.

January 10, 1946
#175 "This Was a Hero"
Phillip Terry plays the role of a rookie cop who takes the heroism reported in the newspapers of his shooting of a safe-cracker. After falling in love with the victim's widow, he suspects that the man he shot to death may not have been a safe-cracker at all.

January 17, 1946
#176 "The Pasteboard Box"
With Joseph Cotten. Jack murders his twin brother, with what he thinks is a foolproof method of an alibi, and then cuts his brother's body into pieces. When he gets a box switched by accident, he tracks down the head before the crime is discovered.

January 24, 1946
#177 "My Dear Niece"
Actress Dame May Whitty writes to her niece, telling her the exciting

story of how she rented out a flat to a mystery writer, only to discover he isn't what he seems. This episode was written by future *Suspense* producer and director Elliott Lewis.

January 31, 1946
#178 "The Long Shot"

With George Coulouris. An Englishman answers a classified, requesting someone to accompany a stranger cross-country so he can deliver some important papers. When he discovers the true motive behind the papers, he commits a murder and assumes the driver's place. This script would later be dramatized on June 8, 1952 on *Hollywood Star Playhouse* with David Niven in the lead and on December 4, 1950 on *Murder by Experts*.

February 7, 1946
#179 "Too Little to Live On"

With George Murphy and Nancy Kelly. Uncle Ed has driven the family to the brink of murder. Switching his medicine, they hope to make it look like an accident.

February 14, 1946
#180 "The Lucky Lady"

With Fay Bainter. An aging actress takes in a new boarder with a mysterious secret. When two of her young actresses die in the house, she starts to suspect her new boarder of foul play.

February 21, 1946
#181 "Consequence"

With Jimmy Stewart. Dr. Martin wants to leave his wife for a younger woman. When a friend of his dies in a fire, and the police mistake the corpse as his, Dr. Martin takes advantage of the opportunity and leaves with the girl.

February 28, 1946
#182 "The Keenest Edge"

Richard Greene plays Jack, a new cook at a diner where his boss is suspected of being the murderer the police are looking for. To prove his theory, he checks the slabs of meat hanging in the freezer, hoping to find fingers attached.

Suspense

March 7, 1946
#183 "The Black Path of Fear"
   With Cary Grant. Same story and script from August 31, 1944.

March 14, 1946
#184 "No More Alice"
   With Paul Henried. A medical doctor hears on the radio reports of a killer on the loose. Picking up a hitch-hiker, he learns of the stranger's identity and hires him to kill his wife.

March 21, 1946
#185 "The Lonely Road"
   Gregory Peck is Steve Gare, who falls for the wiles of his new maid, played by Maria Palmer. The two plot the murder of his wife, but Steve soon finds himself the victim of a grander scheme. This script was originally supposed to air on March 7, 1946. This script would later be dramatized on October 1, 1950 on *Murder by Experts*. Peck reprised his role for the May 15, 1947 broadcast of *The Family Theatre*.

March 28, 1946
#186 "Out of Control"
   Brian Donlevy plays Duncan McClaine, a blind detective. Based on the novel by Baynard Hardwick Kendrick. McClaine receives a visit from a young lady claiming she is being blackmailed, and her husband has been murdered.

April 4, 1946
#187 "Post Mortem"
   With Agnes Moorehead and Howard Duff. Josephine Archer has just learned that she has just won $150,000 in a sweepstakes. The problem is the ticket was in the coat her recently-deceased husband was buried in!

April 11, 1946
#188 "The Name of the Beast"
   Vincent Price plays an artist, who shelters a murderer long enough to use them as a model for his work. After stealing the loot, the artist then turns the murderer in to the police. In real life, Vincent Price

had a passion for art, often buying good paintings to hang around his house. It seemed natural to have him play the role of an artist for this broadcast.

April 18, 1946
#189 "The Night Reveals"
With Keenan Wynn and Howard Duff. Same story and script from December 9, 1943. "Return Trip" was originally scheduled for this date, but later broadcast June 27.

April 25, 1946
#190 "Dark Journey"
Nancy Kelly plays Ann, a young girl whose imagination is running away from her. Believing she has the power to make anyone do anything at her will, she tries to claim ownership of the man of her dreams.

Thursday — 7:00 p.m. to 7:30 p.m. (E.S.T.)

May 2, 1946
#191 "Crime Without Passion"
Joseph Cotten is a criminal attorney, who tries to get away with murder. Based on the screenplay by Ben Hecht and Charles MacArthur. The 1934 movie starred Claude Rains in the lead.

May 9, 1946
#192 "The Clock and the Rope"
Jackie Cooper plays Henry Gilford, accused of a murder and sentenced to hang because the only witness to the crime has vanished off the face of the Earth. This broadcast marked Jackie Cooper's first radio appearance since he was recently released from active duty.

May 16, 1946
#193 "The Plan"
Claire Trevor is a housewife who discovers her husband's dark secret too late. Apparently she has a brother-in-law he never talked about, a brother-in-law who just broke out of a criminally insane sanitarium.

Suspense

May 23, 1946
#194 "Spoils for Victor"
Dane Clark plays the title role, tricked by his agent into falling in love with a wealthy woman. After the marriage, Victor is encouraged by his agent to kill her so the money will be his.

May 30, 1946
#195 "The Leading Citizen of Pratt County"
Alan Hale plays a con artist, who plans the biggest take of his career. Before he can con the inhabitants of a town for their valuable land, he must murder a young boy who stands in his way.

June 6, 1946
#196 "The High Wall"
Robert Young plays Mr. Lewis, who wakes to find himself committed in an asylum and a doctor, played by George Zucco, trying to cure him. Mr. Lewis insists he's innocent but in his present state, fails to help himself. George Zucco makes his fourth and final appearance on *Suspense*.

June 13, 1946
#197 "Too Many Smiths"
Hume Cronyn plays Charles, who discovers early on the winner of a slogan contest. In order to win the prize money, he seeks out the winner, Mr. Pat Smith, and kills the contestant, assuming his identity.

June 20, 1946
#198 "Your Devoted Wife"
June Duprez, as Melissa, is transporting her husband from one medical clinic to another, on board a train. Her husband will try anything he can to escape the strait-jackets, including telling the conductor that his wife is the real insane one.

June 27, 1946
#199 "Return Trip"
With Elliott Reid. A bus driver caught in a snow trap realizes that one of his passengers is an escaped loon from the asylum up the road.

July 4, 1946
#200 "An Evening's Diversion"
　With Leon Ames and Gerald Mohr. A businessman accidentally stumbles on a murder plot. Being the Good Samaritan, he tracks down the intended victim to discover he knows them personally.

July 11, 1946
#201 "Feast of the Furies"
　With Sheldon Leonard and Elliott Reid. Sam wakes to find himself the victim of a kidnapping. His kidnapper is a hired assassin; unarmed, the only way Sam is walking away from this situation is by conversation.

July 18, 1946
#202 "Photo Finish"
　Michael O'Shea plays a photographer who takes a picture and captures a killing on negative. Two criminals disguised as police officers pick him up and stash the body in his trunk. A female steals the negative and the photographer has some answers to give.

July 25, 1946
#203 "Can't We Be Friends"
　With Elliott Reid and Lurene Tuttle. Frances has done her best to keep Michael away from her, but he won't leave her alone. When she rejects his intentions one too many times, he plans her murder. This episode was written by future *Suspense* producer and director Elliott Lewis. Ken Niles replaces Truman Bradley as the commercial spokesman for Roma Wines.

August 1, 1946
#204 "Commuter Ticket"
　With J. Carrol Naish, Jim Backus and Howard Duff. Bert Garvin murders his wife and takes the train to get from his house to work without being seen. He has a theory that so many people ride the train that he's just another face in the crowd, and an alibi is not needed.

Suspense

August 8, 1946
#205 "Dead Ernest"
　With Wally Maher and Walter Tetley. Ernest Bowers is knocked unconscious after a serious auto accident. The attendant in the morgue prepares the body, while he lies in a cataleptic state, aware of his surroundings. This episode won *Suspense* the George Foster Peabody Award in 1946.

August 15, 1946
#206 "The Last Letter of Dr. Bronson"
　With Henry Daniell. Same story and script from July 27, 1943.

August 22, 1946
#207 "The Great Horrell"
　With Joan Lorring and Howard Duff. A mind reader with real talents leaves the country and his wife.

August 29, 1946
#208 "Blue Eyes"
　Hume Cronyn plays Mr. Littlefield, who loses his job and returns home to find his wife committed suicide.

September 5, 1946
#209 "You'll Never See Me Again"
　With Robert Young. Same story and script as September 14, 1944.

September 12, 1946
#210 "Hunting Trip"
　With Vincent Price and Lloyd Nolan. Two men go out on a friendly hunting trip, with loaded rifles, to work out their grievances about the love they have for the same woman. This script would later be dramatized on January 9, 1950 on *Murder by Experts*.

September 19, 1946
#211 "'Til the Day I Die"
　With Dane Clark. Frankie is forced to shoot a police officer

during a high-stakes robbery. Leaving town before the heat gets too hot, he finds himself sitting next to the wife and son of his victim.

September 26, 1946
#212 "Statement of Employee Henry Wilson"
 Gene Lockhart reprises his role from the broadcast of November 2, 1943.

Thursday — 8:00 p.m. to 8:30 p.m. (E.S.T.)

October 3, 1946
#213 "Three Times Murder"
 Rita Hayworth plays a woman who discovers after her new marriage that her brother-in-law is the same Assistant District Attorney who tried to convict her after the death of her first husband.

October 10, 1946
#214 "A Plane Case of Murder"
 John Lund helps a woman murder her husband and then frames it on her. The title "Plane" is the proper spelling since the caper takes place on an airplane. Mark Stevens was originally to play the lead instead of Lund.

October 17, 1946
#215 "The Man Who Thought He was Edward G. Robinson"
 Edward G. Robinson is a meek little man, who can't even harm a house fly. When he wants to murder his wife, he seeks out the only man tough enough to accomplish the task, the actor Edward G. Robinson. Part of the humor is having Edward G. Robinson play dual roles and during one moment, he recites lines from the 1930 Warner Bros. motion picture, *Little Caesar*.

October 24, 1946
#216 "Dame Fortune"
 Susan Hayworth plays a singer with a shady past. When a blackmailer makes her an offer, she confesses her past to her husband. So why did her husband get murdered?

Suspense

October 31, 1946
#217 "Lazarus Walks"
   With Brian Donlevy. Same story and script from October 19, 1943.

November 7, 1946
#218 "Easy Money"
   Jack Carson is a husband who plots the murder of his wife.

November 14, 1946
#219 "The One Who Got Away"
   Hume Cronyn plays a bank employee who discovers one day that another employee has been embezzling money. Rather than turn him in to the authorities, he blackmails the employee into helping assist in the murder of his wife.

November 21, 1946
#220 "Drive-In"
   With Judy Garland. Same story and script from January 11, 1945. Producer and director William Spier was Judy Garland's Godfather in real-life.

November 28, 1946
#221 "The Strange Death of Gordon Fitzroy"
   With Chester Morris and Howard Duff. Safecrackers Johnny and Gordon foil a job and an explosion disfigures Johnny's face. Gordon squealed on his partner and years later, Johnny is released and seeks revenge.

December 5, 1946
#222 "The House in Cypress Canyon"
   With Robert Taylor, Cathy Lewis, Howard Duff and Hans Conried. A real estate agent invites his detective friend to listen to a transcription that defies the imagination. A young couple moves into a newly purchased home and discover a werewolf prowls the grounds. Cary Grant was originally supposed to play the lead, but Robert Taylor took his place.

   This episode is considered by many old-time radio fans as one of the best of the series, and ranked as one of the ten scariest radio programs ever broadcast. The investigating detective in this episode was played by Howard Duff, and his name was referred to only as "Sam." This was an in-joke from William Spier, who was also producing and directing the radio series *The Adventures of Sam Spade*. The original title of this episode was "The House in Cypress Gardens."

December 12, 1946
#223 "They Call Me Patrice"
Susan Peters plays Helen, a young lady who longs for a new life and finds it when she wakes from the train crash and victim of mistaken identity. She now has wealthy parents who care for her.

December 19, 1946
#224 "The Thing in the Window"
Joseph Cotten is a tenant who keeps seeing the mysterious figure of a corpse in another window, but when the police investigate, they find nothing.

December 26, 1946
#225 "Philomel Cottage"
With Lilli Palmer. Same story and script from July 29, 1942.

January 2, 1947
#226 "Tree of Life"
Mark Stevens plays an innocent man who walks into a murder, and rather than be killed, is mistaken for the killers' employer.

January 9, 1947
#227 "The Will to Power"
Dan Duryea murders a man and throws the blame on his female accomplice.

January 16, 1947
#228 "Overture in Two Keys"
Joan Bennett plays a young lady whose husband dies in a horrible accident and her lover gives her the good news. Months later, after their marriage, she has suspicions that her husband did not die in an "accident."

January 23, 1947
#229 "One-Way Street"
　Roddy McDowall, as a prodigal nephew, who returns home and shortly after, begins to suspect his uncle wants to murder his new wife.

January 30, 1947
#230 "Three Blind Mice"
　Van Heflin is one of three business partners who have their life turned upside down. One is found dead, another is the murder suspect, and the third relaxes as he recounts the events of the story.

February 6, 1947
#231 "End of the Road"
　With Glenn Ford as Speed, a car salesman who murders a client's husband so he and his lover can marry. His plan backfires when he learns of her betrayal.

February 13, 1947
#232 "The Thirteenth Sound"
　Agnes Moorehead plays Sally Skinner, who murders her husband and gets away without suspicion from the police. In the tradition of *The Tell-Tale Heart*, she is haunted by her dead husband's fingernails scratching on the window.

February 20, 1947
#233 "Always Room at the Top"
　With Anne Baxter and Jack Webb. A female art director commits suicide by jumping out a window. She returns from the dead to prove it was murder.

February 27, 1947
#234 "Three Faces at Midnight"
　William Bendix plays Muscles, a tough guy hired to play the role of a cop in a blackmailing scam involving the governor. When things go wrong, Muscles is left holding the bag. Jack Webb is among the supporting cast.

March 6, 1947
#235 "Elwood"
  Eddie Bracken stars as Elwood, a boy with a mental problem, who suspects he may be the killer the police are looking for. Mickey Rooney was originally scheduled to play the lead.

March 13, 1947
#236 "You Take Ballistics"
  With Howard da Silva and Jack Webb. A homicide detective sets out to prove that ballistics can be wrong when his department is forced to let the prime suspect go off a murder rap. James Stewart was originally scheduled to play the role Howard da Silva played. Truman Bradley returns as the spokesman for Roma Wines, replacing Ken Niles.

  On November 29, 1948, an audition recording was cut for a proposed radio series titled *The Hunters*. This same script was dramatized for the audition. Victor Jory starred in the cast and the entire production was directed by future *Suspense* producer/director Anton M. Leader.

March 20, 1947
#237 "The Waxwork"
  Claude Rains, in a one-man performance, plays a reporter who gets the opportunity to spend the night in a creepy wax museum for a human interest story. As the hours pass, one of the waxworks takes on a life of his own, as a convicted killer explains his escape route.

March 27, 1947
#238 "Trial by Jury"
  With Nancy Kelly and Howard Duff. A female attorney clears her client of a crime that he was really guilty of. When he won't leave her side for a moment, she commits a murder to get rid of the pest.

April 3, 1947
#239 "The Swift Rise of Eddie Albright"
  With Phil Silvers and Frank Lovejoy. Silvers is an elevator operator, who witnesses two men leaving with a corpse wrapped in carpet. This script would later be dramatized on January 18, 1949 on *The Philip*

Morris Playhouse under the title "Going Down, Please" with Donald O'Connor in the lead.

April 10, 1947
#240 "Community Property"
With Kirk Douglas. After receiving an inheritance of half a million, Kirk Douglas is forced to kill his wife before she makes the divorce final, taking away half of his good fortune.

April 17, 1947
#241 "The Green-Eyed Monster"
Lloyd Nolan plays Mr. Dawson who reports his car stolen, and soon discovers the body of his late wife in the trunk.

April 24, 1947
#242 "Win, Place and Murder"
With Richard Conte. A gambler and his woman are surprised when the local law enforcement has a larger interest in the horse races than the corpse in their office.

Thursday — 7:00 p.m. to 7:30 p.m. (E.S.T.)

May 1, 1947
#243 "Lady in Distress"
With Ava Gardner and Howard Duff. After picking up a hitchhiker, Gardner discovers the man is an escaped con. But since she wants her husband dead, she strikes a deal with the murderer. Years after this broadcast, in 1972, Ava Gardner would star in *The Ballad of Tam Lin*, scripted by William Spier.

May 8, 1947
#244 "Dead Ernest"
With Wally Maher. Same story and script as August 8, 1946. David Niven was originally scheduled to play the lead.

May 15, 1947
#245 "Death at Live Oak"
With Robert Mitchum. Two lovers plot the murder of her husband, since he is a dead ringer for her husband.

May 22, 1947
#246 "Knight Comes Riding"
   With Virginia Bruce and Howard Duff. When a woman discovers her husband is a murderer, she finds her knight in shining armor in the guise of a war veteran.

May 29, 1947
#247 "A Thing of Beauty"
   Angela Lansbury plays the role June Duprez played for episode 123.

June 5, 1947
#248 "Make Mad the Guilty"
   With Hume Cronyn and Howard Duff. A man fakes his death to gain the payoff to a life-insurance policy but finds his payoff in a different form, courtesy of his wife and her lover.

June 12, 1947
#249 "Stand-In"
   June Havoc plays an actress who tries to play hard-to-get after her husband uses her professional stand-in to create a fake murder, fooling the witness and the proper time of death. June Havoc was the girlfriend of producer/director William Spier at the time of this broadcast.

June 19, 1947
#250 "Dead of Night"
   With Elliott Reid. Same story and script from November 16, 1944.

June 26, 1947
#251 "Phobia"
   Eva La Galliene plays wheelchair-bound Emily, who defends herself against a burglar and then confuses the police when they cannot figure out who committed the murder. Emily or her sister? This script would later be dramatized on September 11, 1950 on *Murder by Experts*.

July 3, 1947
#252 "Money Talks"
   With Alan Baxter and Russell Thorson. A young employee at the

bank has been secretly altering the books in his favor. Before he can cash out, the beautiful secretary makes her move.

July 10, 1947
#253 "Murder by the Book"
Gloria Swanson plays a mystery writer who attempts to get involved in a real-life murder mystery. Swanson misses a few of her lines and cues during this broadcast.

July 17, 1947
#254 "Beyond Good and Evil"
With Vincent Price. Same story and script from October 11, 1945.

July 24, 1947
#255 "Murder by an Expert"
With Lynn Bari and Jack Webb. Bari is a professional dancer who kills her husband and attempts to cover the deed by establishing a fake alibi.

July 31, 1947
#256 "Mortmain"
With Jerome Cowan. Two attorneys plan to double cross each other.

August 7, 1947
#257 "Quiet Desperation"
Walter Abel plays Homer, a petty thief who uses a friend's identity to cover his deed.

August 14, 1947
#258 "Smiley"
Donald O'Connor is Smiley, just released from prison for attempted murder. Since he was guilty of the crime accused, he takes his anger out on the first beautiful woman who shows interest toward him.

August 21, 1947
#259 "Murder Aboard the Alphabet"
John Lund plays the captain of a vessel who orders his crew to perform all tasks alphabetically. The crew soon plans mutiny.

August 28, 1947
#260 "Double Ugly"

Lloyd Nolan is Matthew, the ugliest boy in the world. A woman takes pity on him and attempts to find love behind his sick face, but he chooses murder instead. June Havoc, for artistic reasons, chants "Double Ugly" throughout the drama.

September 4, 1947
#261 "The Argyle Album"

With Edmond O'Brien. Same story and script from December 13, 1945.

September 11, 1947
#262 "The Twist"

With Michael O'Shea and Sidney Miller. A radio script writer creates what is considered the perfect murder. Only his job is writing for radio comedy programs. Blaming his error on his partner, he soon discovers a "twist" in his story.

September 18, 1947
#263 "The Visitor"

With Donald O'Connor. Same story and script as performed on May 11, 1944.

September 25, 1947
#264 "The Blue Hour"

Claire Trevor arrives in New York to perform on stage but finds the spotlight on her husband's murder instead.

Thursday — 8:00 p.m. to 8:30 p.m. (E.S.T.)

October 2, 1947
#265 "The Story of Markham's Death"

Kirk Douglas is a mystery writer who discovers an unpublished manuscript written by Edgar Allen Poe. If he plays his cards right, he'll become the next master of mystery and horror.

Suspense

October 9, 1947
#266 "The Man Who Liked Dickens"
Richard Ney is an Englishman who finds himself trapped in the Amazon, and is forced to read Charles Dickens to his captor. This same script would later be dramatized on December 21, 1952 on *Escape*.

October 16, 1947
#267 "Self-Defense"
Marsha Hunt plays a woman who uses her wiles to con a young man into murdering her husband.

October 23, 1947
#268 "The X-Ray Camera"
Dennis O'Keefe wants his wife dead over a divorce. His solution comes in the form of a young love who is tricked into using a "special camera" with a hand grenade.

October 30, 1947
#269 "Subway"
With June Havoc and Lurene Tuttle. After hearing how successful an old school chum is, Paula grabs a pair of scissors and vents with jealousy.

November 6, 1947
#270 "Dream Song"
Henry Morgan suspects every time he hears a specific music bridge, a murder is committed.

November 13, 1947
#271 "Riabouchinska"
With Wally Maher and Lurene Tuttle. When the police question a ventriloquist and his wooden dummy as murder suspects, they discover that the left hand does not know what the right hand is doing. Based on the short story *And So Died Riabouchinska* by Ray Bradbury. This would be Bradbury's first of many short stories dramatized on *Suspense*. Mel Dinelli, who wrote the radio script for this broadcast, also wrote the television script from the same story for the February 12, 1956 broadcast of *Alfred Hitchcock Presents*.

November 20, 1947
#272 "One Hundred in the Dark"
With Howard Duff and June Havoc. This is the same script as episode 14. This was the final episode to be sponsored by Crestra Blanca Wines (Roma Wines). Truman Bradley, the sponsor's pitchman, was not heard on the series after this episode.

Friday — 9:30 p.m. to 10:00 p.m. (E.S.T.)

November 28, 1947
#273 "The Pit and the Pendulum"
With Jose Ferrer and Jeanette Nolan. Same story and script from January 12, 1943. This was the first of five, half-hour episodes that were repeat performances of previously-dramatized episodes, and CBS footed the bill with no sponsor.

December 5, 1947
#274 "The Clock and the Rope"
Jackie Cooper reprises the same role he did for the broadcast of May 9, 1946.

December 12, 1947
#275 "The Man Who Couldn't Lose"
With Dan Duryea and Jack Webb. Same story and script from September 28, 1944.

December 19, 1947
#276 "Wet Saturday"
With Boris Karloff. Same story and script from June 24, 1942.

December 26, 1947
#277 "Too Little to Live On"
With Ozzie and Harriet Nelson. Same story and script from February 7, 1946.

Suspense

Saturday — 8:00 p.m. to 9:00 p.m. (E.S.T.)

January 3, 1948
#278 "The Black Curtain"
With William Conrad. Same story from December 2, 1943, expanded to an hour-long format. This was the first hour-long episode of the series. Robert Montgomery begins hosting the series with this episode. Because the series expanded from a half-hour to an hour, and because the series was not sponsored, the actors all received scale for their work. Anne Nelson, the V.P. of CBS at the time, sent them all a great, big, bulky short-wave overseas radio for a gift.

January 10, 1948
#279 "The Kandy Tooth"
With Howard Duff, Joseph Kearns and Lurene Tuttle. This was the same two-part adventure/script featured on *The Adventures of Sam Spade* as broadcast on November 24, 1946 and December 1, 1946, with the entire cast reprising their roles from the two broadcasts. As a sequel to Dashiell Hammett's *The Maltese Falcon*, Sam receives a return visit from Kasper Gutman, in another search for a priceless treasure. During this drama, Sam actually calls detective Philip Marlowe to verify a witness's story.

January 17, 1948
#280 "Love's Lovely Counterfeit"
James Cagney plays the role Humphrey Bogart played on March 8, 1945. Same story and script, expanded to an hour-long time slot.

January 24, 1948
#281 "Eve" / "The Black Angel"
With June Havoc and Robert Montgomery. The same story from October 19, 1944, but the announcer gives this drama two episode titles instead of one during the broadcast.

January 31, 1948
#282 "A Bet with Death"
With Lee Bowman and Otto Kruger. Same story from November 10, 1942, expanded to an hour-long time slot.

February 7, 1948
#283 "Donovan's Brain"
   John McIntire stars in the role Orson Welles did for the same script dramatized on May 11 and 18, 1944.

February 14, 1948
#284 "The Lodger"
   Robert Montgomery reprises the same role he did for the broadcast of December 14, 1944, expanded for an hour-long time slot. William Spier left the producing and directing duties after this episode.

February 21, 1948
#285 "Beyond Reason"
   With Robert Ryan and Ruth Warrick. Mr. Carr is killed by a hit-and-run driver, leaving behind a fortune to his three daughters. A stranger introduces himself to the women, claiming to be their father's business partner. Beginning with this episode, host Robert Montgomery begins producing the series and Anton M. Leader begins directing.

February 28, 1948
#286 "The House by the River"
   Dan O'Herlihy plays Steven, a young man who murders the family maid. His brother assists in sinking the corpse in the river. Days later the girl returns from the dead to haunt Steven.

March 6, 1948
#287 "In a Lonely Place"
   With Robert Montgomery and Lurene Tuttle. A freelance writer is accused of murdering a woman he spent time with the night before. Based on the novel by Dorothy Belle Hughes.

March 13, 1948
#288 "Nightmare"
   Eddie Bracken plays Vincent, who keeps having strange dreams of having committed a murder. His best friend takes him to the scene of the crime to prove that it was nothing but a nightmare.

March 20, 1948
#289 "Wet Saturday" / "August Heat"
　　With Berry Kroeger, Joseph Kearns and Dennis Hoey. Two separate stories instead of one, hour-long story. The first was the same script dramatized on June 24, 1942. The second was previously dramatized on May 31, 1945.

March 27, 1948
#290 "Night Must Fall"
　　With Heather Angel, Richard Ney and Dame May Whitty. Whitty hires a new servant, played by Richard Ney, for the house chores and her suspicious niece, played by Heather Angel, suspects him of the murder reported in the local papers. Based on the novel by Emyln Williams. Dame May Whitty reprises her film role from the 1937 movie of the same name.

April 3, 1948
#291 "Suspicion"
　　With Sam Jaffe and Alan Reed. Same story previously dramatized on August 12, 1942, but expanded into an hour-long time slot. Robert Montgomery stopped producing the series with this episode, leaving the producing job with director Anton M. Leader.

April 10, 1948
#292 "Crossfire"
　　Adapted from the RKO motion picture of the same name. Robert Young, Robert Mitchum and Robert Ryan reprise their film roles in this *film noir* classic about three good Army buddies suspected of committing a murder.

April 17, 1948
　　Pre-empted due to a Major League Baseball special entitled "Play Ball."

April 24, 1948
#293 "The Search"
　　Howard Culver and Sandra Gare are a young couple accused of murdering a famous cowboy star, and are forced to run from town to town to find the real killer.

May 1, 1948
#294 "The Blind Spot"
   Edmund O'Brien plays a bodyguard, who is hired to protect the life of his employer, played by Jeff Corey. He fails to accomplish this job when his employer is found murdered. The killers then target the bodyguard.

May 8, 1948
#295 "Life Ends at Midnight"
   With Fay Bainter and Tony Barrett. Same story and script from February 17, 1944, expanded to an hour-long time slot.

May 15, 1948
#296 "Deadline at Dawn"
   John Beal plays a young sailor who, upon learning that a young lady stole a large amount of cash, attempts to steal the stolen loot. Instead, he finds himself accused for the girl's murder. Helen Walker also stars. Based on the novel by Cornell Woolrich. This was the final hour-long episode of the series.

Thursday — 9:00 p.m. to 9:30 p.m. (E.S.T.)

July 8, 1948
#297 "The Last Chance"
   With Cary Grant in the lead role. This was the first episode sponsored by Auto-Lite spark plugs. The series returned to the original half-hour time slot. The story and script are the same as the broadcast of November 4, 1948. Supposedly, this episode never aired. There is evidence that contradicts that statement. No recording is known to exist for this broadcast so it is possible that this broadcast never aired. Paul Frees is the announcer for the series beginning with this episode.

July 15, 1948
#298 "Summer Night"
   According to the local news, a "lipstick killer" is on the loose, marking the foreheads of his victims with lipstick. Ida Lupino plays Anna, who murders a rival and throws the blame on the killer, unaware that

she's the next intended victim of the real killer. Based on the short story by Ray Bradbury.

July 22, 1948
#299 "Deep Into Darkness"
   Douglas Fairbanks, Jr. is an ex-con who observes the murder victim he was falsely accused of killing, walking about alive and well.

July 29, 1948
#300 "The Yellow Wallpaper"
   Agnes Moorehead stars as a woman going mad when she claims the patterns on the yellow wallpaper in her new house comes off the wall and tries to come after her. Based on the short story by Charlotte Curtis Stetson Gilman.

August 5, 1948
#301 "An Honest Man"
   Charles Laughton plays Freddie, a young man who steals money from his employer in hopes of impressing a woman.

August 12, 1948
#302 "Beware the Quiet Man"
   With Ann Sothern and William Conrad. A housewife strikes up a conversation with a private investigator in a bar, whose recent employment involves killing a woman if she's found to be unfaithful to her husband. She later learns her husband is the employer.

August 19, 1948
#303 "Crisis"
   With Martha Scott and Frank Lovejoy. An expectant mother-to-be dreams of the horrors her young son may commit when he grows up.

August 26, 1948
#304 "Song of the Heart"
   Van Heflin is a boy named Neal, who brings home his new girlfriend to Aunt Alice, who hates any woman he brings through the front door. If he wants to keep this girl, he'll have to kill the aunt. Van Johnson was originally scheduled to play the lead.

September 2, 1948
#305 "The Morrison Affair"
  With Madeleine Carroll and Gerald Mohr. A young couple on a train suspects a newborn infant, recently kidnapped, to be their own.

September 9, 1948
#306 "The Big Shot"
  Half a million in gold can tempt any thief to murder. Burt Lancaster plays one of a handful of crooks who, one-by-one, kill each other off for the booty. Lancaster appeared courtesy of Paramount, who released the big-screen movie of *Sorry, Wrong Number* just a week before.

September 16, 1948
#307 "Hitch-Hike Poker"
  Gregory Peck picks up a hitch-hiker and discovers his kindness was a mistake when the hitch-hiker attempts to kill him. Surviving the evening, he picks up another hitch-hiker and discovers he's in the same situation again. Also stars Ed Begley.

September 23, 1948
#308 "Celebration"
  To celebrate their eighth wedding anniversary, a married couple, Robert Young and Virginia Bruce, take an outing where the evening will end in suicide.

September 30, 1948
#309 "The Man Who Wanted to be Edward G. Robinson"
  Edward G. Robinson reprises the same role he played for the broadcast of October 17, 1946. The title of this episode was changed slightly from the 1946 episode.

October 7, 1948
#310 "Night Cry"
  Ray Milland plays a homicide detective who murders a man and then throws the blame on an innocent party to keep his perfect record of solved mysteries unsoiled. Based on the novel by William L. Stewart.

October 14, 1948
#311 "A Little Piece of Rope"
    Lucille Ball plays Isabel, a con artist who makes love to men, knocks them out and steals their money. Evidence suggests her latest victim is the "The Strangler," a notorious murderer wanted by the police.

October 21, 1948
#312 "Give Me Liberty"
    William Powell plays an embezzler who is sentenced and found guilty. En route to prison by train, an accident offers him the opportunity for escape but no matter who he meets up with, no one will help him escape from the chains and handcuffs. Ann Morrison co-stars. This episode was scripted by Herb Meadow, who would later co-create the television program *Have Gun — Will Travel*.

October 28, 1948
    Pre-empted due to a speech by Thomas E. Dewey, Governor of New York.

November 4, 1948
#313 "Death Sentence"
    With John Garfield and Raymond Burr. Tommy is given a week to live by a crooked crime boss, and fleeing town, finds true love. Now that he has a reason for living, Tommy tries to find an escape route. See the entry for July 8, 1948 for trivia. This script would later be dramatized on September 21, 1952 on *Hollywood Star Playhouse* with Charlton Heston in the lead.

November 11, 1948
#314 "Muddy Track"
    With Edmond O'Brien and Ann Blyth. A horse player finds himself framed for murder.

November 18, 1948
#315 "Sorry, Wrong Number"
    With Agnes Moorehead and Eleanor Audley. Same story and script from May 25, 1943.

November 25, 1948
#316 "The Screaming Woman"

Margaret O'Brien plays a little girl who hears a woman's screams originating from the ground. The adults dismiss her ramblings as a child's game, but they eventually realize she found a woman buried alive. Agnes Moorehead supplies the voice of the screaming woman from underneath the dirt, and received no on-air credit for her role. Based on the short story by Ray Bradbury, who recalled "*The Screaming Woman*'s finale was changed, because broadcast morality in those days would not allow the sort of unhappy ending I originally had in my story."

December 2, 1948
#317 "The Hands of Mr. Ottermole"

With Claude Rains and Vincent Price. A wisecracking reporter tries to make the police look foolish by showing up at the murder scenes before they do. One detective, with a dislike for being made a fool, decides to take care of the reporter in the same fashion as the murderer-on-the-loose. Based on the short story by Thomas Burke, who was pleased just weeks before to learn that a board of eminent mystery critics and writers cited this story as "the greatest mystery story of all time."

December 9, 1948
#318 "The Sisters"

With Rosalind Russell and Lurene Tuttle. Same story and script from February 3, 1944.

December 16, 1948
#319 "No Escape"

With James Cagney and Lurene Tuttle. In a plea for safe driving, *Suspense* and the sponsor Auto-Lite offer a driver-safety drama about a man who, on the evening he is to be given a safe driver award, drives reckless and causes an accident on the road. This radio script was adapted into a movie script, *Dark City*, released in theaters October of 1950.

December 23, 1948
#320 "Holiday Story"

With Herbert Marshall. Same story and script from December 23,

1943. This episode was billed as "a holiday story" by announcer Paul Frees. Based on the short story "Back for Christmas" by John Collier, the title of the drama was never delivered on the air, but is often referred to in mail order catalogs as "Holiday Story."

December 30, 1948
#321 "Break-Up"
William Bendix is an out-of-work police officer who finds employment as a bodyguard for a drug dealer. When a shootout occurs, Bendix must explain his actions to his friends on the force. Jack Benny makes a guest appearance after the drama.

January 6, 1949
#322 "To Find Help"
With Gene Kelly and Ethel Barrymore. Same story and script from January 18, 1945. Frank Sinatra and Agnes Moorehead were originally supposed to reprise their roles from the 1945 episode.

January 13, 1949
#323 "The Too-Perfect Alibi"
Danny Kaye creates an alibi for a murder case when he sneaks out of and back into a party unnoticed. But since he proves he didn't commit the murder, a close friend takes the rap.

January 20, 1949
#324 "If the Dead Could Talk"
Dana Andrews plays an acrobat who falls in love with the woman of his dreams. After plotting the murder of her lover in the form of an "accident," he changes his mind, causing his own death. Ted de Corsia co-stars.

January 27, 1949
#325 "The Thing in the Window"
With Robert Montgomery. Same story and script from December 19, 1946. Originally the drama "Odd Man Out" was supposed to be dramatized on this date.

February 3, 1949
#326 "Backseat Driver"
   Jim and Marian Jordan (Fibber McGee and Molly) are taken hostage by a fugitive murderer who sits in the backseat with a loaded gun pointed toward their heads.

February 10, 1949
#327 "De Mortius"
   Charles Laughton plays an English professor who discovers his wife's unfaithfulness when two visitors find him digging a grave-sized hole in the basement and mixing cement. Based on the short story by John Collier. Ronald Colman was originally supposed to play the lead.

February 17, 1949
#328 "Catch Me if You Can"
   With Raymond Burr, Jane Wyman and Frank Lovejoy. A scornful wife poisons her husband and before he dies, he confesses he saved and hid evidence against her. Buying on hours, she begins a search that will determine her future.

February 24, 1949
#329 "Where There's a Will"
   With Pamela and James Mason. Aunt Mary's nephew plots her death so he can inherit the money needed to pay off his gambling debts. James Mason wrote a book, *The Cat in Our Lives*, which was pitched on the air after the drama. The original title of this episode was "The Bedford Case."

March 3, 1949
#330 "The Lovebirds"
   A love-sick husband threatens to kill himself if his wife (played by Joan Fontaine) ever leaves him, and make it look like a murder from her own hands.

March 10, 1949
#331 "Three O'Clock"
   Van Heflin is a husband who plants a time bomb in the basement of his house to surprise his wife. Before he can leave, a robber breaks in and

ties the husband up. After he leaves with the loot, the husband is forced to watch the clock tick by as he remains tied.

March 17, 1949
#332 "Murder Through the Looking Glass"
Gregory Peck plays an amnesia victim who is accused of murder. Also stars Ed Begley.

March 24, 1949
#333 "Dead Ernest"
With Pat O'Brien. Same story and script from August 8, 1946.

March 31, 1949
#334 "You Can't Die Twice"
Edward G. Robinson plays Sam Brown, whose wife receives a phone call from the local police asking her to identify the body of her husband. They take advantage of the opportunity to file an insurance claim for a large payout. Robinson plays a role similar to the one he did for the big screen, *Scarlet Street* (1945).

April 7, 1949
#335 "Noose of Coincidence"
Ronald Colman is the owner of a bookstore who receives a visit from a customer who claims he can predict the future, including the store owner's death.

April 14, 1949
#336 "Murder in Black and White"
Edmund Gwenn plays a murderer who shoots his business partner and spends the next few days suspicious of everyone who lays claim that they just spoke to the dead man.

April 21, 1949
#337 "The Copper Tea Strainer"
Betty Grable plays Jeannie, who poisons her mother with enough medicine to knock a horse unconscious. Raymond Burr plays a supporting role in this episode.

April 28, 1949
#338 "The Lie"
　　With Mickey Rooney and Ed Begley. A father confesses to a crime he did not commit, but he does so to protect his son, the guilty party. Based on a short story by Cornell Woolrich.

May 5, 1949
#339 "Death has a Shadow"
　　Bob Hope plays a crooked lawyer who commits a murder and uses the law as a tool for walking away from a murder rap. His problems get worse when other parties get involved. William Conrad co-stars.

May 12, 1949
#340 "The Light Switch"
　　Claire Trevor plays a vengeful wife who plans to murder her unfaithful husband by turning on the gas from the stove, and sealing all the doors and windows. If her husband returns home and flicks on the light switch, an accidental explosion will kill her.

May 19, 1949
#341 "Consequence"
　　Jimmy Stewart plays a doctor who changes his identity and runs off with a younger woman. Stewart was originally supposed to star in a script entitled "Revenge," but did this one instead.

May 26, 1949
#342 "The Night Reveals"
　　With Fredric March and Jeanette Nolan. Same story and script from December 9, 1943.

June 2, 1949
#343 "The Ten Years"
　　With Joan Crawford. Same story and script from February 8, 1945. Joan Crawford was supposed to star in an episode entitled "The Hand," but the sponsors rejected the script.

June 9, 1949
#344 "The Lunch Kit"
John Lund plays a saboteur who plants a bomb in his lunch kit, but discovers events beyond his control are keeping him from leaving the plant while the clock ticks by. This script was written by Larry Marcus, which was originally broadcast on *The Whistler* on October 23, 1944 under the title "Death Carries a Lunch Kit."

June 16, 1949
#345 "The Trap"
Agnes Moorehead portrays Helen Crane, an emotionally distraught spinster who lives alone in her house. That is, until the day she finds evidence that someone is living inside her house without her knowledge.

June 23, 1949
#346 "Ghost Hunt"
Ralph Edwards is Smiley Smith, a local disc jockey, who, for publicity reasons, spends the night in a haunted house. He records his evening's diversion and when the police find his corpse, they play back the recording. This episode is considered by many old-time radio fans as one of the best of the series, and ranked as one of the ten scariest radio programs ever broadcast.

June 30, 1949
#347 "The Day I Died"
Joseph Cotten plays Wells Galaway, a lawyer who learns that his business partner died in a cabin fire. Since the body is mistaken as his, he assumes his partner's identity to claim the insurance money. This was the final episode of the season. This was the final episode produced and directed by Anton M. Leader.

September 1, 1949
#348 "Nightmare"
Gregory Peck plays a vengeful father who takes the law into his own hands when he learns of the identity of the hit-and-run driver who killed his son. Loosely adapted from the short story "Revenge" by Samuel Blas.

This is the first episode of the season. William Spier returns as the producer, and Norman MacDonnell takes over as director.

September 8, 1949
#349 "Chicken Feed"
   Ray Milland is an innocent picked up for robbery, and then freed from jail by the gang responsible for his dilemma.

September 15, 1949
#350 "Last Confession"
   Dorothy McGuire plays a woman in a nervous state who reads the newspaper accounts too closely and starts to suspect that she's the murderer in hiding.

September 22, 1949
#351 "Experiment 6-R"
   With John Lund and William Conrad. An assistant manager of a high-class hotel learns of an experimental powder known as "6-R." After getting a hold of this powder, he slips it in his boss's coffee and waits for the deadly results to kick in effect. William Spier, the producer of the series, did not attend the broadcasts throughout September because he needed time off for his wedding with June Havoc and their honeymoon.

September 29, 1949
#352 "Blind Date"
   With Charles Laughton and June Havoc. A young lady accepts a blind date into her house and when he pulls out a knife, she realizes she made a mistake.

October 6, 1949
#353 "The Defense Rests"
   With Van Johnson. Same story and script from March 9, 1944.

October 13, 1949
#354 "Account Payable"
   With Edward Arnold. Timothy wants happiness for his daughter and when his boss rejects the lovers' intentions, he plans to murder his boss.

October 20, 1949
#355 "Goodnight Mrs. Russell"
   With Bette Davis and Elliott Reid. A dysfunctional young man drugs a woman's food and when she wakes, she finds herself tied to a chair and a victim in her own house.

October 27, 1949
#356 "Momentum"
   Victor Mature plays Richard, an employee cheated out of his wages. When he tries to make back his earnings by robbing a safe, he is caught in the act and forced to kill his greedy boss.

November 3, 1949
#357 "The Search for Isabelle"
   With Red Skelton and Cathy Lewis. A meek bank teller becomes obsessed with finding Isabel LaRue, the former owner of his telephone number, and finds himself involved in an undercover investigation.

November 10, 1949
#358 "Murder of Aunt Delia"
   With Van Heflin and Howard McNear. When a hitch-hiker learns that his driver is a young nephew who is due for an inheritance from of his wealthy old aunt, he kills the nephew and assumes his identity. This script would later be dramatized on December 14, 1952 on *Hollywood Star Playhouse* with Cornel Wilde in the lead.

November 17, 1949
#359 "The Red-Headed Woman"
   With Lucille Ball and Desi Arnaz. Lucille Ball plays an embezzler who tries a new start on life, and meets up with a known fugitive from justice.

November 24, 1949
#360 "The Long Wait"
   Burt Lancaster plays an ex-con named Dan who was recently released from prison. Everyone assumes he'll exact revenge on the woman who set him up, played by Betty Lou Gerson, but is shocked when he helps her grow a successful business instead.

December 1, 1949
#361 "Mission Completed"
　　Jimmy Stewart plays a paralyzed World War II veteran whose sighting of a former P.O.W. torturer drives him back to health and murder. This broadcast is considered by *Suspense* fans as one of the best of the series. Gracie Allen makes a guest appearance after the drama. This episode was broadcast to commemorate the eighth anniversary of the bombing of Pearl Harbor.

December 8, 1949
#362 "For Love or Murder"
　　With Mickey Rooney. A young piano player falls for the wiles of a woman who convinces him to help murder her husband.

December 15, 1949
#363 "The Flame Blue Glove"
　　With Lana Turner. After testifying against a man on a murder charge, Sara falls in love with the accused and marries him. Did he marry her to protect the witness against him?

December 22, 1949
#364 "Double Entry"
　　With Eddie Cantor and Sidney Miller. Same story and script from December 20, 1945.

December 29, 1949
#365 "The Bullet"
　　Ida Lupino plays an emotionally-tormented woman who is fearful for her abusive, ex-con husband who thinks he knows how to run her lucrative business. His method of persuasion is to play Russian Roulette with a handgun. June Foray helps assist in the Auto-Lite commercials.

January 5, 1950
#366 "I Never Met the Dead Man"
　　Danny Kaye plays an innocent man accused of a murder he had no involvement with. As the clues pile up, so do the guilty of suspicion.

Suspense

January 12, 1950
#367 "Four Hours to Kill"
  Robert Taylor plays a murderer who discovers the phone was off the hook at the time of the murder. He has only a few hours to track down the witness before the police learn the truth. Joseph Kearns replaces Paul Frees as the announcer for *Suspense* beginning with this episode. This script would later be dramatized on June 19, 1950 on *Murder by Experts*.

January 19, 1950
#368 "The Escape of Lucy Abbott"
  William Powell plays an escaped inmate of the local sanitarium who tracks down the man responsible for his wife's death, and holds the victim's family hostage.

January 26, 1950
#369 "Mr. Diogenes"
  With Ozzie and Harriet Nelson. A prediction from a carnival scale comes true when Ozzie Nelson finds himself the possible winner of a contest with prize money.

February 2, 1950
#370 "Consideration"
  Rosalind Russell suspects her husband plans to kill her for insurance money.

February 9, 1950
#371 "The Butcher's Wife"
  Kirk Douglas is a playboy who falls for the wiles of a butcher's wife.

February 16, 1950
#372 "Murder Strikes Three Times"
  With Marlene Dietrich and Hans Conried. Same story and script from October 3, 1946.

February 23, 1950
#373 "Slow Burn"
  Dick Powell plays Johnny Wilson, a professional boxer, who can't

sustain his jealousy when he suspects a young rival of flirting with his wife. Richard Widmark was originally scheduled to play the lead.

March 2, 1950
#374 "Lady Killer"
Loretta Young is a female insurance inspector who is rescued by a man who might just be a killer.

March 9, 1950
#375 "Banquo's Chair"
With James Mason and Hans Conried. Same story and script from June 1, 1943. The drama "Crime Without Passion" was originally planned for this date.

March 16, 1950
#376 "Motive for Murder"
Alan Ladd plays the role of a detective, who sets out to prove his wife, accused of murder, innocent of the charges against her. John Dehner plays a supporting role. This script would later be dramatized on September 11, 1952 on *Jurgen's Hollywood Playhouse*.

March 23, 1950
#377 "One and One's a Lonesome"
Actor and future President Ronald Reagan plays the role of a war vet who returns to his old job at a lumberyard, and begins to make changes to the layout, including an illegal gambling hall. When the owner of the yard protests, Reagan plans to eliminate the protesting factor.

March 30, 1950
#378 "Blood Sacrifice"
Joseph Cotten is a playwright who has second thoughts about participating in a blood transfusion when be becomes an unwilling donor for a dying actor.

April 6, 1950
#379 "Salvage"
With Van Johnson and William Conrad. An unscrupulous wife plots the murder of her husband with a stranger, and the men face

off in a deadly game of cat and mouse. Cary Grant was originally scheduled to play the lead.

April 13, 1950
#380 "Six Feet Under"
Dan Dailey plays a traveling circus performer whose gift for being buried alive and surviving is legendary. When his wife wants to eliminate her husband, she arranges for an accident six feet under.

April 20, 1950
#381 "Pearls are a Nuisance"
With Ray Milland. Same story and script from April 19, 1945. Arthur Godfrey was originally scheduled to play the lead.

April 27, 1950
#382 "The Chain"
Agnes Moorehead guest stars as Lenora, who sends a vile chain letter to a rival that may or may not have caused his death. When her husband leaves her for what she's done, she finds herself alone in a house with a madman wanting to kill her.

May 4, 1950
#383 "Statement of Mary Blake"
Joan Bennett plays the title role, an assistant to a famous scientist, who just created a poison that kills instantly. After he uses his wife as a human guinea pig, the scientist informs the police that his new employee was responsible for his wife's death.

May 11, 1950
#384 "The Man in the Room"
John Lund plays a mystery writer who creates a fictional tale about a magazine editor who is murdered, and soon finds the facts of the story coming true.

May 18, 1950
#385 "Angel Face"
Claire Trevor portrays a nightclub singer who goes to extreme lengths

to find the proof that will clear her brother's name before his execution. Based on a short story by Cornell Woolrich.

May 25, 1950
#386 "Very Much Like a Nightmare"
Dennis O'Keefe is a dedicated employee who falls asleep at his desk, and wakes in the middle of the night to find robbers breaking into the building. Donald O'Connor was originally scheduled to play the lead.

June 1, 1950
#387 "A Case of Nerves"
Edward G. Robinson guest stars as Mr. Baker, who cleverly fakes a case of nerves so he can gain access to toxic medicine that he can use to murder his wife.

June 8, 1950
#388 "The Case of Henri Vibard"
Charles Boyer plays an unarmed man suffering from a case of amnesia, holding $20,000 in cash. When they learn his identity, he only adds more pieces of a puzzle when they discover his wife was convicted of his murder two years before.

June 15, 1950
#389 "Deadline"
With Broderick Crawford and John Hoyt. A crooked businessman in town agrees to help a newspaper editor build circulation on consideration of removing all scandalous print in future issues.

June 22, 1950
#390 "The One-Millionth Joe"
Jack Carson stars in a confusing comedy about a Hollywood airline that awards their one-millionth passenger prize money. A woman files suit when she claims she was pushed out of line, and the man who won the prize money is wanted for robbery.

June 29, 1950
#391 "Love, Honor, or Murder"
With Cathy and Elliott Lewis. Harry returns home one evening

with his boss's wallet in his hands. His wife gives him an ultimatum. If he doesn't keep the cash, she'll leave him for good. This was the final episode produced by William Spier. Norman MacDonnell stopped directing the series after this episode.

August 31, 1950
#392 "True Report"

Pat O'Brien plays an inspector who discovers that his son was involved with an auto accident, and files a false report to cover his kin's mistake. An old woman, who was a witness to the crime, may prove his downfall. Elliott Lewis takes over as producer and director beginning with this episode. The President of Auto-Lite makes a speech after the drama.

September 7, 1950
#393 "The Tip"

Ida Lupino is a housewife who is being held hostage by a gunman, waiting for her husband to come home so he can kill him. She has only a few hours to get a message out in hopes of saving her husband's life without the killer knowing.

September 14, 1950
#394 "Over the Bounding Main"

Dan Dailey is the unwilling victim of a murder plot conjured by his wife and her lover, the captain of a boat. He has no other choice but to survive on board the vessel until it docks.

September 21, 1950
#395 "The Crowd"

Dana Andrews plays a police lieutenant who discovers a killer's motive for getting away from the scene of a crime is to blend in with the on-looking crowd at each murder scene. Loosely adapted from the short story by Ray Bradbury, who recalled that he was not informed of the changes in "The Crowd." "I simply don't know why certain things were put into the story. I imagine they made the changes because they were afraid of fantasy, so they wrote in a real killer."

September 28, 1950
#396 "Fly-By-Night"
   Joseph Cotten is an innocent man who is forced to confess to a crime he did not commit, courtesy of third-degree methods by the local police.

October 5, 1950
#397 "The Rose Garden"
   With Miriam Hopkins and Jeanette Nolan. An old spinster scares a young tenant to death with stories and talk about murder and poison. The original title of this episode was "Miss Bone."

October 12, 1950
#398 "Rave Notice"
   Milton Berle plays an actor who commits murder and then applies his trade by acting insane to walk from a murder rap.

October 19, 1950
#399 "The Wages of Sin"
   Barbara Stanwyck plays Ruby Miller, an older woman, who was paid to have a murder occur in her house. The investigating detective knows her alibi will stick, but hoping to catch the real murderer, he keeps an eye out on the house to see when the payoff occurs.

October 26, 1950
#400 "Too Hot to Live"
   Richard Widmark plays a murderer who, after taking off his socks and shoes because of the summer heat, is forced to run for his life barefoot when he escapes police custody.

November 2, 1950
#401 "The Victoria Cross"
   Herbert Marshall is an English Schoolmaster who falls victim to a young student's blackmail when the child learns of his personal affections with a young female student.

November 9, 1950
#402 "Blood on the Trumpet"
   With William Holden and Barton Yarborough. A wannabe trumpet

player in New Orleans finds himself playing the blues when his wife is murdered. Ziggy Elman, who played with Tommy Dorsey, supplies the trumpet music for this episode.

November 16, 1950
#403 "On a Country Road"

Cary Grant and Cathy Lewis play a loving couple trapped in their stalled car while the radio reports a mad woman on the loose murdering people. One woman screams outside the window asking to be brought in for safety. Is she the murderer they fear?

November 23, 1950
#404 "Going, Going, Gone"

Ozzie and Harriet Nelson play a couple who purchase a locked trunk at an auction. When they open their treasure chest back at the house, they find a collection of valuable diamonds and rubies.

November 30, 1950
#405 "The Lady in the Red Hat"

With Van Heflin and Joan Banks. A reporter receives a note from a man who claims to be the "Thirteenth Apostle," a killer on the loose that has avoided the police. If he meets the stranger at the rendezvous, who can he expect to see? The original title of this drama was "The Thirteenth Apostle."

December 7, 1950
#406 "After the Movies"

Ray Milland is a juror who finds an envelope containing enough cash to warrant a "fix" in the verdict of a court case. When he rejects the offer, he learns his wife has been kidnapped to influence the verdict.

December 14, 1950
#407 "A Killing in Abilene"

With Alan Ladd, Parley Baer and Barton Yarborough. A western story about a stranger who rides into town searching for the killer of his brother, only to learn the killer is already dead.

December 21, 1950
#408 "Christmas for Carol"
   Dennis Day plays a father-to-be who needs money for his wife and baby, so he takes advantage of the holiday festivities to commit a theft.

December 28, 1950
#409 "A Ring for Marya"
   Cornel Wilde plays John, who proposes to his fiancée, played Irene Tedrow, and shortly after, asks her to commit an arson for an insurance payoff. When something goes wrong and his fiancée gets seriously burned, he disregards her existence.

January 4, 1951
#410 "Alibi Me"
   With Mickey Rooney and Tommy Bernard. Mickey Rooney plays George, a young street punk who commits a murder and spends the rest of the day finding someone who'll front him an alibi before the detectives catch up to him.

January 11, 1951
#411 "Vamp Till Dead"
   Ginger Rogers plays Amy, hired by a writer to take dictation. The writer was once accused of murdering his wife but the case was never proven. Amy happens to be the sister of the dead wife. Also stars Jeanette Nolan.

January 18, 1951
#412 "The Well-Dressed Corpse"
   Eve Arden stars as Ruth Franklin, voted the best-dressed woman in town. When she meets the love of her life, she finds herself committing a murder to cover her mistake.

January 25, 1951
#413 "Aria for Murder"
   With Ezio Pinza and Howard McNear. An opera singer confesses to murdering his boss. When the police investigate, they find blackmail as a motive. Ezio Pinza was a celebrated opera singer whose claim to fame came when he starred in a production of *Don Giovanni* for the Metropolitan Opera.

February 1, 1951
#414 "Fragile. Contents: Death"
Paul Douglas plays a postmaster in search of a package with a time bomb. Could the package have already been delivered to its destination?

February 8, 1951
#415 "The Windy City Six"
Fred MacMurray is a musician who witnesses a murder during a police raid, and finds himself the victim of the murderer. To help set the mood for this episode, Red Nichols and his Five Pennies supplies jazz music of the "Roaring Twenties." Fred MacMurray played the baritone sax in high school and with a Big Band, years before this broadcast.

February 15, 1951
#416 "The Death Parade"
Agnes Moorehead plays Ellen Johnson, a woman who finds a letter warning of a murder. In the tradition of *Sorry, Wrong Number*, she sets out to seek the victim before the murder occurs.

February 22, 1951
#417 "Backseat Driver"
Jim and Marian Jordan (Fibber McGee and Molly) reprise their roles from the February 3, 1949 broadcast.

March 1, 1951
#418 "The Gift for Jumbo Brannigan"
William Bendix plays the title character, an ex-safe cracker who is released from prison. After meeting with the son he never saw in years, he discovers the son took after his trade.

March 8, 1951
#419 "A Vision of Death"
Ronald Colman plays a stage mentalist who discovers his assistant has the gift for reading minds. No sooner does he discover this fact, than she gives him a prediction of his death. Charles Calvert and Cathy Lewis are in the supporting cast.

March 15, 1951
#420 "Strange for a Killer"
   Van Johnson returns home to find his wife and son being held hostage. The police want to handle the situation without gunplay, but Johnson eventually enters the house to talk to the escaped killer.

March 22, 1951
#421 "Three Lethal Words"
   With Joan Crawford and Don Diamond. A woman scorned decides to have a jar of acid scar her boyfriend's face.

March 29, 1951
#422 "Death Notice"
   Jack Carson plays the owner of a traveling circus, who tricks a drunken lion tamer to enter the cage, unarmed. With the boyfriend gone, he now has a chance with Annette.

April 5, 1951
#423 "Murder in G-Flat"
   Jack Benny plays Hercules Remmington, professional piano tuner, who accidentally switches bags with a subway passenger and soon finds himself $25,000 richer. With Clayton Post and Paul Frees in the cast.

April 12, 1951
#424 "Early to Death"
   Husband-and-wife team Lucille Ball and Desi Arnaz guest as a clever couple who steal a $300,000 bankroll and sky dive out of an airplane with the loot. After hiding the money and clearing their name with law authorities, they find a blackmailer in the scheme.

April 19, 1951
#425 "The Rescue"
   Jimmy Stewart is Lee, a man trying to talk a woman off the ledge.

April 26, 1951
#426 "The Thirteenth Sound"
   Anne Baxter shoots her husband and then throws the guilt on another party.

May 3, 1951
#427 "When the Bough Breaks"
  Rosalind Russell guests. A reporter suspects a husband of killing his wife.

May 10, 1951
#428 "Death on My Hands"
  Phil Harris and Alice Faye star in this top-notch John Michael Hayes script about a musician who accidentally shoots a fan and is forced to deal with a mob outside the hotel that wants to hang him. Film director Alfred Hitchcock was a fan of this radio program and listened faithfully weekly. This episode caught his attention and shortly after, Hitchcock hired John Michael Hayes as a scriptwriter for eight of his films including *Rear Window* (1954). Barbara Whiting has a small role as the murdered fan.

May 17, 1951
#429 "Another Man's Poison"
  Charles Boyer plays the role of Claude, who finds a package containing $100,000 and as a Good Samaritan, turns it over to the police. The police then arrest him for theft and a murder charge. Also in the cast, Herb Butterfield and Paul Frees. This drama was originally scheduled to be broadcast the week before.

May 24, 1951
#430 "Fresh Air, Sunshine and Murder"
  With Jeff Chandler and Clayton Post. A health studio is the setting for jealousy and murder.

May 31, 1951
#431 "Overdrawn"
  Dick Powell is Mr. Farley, a bank teller, who takes advantage of a bank robbery by pocketing some of the money for himself.

June 7, 1951
#432 "Tell You Why I Shouldn't Die"
  Richard Widmark is Charlie, who holds a former love rival at gunpoint.

June 14, 1951
#433 "The Truth About Jerry Baxter"
   With Gregory Peck and John Dehner. Jerry Baxter is released from custody after he turns state's evidence, given a second chance for a new life. When he is picked up for possession of narcotics, the police suspect he's being framed.

June 21, 1951
#434 "The Greatest Thief in the World"
   With Pamela and James Mason. Scotland Yard is baffled regarding the identity of "The Squire," a jewel thief who has been successful so far. James Mason plays the role of Peter Mariot, a suspect in the case.

June 28, 1951
#435 "The Case for Dr. Singer"
   With Edgar Barrier, Larry Thor and Lawrence Dobkin. A man is shot down in front of the U.S. Embassy in Sweden and before he dies, reveals a top secret project involving a Nuclear-Thermal device. This script was written by Blake Edwards, who would later direct the Pink Panther movies and *Breakfast at Tiffany's* (1961).

Monday — 8:00 p.m. to 8:30 p.m. (E.S.T.)

August 27, 1951
#436 "Report on the Jolly Death Riders"
   With William Holden and Sam Edwards. A gang of teenagers is suspected in a crime involving the death of a woman in an auto wreck. The President of the National Safety Council speaks after the drama. Beginning with this new season, the sponsor, Auto-Lite, and the producer, Elliott Lewis, agreed to offer more episodes based on true crime stories rather than fiction.

September 3, 1951
#437 "The Steel River Prison Break"
   With Jeff Chandler and Barton Yarborough. Three convicts take advantage of the rising flood waters to escape from prison, but fail to co-operate together when it comes to covering their tracks.

September 10, 1951
#438 "The Evil of Adelaide Winters"
   Agnes Moorehead stars in the title role of a fake medium, who creates séances bringing back dead war soldiers for grieving parents. When she cons the wealthiest customer into marrying her, she expects a big reward for her services.

September 17, 1951
#439 "Neil Cream, Doctor of Poison"
   With Charles Laughton and Charles Davis. A dramatization of the famed Neil Cream, who poisoned three women and threw the blame on another man.

September 24, 1951
#440 "The McKay College Basketball Scandal"
   Tony Curtis plays Fred Hudson, a star player for the college basketball team, who accepts a bribe to ensure the outcome of a big game. The original title of this episode was "The Losing Game of Frederick Hudson."

October 1, 1951
#441 "The Case Study of a Murderer"
   With Jeanne Crain, Howard McNear and William Conrad. The newspaper reports of a murderer, who strangles pregnant women and their husbands, fascinated with the articles, starts to suspect he is the killer. Especially since his wife just discovered that she's pregnant. This episode was based on actual medical reports.

October 8, 1951
#442 "Betrayal in Vienna"
   With Herbert Marshall and Herb Butterfield. A spy for a foreign country harbors a secret that is used against him during a blackmail scheme.

October 15, 1951
#443 "The Flame"
   With Cornel Wilde and Sidney Miller. Andy is a pyromaniac who is just looking for an excuse to set a house or building on fire. His

deliverance comes in the form of a neighbor who needs insurance money to pay the medical bills.

October 22, 1951
#444 "The Log of the Marne"
With Ray Milland and Anthony Ellis. A British naval ship is attacked by Chinese communists. Based on the famous book *Yangste Incident* by Lawrence Earl.

October 29, 1951
#445 "The Hunting of Bob Lee"
With Richard Widmark and Cathy Lewis. Bob Lee finds himself hunted by a friend and witness to the man he killed. The game of cat and mouse during the Civil War concludes with a fight to the death.

November 5, 1951
#446 "The Trials of Thomas Shaw"
With Joseph Cotten, Irene Tedrow and Lou Krugman. An innocent man is released from custody and persecuted by the town folk who feel he is guilty of murder.

November 12, 1951
#447 "The Mission of the Betta"
With John Hodiak and Charles Calvert. Months before our entry into World War II, a United States submarine is given the task of transporting a dozen Australians from Japanese territory.

November 19, 1951
#448 "The Embezzler"
With John Lund, Joseph Kearns and Mary Jane Croft. John Lund plays the role of a con artist who profiles the employees of the largest banks and centers his "land deals" on the man they chose as their victim to take the fall.

November 26, 1951
#449 "A Misfortune in Pearls"
With Frank Lovejoy, Joan Banks and Charles Calvert. Mark steals

a valuable necklace too high for the price range of most black market operators, so he returns it to the owner for the reward money.

December 3, 1951
#450 "A Murderous Revision"
   With Richard Widmark and Charlotte Lawrence. A scriptwriter for radio mystery programs takes his revenge against the producer and director who bosses him around like a shepherd with a flock of sheep.

December 10, 1951
#451 "Blackjack to Kill"
   With Victor Mature and Clayton Post. A hired assassin travels to Havana to perform a job and discovers his intended target is on to him. Gene Kelly was originally scheduled to play the lead. The original title of this episode was "Assassin."

December 17, 1951
#452 "The Case History of a Gambler"
   With John Hodiak, Lillian Buyeff and Clayton Post. Matthew Miller establishes an illegal gambling ring and makes many enemies in the process. This episode was scripted by sound man Ross Murray.

December 24, 1951
#453 " 'Twas the Night Before Christmas"
   With Greer Garson and Anne Whitfield. Kathy stays up late on Christmas Eve, waiting the arrival of her parents who are flying in from Paris during a snowstorm. What no one has told Kathy is the plane crashed the night before.

December 31, 1951
#454 "Rogue Male"
   With Herbert Marshall. After failing to assassinate Adolf Hitler, an English hit-man is apprehended and hunted down for sport. Based on the novel by Geoffrey Household.

January 7, 1952
#455 "The Case Against Loo Doc"
   With Jeff Chandler and Sam Edwards. Loo Doc is the leader of a

Tong who strikes a friendship with a reporter for a local newspaper. The police want to arrest Loo Doc but the reporter is willing to test the bounds of his friendship to ensure the safety of his friend. The original title of this episode was "Chinatown."

January 14, 1952
#456 "The Fall River Tragedy"
 With Agnes Moorehead and Peggy Webber. Testimony during the trial of the murder of Lizzie Borden's parents sheds light on what would become the crime of the century.

January 21, 1952
#457 "The Perfectionist"
 With Richard Basehart and Charlotte Lawrence. A hired killer goes from professional to amateur when his recent cadaver victim disappears without his knowledge. Clifton Webb was originally scheduled to star in the lead.

January 28, 1952
#458 "Carnival"
 Joseph Cotten plays a mechanical man in a carnival that has been under the spell of his crooked boss. In order to leave his job, the boss has to be killed. Charles Boyer was originally supposed to play the lead.

February 4, 1952
#459 "The Treasure Chest of Don Jose"
 With J. Carrol Naish and Clayton Post. The lost treasure of Don Jose has been unearthed by a hurricane and the treasure hunt is on. But the treasure has a curse to anyone who finds it.

February 11, 1952
#460 "Odd Man Out"
 With James Mason and Ben Wright. Based on the novel by Frederick Lawrence Green. A wounded member of the Irish Republican Army has to decide whether to trust an Englishman offering assistance. James Mason reprises the same role he played on the 1947 movie.

February 18, 1952
#461 "The Track of the Cat"

With Richard Widmark and Sharon Douglas. Two men track through the snowy mountains in search of the large black panther rumored to trek a killing spree on the first snowfall of the winter. Based on the Walter Van Tilburg Clark novel.

February 25, 1952
#462 "A Killing in Las Vegas"

With Linda Darnell. Dixie's life has been attempted twice in the same week and it doesn't take long for her to discover that her husband has been behind the attempts. Barbara Stanwyck was originally scheduled to play the lead.

March 3, 1952
#463 "The Thirty-Nine Steps"

With Herbert Marshall, Tudor Owen and Ben Wright. A tourist in London must prove his innocence of the murder of a female spy. His chase through the London streets leads to the discovery of secret documents and codes being smuggled out of the country. Based on the novel by John Buchan.

March 10, 1952
#464 "A Watery Grave"

With Joseph Cotten and Mary Jane Croft. A district attorney accepts a lucrative offer in exchange for the name of a silent witness. When the murder attempt is foiled, he suspects his life is in danger. Ray Milland was originally scheduled to play the lead.

March 17, 1952
#465 "The Wreck of the Old '97"

Frank Lovejoy plays Joseph A. Brody in an exceptional production that blends the folk ballad "The Ship That Never Returned," with a dramatic recreation of a real train wreck. One of the most exciting episodes of the series, this episode caused the network to receive a number of compliments by postal mail. As a result, producer/director Elliott Lewis offered a number of musical productions for the series.

March 24, 1952
#466 "A Murder of Necessity"

With Robert Young and Paula Winslowe. The plot is almost the same as the broadcast of January 12, 1950. The original title of this episode was "Backfire" and "Frame Up."

March 31, 1952
#467 "The Lady Pamela"

With Deborah Kerr and Peter Leeds. Kerr plays the role of Pamela, a customer who happens to be in the same store when a robbery occurred, and is accused of the crime. Two years later, released from prison, she seeks out those responsible for her incarceration. This radio drama was originally titled "The Colonel's Lady."

April 7, 1952
#468 "Remember Me?"

With Dan Duryea and Charlotte Lawrence. A young punk robs a store and shoots the owner. When he follows the witness to the crime to her house, he discovers she had a school-girl crush on him years back.

April 14, 1952
#469 "Mate Bram"

With Richard Widmark and Joan Banks. The crew on board a sailing vessel is frightened of a hatchet murderer, who has already taken the life of the Captain, his wife and another crew member.

April 21, 1952
#470 "The Diary of Captain Scott"

With Herbert Marshall, Charles Davis and June Whitley. Captain Scott leads an expedition through the frozen land of the arctic. Told through the diary entries of his journal, his men are growing weaker by the day. The original title of this episode was "Scott's Last Expedition."

April 28, 1952
#471 "The Shooting of Billy the Kid"

With Frank Lovejoy, Parley Baer and William Conrad. A biography of the famed fugitive, who killed sixteen men while trying to outrun the law. Just two days before this broadcast, William Conrad and Parley Baer starred as Marshal Matt Dillon and Deputy Chester in the premiere radio episode of *Gunsmoke*, and the plot concerned their discovery and "naming" of a young criminal known as Billy the Kid.

May 5, 1952
#472 "Frankie and Johnny"
With Dinah Shore and Lamont Johnson. A musical presentation, based on the folk song of the same name. Johnny feels scorned when she learns that her man done her wrong, and shoots him to death. Singer Dinah Shore contributes her talents for this production. Elliott Lewis, the producer and director, recalled, "It was the first time Dinah Shore has done anything of this type. When we asked her if she'd like to play the lead she said she'd love it. Our only problem at all on the show was asking Dinah in what key she'd like to sing the role. She said E flat. That was the last word we had with her until she did the production."

May 12, 1952
#473 "The Missing Person"
With Macdonald Carey and Paula Winslowe. A crusading newspaper reporter smells a human interest story when a concert violinist vanishes.

May 19, 1952
#474 "The Flight of the Bumble Bee"
With Fred MacMurray and Edgar Barrier. Low on fuel and one man wounded, the crew of a B-29 flier is forced to strip the plane to the bare necessity in hopes of arriving home safely, after having been attacked by the Japanese during World War II.

May 26, 1952
#475 "The Death of Me"
With George Murphy, Irene Tedrow and Charlotte Lawrence. Harry Sawyer witnesses a murder at the lumberyard. After discovering that the victim was intended to be him, Harry discovers that his wife and the foreman are responsible for a second attempt on his life.

June 2, 1952
#476 "A Good and Faithful Servant"

Jack Benny plays Mr. Fenton, a bank employee, who overnight becomes the most respected and popular employee when he is found alive and well, after having been locked inside the vault by bank thieves.

June 9, 1952
#477 "Concerto for a Killer and Eye-Witnesses"

Edward escapes police custody and after purchasing a gun, seeks out the men responsible for his present-day situation. Elliott Lewis, the producer and director of the radio series, stars in the lead. William Conrad plays a supporting role.

September 15, 1952
#478 "Sorry, Wrong Number"

With Agnes Moorehead. Same story and script from August 21, 1943.

September 22, 1952
#479 "Jack Ketch"

With Charles Laughton and Joan Banks. A biographical drama based on the life of Jack Ketch, also known as John Price, a barbaric hangman who became synonymous with a hangman.

September 29, 1952
#480 "Vidocq's Final Case"

With Charles Boyer, Parley Baer and Ben Wright. Francois Eugene Vidocq is called in by the French police to help assist in solving the plague of robberies that have the police baffled.

October 6, 1952
#481 "The Diary of Doctor Pritchard"

With Sir Cedric Hardwicke. Doctor Pritchard attempts to poison his wife but his mother-in-law stands between him and his success. The original title of this episode was "Dr. Pritchard."

October 13, 1952
#482 "How Long is the Night"

With Richard Widmark and Jack Kruschen. A photographer

stranded on a radioactive island finds himself haunted by the moaning sounds of a beast that can't be seen after sunset.

October 20, 1952
#483 "The Death of Barbara Allen"

With Anne Baxter and Jeanette Nolan. A musical presentation bridged with the folk song of the same name. Shawn shoots Willie out of jealousy and Barbara Allen takes the law into her own hands.

October 27, 1952
#484 "Allen in Wonderland"

With Cornel Wilde and Edgar Barrier. A lawyer is forced into committing an assassination by a gang of influential killers. Larry Thor and Charles Calvert, who played the roles of Danny Clover and Sgt. Gino Tartaglia on the radio program *Broadway is My Beat*, played the same characters for this episode.

November 3, 1952
#485 "Frankenstein"

With Herbert Marshall and Paul Frees. A scientist creates life from the remains of dead humans. When the creature wants him to make a wife, the scientist rejects the offer. Soon after his marriage, the scientist discovers his wife the victim of his monster.

November 10, 1952
#486 "The Frightened City"

Frank Lovejoy plays Nick, a war vet who returns home and starts asking questions about the whereabouts of his brother, who was also in the service. No one cooperates with his questioning, except for a young woman, played by Lovejoy's real-life wife, Joan Banks.

November 17, 1952
#487 "Death and Miss Turner"

With Agnes Moorehead, Paul Frees and Jeanette Nolan. Amnesia victim Miss Turner is encouraged by her doctor to continue her hobby of painting, in hopes of remembering why she is in her present state. This script was written for *Suspense* by William Spier.

November 24, 1952
#488 "Man Alive"

With Paul Douglas and William Conrad. An investigative reporter close to the heels of Communist spies is murdered for learning too much. He returns from the dead long enough to assist the F.B.I. in arresting the foreign spies. This script was written for *Suspense* by William Spier.

December 1, 1952
#489 "The Big Heist"

With John Hodiak, Charles Calvert and Herb Butterfield. A pool hustler is given an offer to perform the biggest hustle of his career, by distracting a security officer at the bank where his friends commit the largest heist in the city's history.

December 8, 1952
#490 "Joker Wild"

With Cathy and Elliott Lewis. A comedian who isn't taken seriously picks up a female hitch-hiker and kills her in cold blood. Even when he confesses the crime to the local police, he still finds himself laughed at.

December 15, 1952
#491 "The Man with Two Faces"

With Lloyd Nolan and Martha Wentworth. A detective is puzzled when he finds the remains of a dead man with more teeth than a normal man his age, fake hair and an awful suit. Why disguise a corpse when it wasn't meant to be found in the first place?

December 22, 1952
#492 "Arctic Rescue"

With Joseph Cotten and Clayton Post. A sailing vessel charts the unexplored frozen north in search of a previous expedition, hoping to find survivors. After getting trapped in the ever-growing icebergs, they find a means of escape from the Christmas star. This episode was written by one of the sound technicians at CBS.

December 29, 1952
#493 "Melody in Dreams"

With John Lund, Anne Whitfield and Sam Edwards. A concerned

father turns his daughter over to the narcotics division when he discovers she has illegal drugs on her possession.

January 5, 1953
#494 "The Mystery of Edwin Drood" Part One
Charles Dickens' unfinished novel receives an impressive treatment for this two-part presentation, with Herbert Marshall and Betty Hartford in the cast. Edwin Drood returns to town with a bright future ahead of him, and is engaged to be married. His uncle, John Jaspar, a music teacher, is determined to find out who murdered his nephew.

January 12, 1953
#495 "The Mystery of Edwin Drood" Part Two
With Herbert Marshall and Betty Hatrford. John hides the corpse of his nephew to eliminate suspicion of his involvement, and begins questioning the only possible suspect for the crime.

January 19, 1953
#496 "Gold of the Adomar"
With John Hodiak. The great sailing vessel known as *The Adomar* sunk over 30 years ago, taking to the bottom of the sea the largest gold shipment known to man. An old man, dying from a bad heart, reveals the location of the *Adomar* to a deep sea diver. This episode was scripted by sound man Ross Murray.

January 26, 1953
#497 "The Spencer Brothers"
With Richard Widmark and John Dehner. Months after the Civil War, three brothers return from the battlefield to find themselves homeless without a dollar to their name. After killing a man while robbing a bank, they become fugitives from the law.

February 2, 1953
#498 "Plan X"
In the year 2053, an Earth spaceship lands on the red planet Mars to discover the Martians friendly and hospitable. Radio comedian Jack Benny plays the role of a Martian in this episode.

February 9, 1953
#499 "The Man Who Cried Wolf"
  With William Powell and John Dehner. When a Russian is threatened with deportation, he claims he possesses papers from the Russian Embassy that prevents them from doing so. Having applied this tactic more than once, the police do not believe him. Jeff Chandler was originally scheduled to play the lead.

February 16, 1953
#500 "The Love and Death of Joaquin Murieta"
  With Victor Mature, Parley Baer and Harry Bartell. A Texas Ranger is determined to apprehend the Mexican outlaw who has been responsible for robbing stagecoaches in the territory. He succeeds in his task, and preserves the head of the bandit in a glass jar.

February 23, 1953
#501 "The St. James Infirmary Blues"
  Set in the roaring twenties, Rosemary Clooney guests as Sheela, a singer who wants to get in on the ground floor with a gangster so she can steal his money. Clooney had just appeared on the cover of *Time* the same week of this broadcast.

March 2, 1953
#502 "The Storm"
  With Frank Lovejoy and Joan Banks. Larry Weston and his wife are stage performers who are asked to leave when a hurricane makes landfall. Against his wife's wishes, Larry remains to prove to himself that he is stronger than Mother Nature. This was one of many episodes to star real-life husband and wife Frank Lovejoy and Joan Banks. Joan was often a guest in a supporting role when her husband appeared on *Suspense*.

March 9, 1953
#503 "The Dead Alive"
  With Herbert Marshall, Mary Jane Croft and Jeanette Nolan. Based on the story by Wilkie Collins. Philip visits his cousins in New England and stumbles on a crime of murder.

March 16, 1953
#504 "The Mountain"

With John Hodiak. Three mountain climbers brave the treacherous slopes of the tallest mountain in the world. When one of the climbers plunges to his death, another suspects it wasn't an accident.

March 23, 1953
#505 "The Signalman"

With Joseph Kearns and Agnes Moorehead. A magazine writer returns to her old hometown and meets a railroad signalman who tells her of the haunting he receives from the ghost trains of the past. When she laughs at his story, he invites her to stay the night and see for herself. Based on a short story by Charles Dickens.

March 30, 1953
#506 "Tom Dooley"

With Joseph Cotten and Lt. Colonel Sherman D. Cosgrove of the U.S. Army. Based on the folk song of the same name, this musical drama tells the story of young Tom Dooley, who returned from the war (the Civil War) to find his woman in love with another man. Jealous, he kills his old flame and flees the law.

April 6, 1953
#507 "Around the World"

In 1908, the first International auto race became a landmark in Olympic achievement. Every nation of the world wanted to compete and this story about hot engines and danger on the race track gains momentum with a cast that includes Van Heflin, Alan Hewitt and Steve Roberts.

This episode aired "live" from the Grand Ballroom of the Waldorf Astoria Hotel in New York City to commemorate the auto show held there. This episode was originally titled "The Great Auto Race Around the World" and "The Auto Race That Stirred the World."

April 13, 1953
#508 "The Great Train Robbery"

With Fred MacMurray and Hy Averback. In need of quick cash, Walter and his friend rob a train hundreds of miles away from town, and return in time to carry the alibi of a business trip to his wife.

April 20, 1953
#509 "Public Defender"
   With Frank Lovejoy and Whitfield Connor. A killer is picked up by the police for a crime he did not commit, but cannot fess his true alibi because he killed a young lady at the same time. In a strange twist of fate, his public defender turns out to be the father of his victim. Robert Ryan was originally scheduled to play the lead. This episode was interrupted for a special CBS News bulletin regarding the present status of the Korean War.

April 27, 1953
#510 "The Man Within"
   With Herbert Marshall and Ben Wright. A witness to an unspeakable crime agrees to testify in court, and soon finds himself on the run from people who want him silenced. He seeks shelter from the killers but the young lady suspects he has an ulterior motive. Based on the novel by Graham Greene.

May 4, 1953
#511 "Othello" Part One
   With Richard Widmark, Cathy and Elliott Lewis. The first of a two-part presentation adapted from the stage play by William Shakespeare. Iago is upset when Othello, the moor of Venice, marries Desdemona, a young lady from a wealthy class family. He sets plans in motion that will result in the demise of Othello.

May 11, 1953
#512 "Othello" Part Two
   With Richard Widmark, Cathy and Elliott Lewis. The concluding chapter of this two-part drama. Iago plants Desdemona's handkerchief in Cassio's possession, and then retrieves it to prove to Othello that his best friend has been cheating on him. Out of anger, Othello strangles the life out of Desdemona.

May 18, 1953
#513 "Vial of Death"
   With Lloyd Nolan, Howard McNear and Joseph Kearns. A scientist reports his car stolen to the police, and explains the urgent need to retrieve the vehicle before the vial of Cholera in the backseat is discovered and opened by the thief.

May 25, 1953
#514 "Pigeon in the Cage"
   With Dick Haymes and Charlotte Lawrence. A witness to a murder finds himself caught between floors in an elevator when the power goes out. The murderers make one attempt after another to silence the witness while he is trapped with no way out.

June 1, 1953
#515 "A Vision of Death"
   With Ronald Colman and Mary Jane Croft. Same story and script from March 8, 1951.

June 8, 1953
#516 "The Mystery of the Marie Celeste"
   With Van Heflin, William Conrad and Jeanette Nolan. One of the world's greatest unsolved mysteries, the *Marie Celeste* was found drifting off the coast of North Africa in 1872, with no crew on board and no evidence to suggest why. Van Heflin enjoyed sailing so he was chosen to star for this episode.

September 14, 1953
#517 "A Message to Garcia"
   With Richard Widmark and Lillian Buyeff. An American agent travels to Jamaica and Cuba to gain information for the Government regarding the political status of General Garcia, who may help in the cause of freedom with an impending war brewing between Spain and the U.S.

September 21, 1953
#518 "The Empty Chair"
   With Agnes Moorehead and Joseph Kearns. A teacher observes the tell-tale signs of one of her students being careless on the road, and

pleads a concern for traffic safety. The President of Auto-Lite makes a speech after the drama.

September 28, 1953
#519 "Hellfire"
   With John Hodiak and Dick Ryan. A fire breaks out on an oil field and the firemen are powerless to stop the blaze since the oil continues to fuel the fire.

October 5, 1953
#520 "Action"
   With Herbert Marshall and Ellen Morgan. After receiving the fatal diagnosis from his doctor, a man with nothing left to live for decides to brave the steepest slope on an ice-covered mountain. Based on the story by Charles Edward Montague. Due to a malfunction in the studio, part of the country was unable to hear the conclusion of this episode. This same script was previously dramatized on July 21, 1949 on *Escape*.

October 12, 1953
#521 "The Shot"
   With Van Heflin and Jack Webb. Two young men settle their differences with a duel. When one man misses, his opponent chooses to take his shot at a later date. There are no women in the cast of this episode.

October 19, 1953
#522 "My True Love's Hair"
   With Jeff Chandler and Martha Wentworth. Based on the folk ballad of the same name, a young man falls in love with a woman who gets her just desserts when she tosses him aside like scraps at the dinner table.

October 26, 1953
#523 "Dutch Schultz"
   With Broderick Crawford and Jay Novello. A biographical dramatization on the life of a notorious gangster, who meets his match when he faces the Syndicate.

November 2, 1953
#524 "Ordeal in Donner Pass"
   With Edmond O'Brien and Paula Winslowe. The true events of the Donner Party are dramatized without too much of the gory details. A covered wagon gets caught in a mountain-peak blizzard and when the food gets low, members of the party are forced to turn to cannibalism.

November 9, 1953
#525 "Needle in a Haystack"
   With William Holden and Steve Roberts. The crew of a U.S. Navy boat is forced to swim to shore and find a way to clear a Korean harbor when explosive mines floating in the water pose a threat to the boat. Based on a story by Captain Walter Karig. There are no women in the cast of this episode.

November 16, 1953
#526 "The Moonstone" Part One
   With Peter Lawford. A woman inherits "The Moonstone," a huge diamond that supposedly places a curse on the owner. When the diamond is stolen, everyone is suspect. Film director Alfred Hitchcock's daughter, Patricia Hitchcock, plays the role of Miss Bettredge. Based on the novel by Wilkie Collins.

November 23, 1953
#527 "The Moonstone" Part Two
   With Peter Lawford and Ben Wright. One year after the theft, new clues shed light on the unsolved mystery, and a corpse proves to be the solution to the caper.

November 30, 1953
#528 "The Wreck of the Maid of Athens"
   With Agnes Moorehead and Joseph Kearns. The crew on board the *Maid of Athens* feels it's a bad omen to have a woman on board, even if she is the Captain's wife. When the ship catches on fire, the crew wants to kill her before they reach dry land. Based on the personal diary of Emily Wooldridge.

December 7, 1953
#529 "Trent's Last Case"
   With Ronald Colman and Gloria Ann Simpson. A British newspaper reporter sets out to solve a murder case without the assistance of the police detectives.

December 14, 1953
#530 "The Mystery of the Marie Roget"
   With Cornel Wilde and John Dehner. Based on the short story by Edgar Allen Poe. A young lady named Mary Cecilia Rogers is murdered.

December 21, 1953
#531 " 'Twas the Night Before Christmas"
   With Greer Garson and Anne Whitfield. Same story and script from December 24, 1951. A repeat performance of "On a Country Road" with Frank Lovejoy was originally scheduled for this date, but dramatized two weeks later.

December 28, 1953
#532 "The Queen's Ring"
   With Pamela and James Mason. Lord Essex attempts to overthrow the Queen and is soon apprehended and found guilty of treason. Awaiting his execution, his chance of escape comes in the form of the Queen's ring.

January 4, 1954
#533 "On a Country Road"
   With Frank Lovejoy and Joan Banks. Same story and script from November 16, 1950. This drama was originally scheduled for broadcast on December 21, 1953.

January 11, 1954
#534 "One Man Crime Wave"
   With Dana Andrews and Charlotte Lawrence. A killer is roaming the streets and the police have very few clues to work with.

January 18, 1954
#535 "The Face is Familiar"
   With Jack Benny and Sheldon Leonard. Radio comedian Jack Benny plays Tom Jones, a man who looks so plain that no one can describe his physical features or attire. Bank thieves take advantage of Tom Jones by using him in a robbery. This episode was adapted for a television episode of *The General Electric Theater* with Jack Benny reprising the same role.

January 25, 1954
#536 "Want Ad"
   With Robert Cummings and Mrs. Cornelius Vanderbilt Whitney. A burglar makes his trade by reading the classifieds for valuable sale items.

February 1, 1954
#537 "Never Follow a Banjo Act"
   Singer Ethel Merman plays Rosie, a stage performer hired to take on a young apprentice who turns out to be a psycho in disguise.

February 8, 1954
#538 "Death at Skirkerud Pond"
   With Jeff Chandler and Paula Winslowe. A member of the secret underground is responsible for the murder of an old couple.

February 15, 1954
#539 "The Outer Limit"
   With William Holden, Hy Averback and Edgar Barrier. An experimental rocket ship returns to Earth with the astronaut in hysterics, claiming the Earth will be destroyed within the next few hours. Based on the short story by Graham Doar.

February 22, 1954
#540 "Murder by Jury"
   Herbert Marshall plays the role of Edmund Mason, who is put on trial for the murder of his wife, and walks due to lack of evidence. Years later, the District Attorney finds the evidence he needs to convict Mason.

March 1, 1954
#541 "The Barking Death"
   With William Powell and Dick Beals. A sick dog escapes a scientific laboratory and the authorities race against time to find the pooch. A young child finds the dog and befriends it, unaware of how sick the dog is.

March 8, 1954
#542 "Circumstantial Terror"
   With Ronald Reagan and Howard McNear. An unemployed factory worker returns to a liquor store to apologize for yelling at the clerk, only to find the clerk dead.

March 15, 1954
#543 "The Girl in Car Thirty-Two"
   With Victor Mature and William Conrad. An undercover detective strikes an acquaintance with a beautiful young lady whose boyfriend is suspected of participating in a jewel heist. Based on the story by Thomas Walsh.

March 22, 1954
#544 "The Guilty Always Run"
   With Tyrone Power and William Conrad. A married man, who surfs along the beach, flirts with a woman, who is found dead the next day. His best friend testifies with a fake alibi.

March 29, 1954
#545 "Somebody Help Me"
   Cornel Wilde plays Ed, a lonely man, who makes it a living picking up strange women, befriending them, and then hiding the bodies. Georgia Ellis plays an old flame from his school days who is about to discover his secret.

April 5, 1954
#546 "Grand Theft"
   With David Niven and Vic Perrin. A jeweler in need of money stages a fake robbery to fool the insurance company with a false claim.

April 12, 1954
#547 "Parole to Panic"
Broderick Crawford plays Paul, an ex-con recently released on parole and scared that members of the old gang will be gunning for him.

April 19, 1954
#548 "The Card Game"
With Richard Widmark and Cathy Lewis. A gambler with an addiction with playing card games loses his paycheck to a crooked gambler and in desperation, gambles his life on a turn of a card.

April 26, 1954
#549 "The Bertillion Method"
Charles Boyer plays Alphonse Bertillion, a Frenchman responsible for proving and establishing the methods that police use for fingerprinting, and thus solving many crimes that people would normally get away with. Boyer played the role of Bettillion on other anthologies such as radio's *The Hallmark Hall of Fame* and television's *Reader's Digest*.

May 3, 1954
#550 "The Giant of Thermopylae"
With Frank Lovejoy, Charlotte Lawrence and Paul Frees. Walter goes to the local fun house carnival hoping to meet the man responsible for his stay behind bars.

May 10, 1954
#551 "The Last Days of John Dillinger"
With Van Heflin, Parley Baer and Jimmy Eagles. Notorious gunman John Dillinger has his face surgically altered and fingerprints burned to evade police while two women fight over the love of the man who was destined to become Public Enemy Number One.

May 17, 1954
#552 "The Revenge of Captain Bligh"
Charles Laughton plays the role of Captain William Bligh, who kept his loyal men alive after a mutiny on a sailing vessel called *The Bounty*. Laughton reprises his film role 1935's *Mutiny on the Bounty*.

May 24, 1954
#553 "Weekend Special — Death"
   Agnes Moorehead plays a woman trapped in a food store who witnesses two burglars trying to crack open the safe.

May 31, 1954
#554 "Listen, Young Lovers"
   Robert Wagner and Mona Freeman are a young couple who risk their lives while trying to escape from Czechoslovakia because of the Iron Fist of Communism.

June 7, 1954
#555 "A Terribly Strange Bed"
   Based on the short story by Wilkie Collins, Peter Lawford guests as a police officer who wins a considerable sum at the gambling tables, and takes lodging at a hotel for the night. As he sleeps, he discovers his bed is actually an elaborate death trap. This was the final episode sponsored by Auto-Lite.

Tuesday — 8:30 p.m. to 9:00 p.m. (E.S.T.)

June 15, 1954
#556 "The Earth is Made of Glass"
   With Joseph Kearns and Herbert Butterfield. Same story and script from September 27, 1945.

June 22, 1954
#557 "Sequel to Murder"
   With Whitfield Connor and Charlotte Lawrence. A magazine editor reads a mystery about a man who suffocated his wife with the pillow and then set fire to the bed to cover up his crime. After recreating the same method for himself, the editor receives a visit from the mystery writer.

June 29, 1954
#558 "Too Hot to Live"
   With Sam Edwards, Paul Frees and Jean Wood. Same story and script from October 26, 1950.

July 6, 1954
#559 "The Tip"
   With Lurene Tuttle and Howard McNear. Same story and script from September 7, 1950.

July 13, 1954
#560 "Run, Sheep, Run"
   With Cathy and *Suspense* director Elliott Lewis. When Joe accidentally runs over a man on a foggy evening, he telephones his wife to confess his crime. She mistakes him for drunk, so he finds himself fending the police and his girlfriend.

July 20, 1954
#561 "Telling"
   With Anthony Ellis and Richard Peel. Terry is in love with a woman who tosses him aside with no respect. When the girl turns up dead, the town folk dismiss Terry's confessions as heartbroken sorrow and self-pity. This was the final episode produced and directed by Elliott Lewis.

July 27, 1954
#562 "Destruction"
   With Lawrence Dobkin and Paula Winslowe. Little Joe has a bad day when he loses his job, gets in a fight at the bar and tossed out in the streets. Norman MacDonnell replaces Elliott Lewis as producer and director beginning with this episode.

August 3, 1954
#563 "Goodnight Mrs. Russell"
   With Virginia Gregg and Vic Perrin. Same story and script from October 20, 1949.

August 10, 1954
#564 "Never Steal a Butcher's Wife"
   With Hy Averback, Lawrence Dobkin and Paula Winslowe. Same story and script from February 9, 1950.

Thursday — 8:00 p.m. to 8:25 p.m. (E.S.T.)

September 30, 1954
#565 "A Little Matter of Memory"
With Edgar Barrier and Joseph Kearns. A young couple must make a decision whether or not to open the door, when a madman who poses as a police detective roams the streets.

October 7, 1954
#566 "Chicken Feed"
With Harry Bartell and Vic Perrin. Same story and script from September 8, 1949.

October 14, 1954
#567 "Lost"
With William Conrad and John Dehner. Alice suffers from a case of amnesia, but this doesn't stop the police from learning her identity, and the woman she apparently killed.

October 21, 1954
#568 "Rave Notice"
With Hans Conried and Parley Baer. Same story and script from October 12, 1950.

October 28, 1954
#569 "The Shelter"
With Vic Perrin and Joyce McCluskey. A young woman waits at a bus terminal alone with a man who talks very strangely. A killer is loose in the streets and she wonders if this man is the same.

November 4, 1954
#570 "The Last Letter of Dr. Bronson"
With John Dehner and Parley Baer. Same story and script from July 27, 1943.

November 11, 1954
#571 "The Sure Thing"
With Hy Averback and Clayton Post. A hot-shot rookie attempts

to buy himself into the Syndicate when he receives a tip on what appears to be a sure thing. When the fix doesn't go as planned, he is forced to pay up. This same script was previously dramatized on October 15, 1949 on *Escape*. The original title of this episode was "The Fix."

November 18, 1954
#572 "Blind Date"
With Shirley Mitchell and Vic Perrin. Same story and script from September 29, 1949.

November 25, 1954
#573 "Shooting Star"
With Virginia Christine, John Dehner and Joseph Kearns. An actress makes a desperate attempt to prove to a motion picture producer that she has what it takes to be a shooting star, by holding him hostage at the point of her gun.

December 2, 1954
#574 "The Shot"
With William Conrad and John Dehner. Same story and script from October 12, 1953.

December 9, 1954
#575 "On a Country Road"
With Harry Bartell and Virginia Gregg. Same story and script from November 16, 1950.

December 16, 1954
#576 "Pretty Girl"
With Lynn Allen, Ann Morrison and Vic Perrin. Emmy Carter is the love of all men's dreams. On the college campus, she enjoys toying with one man who won't bend toward her affections, even when she makes threats against him. Norman MacDonnell makes his final producing and directing job for *Suspense* with this episode. The original title of this episode was "Baby Sitter."

December 23, 1954
#577 "Premonition"
  With Lawrence Dobkin and Charlotte Lawrence. During their vacation in the snowy mountains, a premonition suggests everyone in the ski lodge will be dead before the weekend is over. But no one will listen to their ravings. Anthony Ellis replaces Norman MacDonnell as producer and director with this episode. Bernard Herrmann steps in to conduct the music for this episode.

December 30, 1954
#578 "Odd Man Out"
  With Ben Wright. Same story and script from February 11, 1952.

January 6, 1955
#579 "Murder Aboard the Alphabet"
  With William Conrad. Same story and script from August 21, 1947.

January 13, 1955
#580 "Final Payment"
  With Harry Bartell and Peter Leeds. Two men fake an auto accident to cash in on an insurance scam, but fail to fool the insurance investigator.

January 20, 1955
#581 "Study of a Murderer"
  With Charlotte Lawrence and William Conrad. Same story and script from October 1, 1951.

January 27, 1955
#582 "The Operation"
  With Hy Averback and Sam Edwards. A burglar robbing a doctor's office is mistaken as a medical man and forced at gunpoint by two crooks, to mend a gunshot wound.

February 3, 1955
#583 "A Killing in Abilene"
  With Parley Baer and Vic Perrin. Same story and script from December 14, 1950.

February 10, 1955
#584 "Diagnosis of Death"
With Dick Beals and Helen Kleeb. A patient mistakes another man's diagnosis as his and assumes he has a few days to live. The doctor races against time to track down the patient before he does something death-defying.

February 17, 1955
#585 "The Man with the Steel Teeth"
With Richard Boone, John Dehner and Maria Palmer. A man is thrown into prison for a crime he is found guilty of without a judge or jury or a fair trial. When he escapes, he finds himself hunted by his captures. Actor Richard Boone was billed as "Robert Boone" for this broadcast. This same script was previously dramatized on March 15, 1953 on *Escape*.

Tuesday — 8:00 p.m. to 8:25 p.m. (E.S.T.)

February 22, 1955
#586 "Waiting"
With Vivi Jannis, Helen Kleeb and Charlotte Lawrence. The family of a man on death row sits by the radio, counting the minutes down before his execution.

March 1, 1955
#587 "The Screaming Woman"
With Sherry Jackson and Paula Winslowe. Same story and script from November 25, 1948.

March 8, 1955
#588 "Nobody Ever Quits"
With Tom McKee and Peter Leeds. A family man receives a phone call from his past, exacting revenge on a crime he turned against them. Even with a blizzard outside, he attempts to get his wife and son to safety before too late.

March 15, 1955
#589 "The Game"

With Sam Edwards and Gil Stratton, Jr. Two young boys, drunk on a hot summer day, play a deadly game of Russian Roulette in the living room. John Dehner narrates. This same script was previously dramatized on August 30, 1953 on *Escape*.

March 22, 1955
#590 "The Cellar"

With Eric Snowden and Jeanette Nolan. Oscar murders his wife, throws the mother-in-law out of the house and runs off with a younger woman.

March 29, 1955
#591 "Give Me Liberty"

With Dick Beals and Michael Ann Barrett. Same story and script from October 21, 1948.

April 5, 1955
#592 "Zero Hour"

With Parley Baer and John Dehner. "Zero Hour" refers to the time when all the children of the world play a new game called "Invasion." Grownups have no idea what's about to happen to them. When this script was dramatized for the October 4, 1953 broadcast of *Escape*, the network received a large number of pieces through the mail both praising and criticizing the program's content. With Anthony Ellis now producing and directing, he chose to reprise a number of scripts from *Escape*, including this one.

April 12, 1955
#593 "The Lunch Kit"

With Harry Bartell, Parley Baer and Tom Hanley. Same story and script from June 9, 1949.

April 19, 1955
#594 "Speed Trap"

With Eddie Firestone and Ted Bliss. Two police officers are involved in a high-speed pursuit when one of the officers discovers that his wife is inside.

April 26, 1955
#595 "Sight Unseen"
With Terrence de Marnay and Ben Wright. A man recounts the year 1926, when he was accused of a crime he never committed.

May 3, 1955
#596 "Remember Me?"
With Tony Barrett and Charlotte Lawrence. Same story and script from April 7, 1952.

May 10, 1955
#597 "Going, Going, Gone"
With John Dehner and Joseph Kearns. Same story and script from November 23, 1950.

May 17, 1955
#598 "Lily and the Colonel"
With Ramsey Hill, Joan Alderson and Paula Winslowe. An old man, his young wife and a young Lieutenant attempt to escape from Kenya, Africa after the natives get restless regarding the British occupation. This same script was previously dramatized on May 3, 1953 on *Escape*.

May 24, 1955
#599 "I Saw Myself Running"
With Charlotte Lawrence and John Dehner. Terrified of her nightmares, a woman decides the only way to escape the dreams is to stay awake and never sleep again. This same script was previously dramatized on February 22, 1953 on *Escape*.

May 31, 1955
#600 "Beirut by Sunrise"
With Mary Jane Croft, Ben Wright and Hy Averback. An American school teacher in Beirut finds a wounded soldier, and finds herself involved in a cat-and-mouse chase through the streets. This radio script was previously dramatized on January 8, 1953 on *On Stage*.

June 7, 1955
#601 "Frankenstein"
With Stacy Harris and Herb Butterfield. Same story and script from November 3, 1952.

June 14, 1955
#602 "The Whole Town's Sleeping"
A strangler nicknamed "The Lonely One" is wandering the city streets. Women fear to walk the streets after dark, except Lavinia Nebbs, played by Jeanette Nolan, who proves to herself that there is nothing to be afraid of. William Conrad narrates. Based on the short story by Ray Bradbury. This drama was originally scheduled for broadcast the week before.

June 21, 1955
#603 "Over the Bounding Main"
With Jack Kruschen and Charlotte Lawrence. Same story and script from September 14, 1950.

June 28, 1955
#604 "The Hold Out"
With Harry Bartell and Parley Baer. During deliberation, one member of the jury insists the defendant is not guilty, and attempts to persuade the others to see it his way.

July 5, 1955
#605 "The Cave-In"
With Ben Wright and John Dosworth. Four men find themselves victim to a cave-in and when one of the men is murdered, the survivors have to figure out which of them is the killer.

July 12, 1955
#606 "Kaleidoscope"
With William Conrad, Parley Baer, Howard McNear and Georgia Ellis, the primary cast of radio's *Gunsmoke*. A spaceship blows up, sending the five astronauts drifting in separate directions. One-by-one they lose communication with each other as they continue to drift apart, and each facing their demise while gaining a bit of sanity in the process.

Producer and director Anthony Ellis recalled, "This is the story of six men blown out of a rocket ship who float about in outer space. Each philosophizes what will happen to him. To help create the desired effect, we had our six actors play their roles in six different isolated booths so that they were entirely alone. They couldn't even see each other. This helped to give them the proper mood and it made for a highly successful show. This sort of thing — even this type of production — could not have been done half as well on television."

July 19, 1955
#607 "Backseat Driver"
With Vivi Jannis and Parley Baer. Same story and script from February 3, 1949. The original title of this episode was "The Case of the Backseat Driver."

July 26, 1955
#608 "The Greatest Thief in the World"
With Ben Wright and John Dodsworth. Same story and script from June 21, 1951.

August 2, 1955
#609 "Black Death"
With Edgar Barrier and William Conrad. A black cat escapes a scientific laboratory and when scientists discover the cat ate a specimen infected with the black plague, the authorities race against time to catch the hissing beast. This script was previously dramatized on October 30, 1950 on *Hollywood Star Playhouse*.

August 9, 1955
#610 "Love, Honor, or Murder"
With Charlotte Lawrence and William Conrad. Same story and script from June 29, 1950.

August 16, 1955
#611 "A Study in Wax"
With William Conrad and Stacy Harris. Two men stationed overseas must learn to live with each other's habits and annoyances if they stand

a chance of living a long life. This same script was previously dramatized on February 1, 1953 on *Escape*.

August 23, 1955
#612 "The Beetle and Mr. Bottle"
With Eric Snowden as Mr. Bottle, who discovers his wife is a true shrew, and swears to himself that if she touches his garden, he'll bury her in it.

August 30, 1955
#613 "The Lady in the Red Hat"
With Vic Perrin and Virginia Gregg. Same story and script from November 30, 1950.

September 6, 1955
#614 "Strange for a Killer"
With John Dehner and Jack Kruschen. Same story and script from March 15, 1951.

September 13, 1955
#615 "A Story of Poison"
With Joseph Kearns and Paula Winslowe. Same story and script from September 17, 1951.

September 20, 1955
#616 "The Stool Pigeon"
With John Dehner, Parley Baer and Joseph Kearns. Prisoners on Devil's Island plan the perfect escape but before they put their plan into motion, they must route out the informant. This drama was originally scheduled for broadcast of August 9, 1955.

September 27, 1955
#617 "The Frightened City"
With Harry Bartell and Charlotte Lawrence. Same story and script from November 10, 1952.

October 4, 1955
#618 "Goodbye, Miss Lizzie Borden"
With Dick Beals, Paula Winslowe and Irene Tedrow. A nosy reporter

Suspense

snoops too close to the scene of the crime and discovers the solution to the greatest hatchet murder mystery.

Tuesday — 8:30 p.m. to 9:00 p.m. (E.S.T.)

October 11, 1955
#619 "Heavens to Betsy"

With Barbara Eiler, Hy Averback and Dick Beals. A flying saucer lands in the Doyle family's backyard and when the Government comes to claim it, Mr. Doyle holds his ground claiming ownership first. This script was previously dramatized on March 24, 1954 on *On Stage*.

October 18, 1955
#620 "Life Ends at Midnight"

With Paula Winslowe and Stacy Harris. Same story and script from February 17, 1944.

October 25, 1955
#621 "To None a Deadly Drug"

With Hy Averback and Jack Kruschen. A druggist gives the wrong prescription to the wrong customer and races against time to correct his mistake.

November 1, 1955
#622 "The Mountain"

With Parley Baer and Ben Wright. Same story and script from March 16, 1953.

November 8, 1955
#623 "Report on the X-915"

With Stacy Harris and Jack Kruschen. A 15-million-dollar submarine on its maiden voyage has a saboteur on board, who has already stolen the nuclear missiles.

November 15, 1955
#624 "Once a Murderer"

With Joseph Kearns and Betty Harford. Thomas Shaw is found not-guilty on a murder charge and believing that he is unstoppable, accepts payments from clients to commit more murders.

November 22, 1955
#625 "Classified Secret"
   With Howard McNear and Dick Beals. A spy named Charlie possesses papers any foreign Government would kill for. After boarding a bus, a number of suspicious passengers could be an enemy faction. This same script was previously dramatized on April 12, 1953 on *Escape*.

November 29, 1955
#626 "This Will Kill You"
   With Sam Edwards and Barney Phillips. Same story and script from August 23, 1945.

December 6, 1955
#627 "When the Bough Breaks"
   With Virginia Gregg and Stacy Harris. Same story and script from May 3, 1951.

December 13, 1955
#628 "A Present for Benny"
   With Jack Kruschen and Junius Matthews. Rick attempts to kill a rival named "Machine Gun" Benny by planting a bomb in a goodwill Christmas package. But when he discovers that his rival sends him good tidings, he regrets his decision and attempts to call the package back.

December 20, 1955
#629 "The Cave"
   With Dick Beals, Billy Chapmin, and John Dehner. Two young boys enter a cave and find themselves magically whisked away into a world of pirates and a beautiful princess. This same script was previously dramatized on December 24, 1950 on *Escape*.

December 27, 1955
#630 "The Mystery of the Marie Celeste"
   With John Dehner and Vic Perrin. Same story and script from June 8, 1953.

January 3, 1956
#631 "The Eavesdropper"
   With Parley Baer, Herb Ellis and Charlotte Lawrence. A plumber eavesdrops on the conversation between a young couple and their blackmailer. After the couple kills the blackmailer, they discover that they have to eliminate the plumber as he witnessed the killing.

January 10, 1956
#632 "Two Platinum Capsules"
   With Dick Beals, Stacy Harris and Edgar Barrier. An employee from the local hospital assists authorities with his Geiger-counter in the search for two platinum capsules that can cause serious radiation burns with anyone who comes in contact with them.

January 17, 1956
#633 "The End of the String"
   With Stacy Harris and Benny Rubin. Same story and script from November 26, 1951. This episode was scripted by David Williams, an alias for producer and director Anthony Ellis.

January 24, 1956
#634 "The Cellar Door"
   With Paula Winslowe, Parley Baer and Byron Kane. This script was previously dramatized on October 28, 1953 on *On Stage*.

January 31, 1956
#635 "Arctic Rescue"
   With John Stevenson and Clayton Post. Same story and script from December 22, 1952.

February 7, 1956
#636 "Variations on a Theme"
   With Parley Baer and Sam Edwards. Herman leaves for his routine fishing trip with an extra bit of cargo. A large trunk where he tied, gagged and bound his wife so he can toss her in the center of his favorite fishing spot.

February 14, 1956
#637 "Listen, Young Lovers"
   With Charlotte Lawrence, Sam Edwards and Jack Kruschen. Same story and script from May 31, 1954.

February 21, 1956
#638 "Hollywood Hostages"
   With Don Diamond. Two Hollywood filmmakers visit a real live ghost town to scout the location of their next motion picture. A killer shows up and steals their vehicle for his getaway.

February 28, 1956
#639 "The Diary of Captain Scott"
   With Ben Wright and Hans Conried. Same story and script from April 21, 1952.

March 6, 1956
#640 "Quiet Night"
   With Stacy Harris and George Walsh. A plane crashes in the Florida everglades and three fugitives running from the law have to choose between staying with the wounded passenger, a young boy, or the money contained in the wreckage.

March 13, 1956
#641 "The Groom of the Ladder"
   With Hans Conried and Ben Wright. Same story and script from September 22, 1952.

March 20, 1956
#642 "Gallardo"
   With Vic Perrin and Virginia Gregg. Circus acrobats vie for the affections of the new addition to their act. One of them goes so far as to plan murder to eliminate the competition.

March 27, 1956
#643 "The Murderess"
   With Cathy Lewis, Dick Beals and Paula Winslowe. After a woman kills a man in cold blood, she reads in the papers about

Suspense

another woman who has been picked up by the police for the same crime.

April 3, 1956
#644 "Game Hunt"
With Joseph Kearns, Stacy Harris and Jack Kruschen. A game hunter in Kenya wounds a lion and treks his way through the deepest part of unexplored territory like a blind prey, for the wounded beast.

April 10, 1956
#645 "The Lonely Heart"
With Ben Wright and Joseph Kearns. A rookie Scotland Yard Inspector uses new evidence on an already closed case to prove Mr. Leach murdered his wife.

April 17, 1956
#646 "The Seventh Letter"
With Stacy Harris and Parley Baer. A mailman is murdered because of a letter he did not deliver. The detective investigating the case discovers his wife was involved.

April 24, 1956
#647 "A Case of Nerves"
With Parley Baer. Same story and script from June 1, 1950.

May 1, 1956
#648 "The Waxwork"
With William Conrad. Same story and script from March 20, 1947.

May 8, 1956
#649 "The Phones Die First"
With Richard Crenna and Jack Kruschen. A man on death row receives a number of visits from friends, but none of them bring good news about a pardon and his execution is only hours away.

May 15, 1956
#650 "The Death Parade"
With Howard McNear. Same story and script from February 15, 1951.

May 22, 1956
#651 "Fragile: Contents Death"
　With John Larkin and Herb Ellis. Same story and script from February 1, 1951.

May 29, 1956
#652 "The Flame"
　With Tony Barrett. Same story and script from October 15, 1951.

June 5, 1956
#653 "The Twelfth Rose"
　With Don Diamond and Miriam Wolfe. A florist starts to suspect one of her customers as the murderer reported in the newspapers. The method of strangulation is with a single-stem rose and she has a customer who purchases a number of roses every week.

June 12, 1956
#654 "A Matter of Timing"
　With William Conrad and Parley Baer. A hired assassin questions his employer regarding the motives for his next job, hoping to get out of the contract. The employer wants his best friend dead and the assassin is having second thoughts.

June 19, 1956
#655 "A Sleeping Drought"
　With Hans Conried and Abraham Sofaer. The captain of a prison ship discovers the criminals have broken free and armed themselves. The only way he can survive the remainder of the trip is to strike a deal with them. This same script was previously dramatized on October 1, 1950 on *Escape*.

June 26, 1956
#656 "The Treasure Chest of Don Jose"
　With Edgar Barrier and Joseph Kearns. Same story and script from February 4, 1952.

July 3, 1956
#657 "The Music Lovers"
   With Stan Jones and Ben Wright. A Scotland Yard inspector discovers that the most respectable men of society, music lovers, are responsible for the murder of a secret agent and the theft of Government papers.

Wednesday — 8:30 p.m. to 8:55 p.m. (E.S.T.)

July 11, 1956
#658 "Want Ad"
   With Stacy Harris and Mary Jane Croft. Same story and script from January 25, 1954.

July 18, 1956
#659 "The Man Who Threw Acid"
   With William Conrad and John Dehner. A young punk tries to gain a position with the crime community by throwing a jar of acid in the face of a prominent citizen. After he accomplishes his mission, the punk discovers his disassociation among society.

July 25, 1956
#660 "The Tramp"
   With Ben Wright. Arthur is hired to board a sailing vessel where he plans to murder the Captain and commandeer the ship worth a small profit. This same script was previously dramatized on March 1, 1953 on *Escape*.

August 1, 1956
#661 "Massacre at Little Big Horn"
   With Stacy Harris. A dramatization based on the Seventh U.S. Calvary, led by General Custer in 1876. The slaughter will go down as a massacre for the history books.

August 8, 1956
#662 "Double Identity"
   With Vic Perrin. An embezzler succeeds in stealing a large sum of money from his employer, and through a twist of fate, escapes town by plane with his boss as a passenger.

August 15, 1956
#663 "A Friend to Alexander"
   With John Dehner and Miriam Wolfe. Same story and script from August 3, 1943.

August 22, 1956
   Pre-empted due to the Republican National Convention.

August 29, 1956
#664 "Hold-Up"
   With Frank Gerstle. A bloodthirsty storekeeper with an itchy trigger finger gets his kicks in defending himself when young punks attempt to rob him of his hard-earned money.

September 5, 1956
#665 "The Security Agent"
   With Parley Baer and Howard McNear. Three men make plans to escape the country by plane and shortly before boarding, learn that one of the passengers is a security agent. The music for this episode was composed by Jerry Goldsmith, who would later rise in fame as a composer of numerous movie and television theme songs.

Tuesday — 8:30 p.m. to 8:55 p.m. (E.S.T.)

September 25, 1956
#666 "A Case of Identity"
   With Parley Baer and Joseph Kearns. After signing for a life-insurance policy, a couple fakes the death of her husband to collect the money. When the job succeeds, the wife won't agree to hand over his share and sets out to keep the money for herself.

October 2, 1956
#667 "Waiting"
   With Paula Winslowe, Vivi Jannis and Charlotte Lawrence. Same story and script from February 22, 1955.

October 9, 1956
#668 "The Digger"
With Torin Thatcher. Making his way through the African jungle, a businessman searches f=or the legendary "Digger," who can help his business grow prosperous with an expert mine shaft digger.

October 16, 1956
#669 "The Prophecy of Bertha Abbott"
With Richard Crenna and Peggy Webber. Two young boys are hexed by a wicked witch when they are caught stealing apples from her tree. The youths laugh it off at first, but as the years pass they discover the prophecy coming true. This was the final episode produced and directed by Anthony Ellis, and the final episode to feature Larry Thor as the announcer.

October 23, 1956
#670 "The Doll"
With Patty McCormack and Richard Beals. A little girl receives the gift of a doll with a wind-up mechanical heart. Soon after the young girl makes a connection with her new friend, she lays claim that if the heart stops ticking, so will hers. This was the first episode produced and directed by William N. Robson. George Walsh replaces Larry Thor as the announcer.

October 30, 1956
#671 "Red Cloud Mesa"
With Reed Hadley. A trader on the Indian reservations is forced to decide between moral obligations and the law when an Indian who escaped an asylum pleads to die out in the open fields like Mother Nature intended.

Sunday — 4:30 p.m. to 4:55 p.m. (E.S.T.)

November 4, 1956
#672 "The Signalman"
With Sarah Churchill and Ben Wright. Same story and script from March 23, 1953.

November 11, 1956
#673 "Three Skeleton Key"

With Vincent Price, John Dehner and Ben Wright. An invading army of rats makes their way to a lighthouse, where three men must fight for survival. The sound of the rats was simulated by rubbing a wet cork on glass (squeaking), and the crunching of berry baskets (chewing). Re-recording the same sound effect over and over created the illusion of thousands of rats. This same script was previously dramatized on November 15, 1949 on *Escape*.

November 18, 1956
#674 "The Long Night"

With Frank Lovejoy. An air traffic controller receives a call from an inexperienced pilot on a dark and foggy night. With the airplane running low on gas, the air traffic controller has to make a frantic decision to talk the passenger into landing. Frank Lovejoy was in reality a licensed pilot.

November 25, 1956
#675 "The Man Who Stole the Bible"

With John Lund and June Foray. After picking up a Bible in his hotel room, a man finds himself the victim of a lengthy chase through the streets of New Orleans during Mardi Gras. This same script was previously dramatized on May 5, 1950 on *Escape*.

December 2, 1956
#676 "Rim of Terror"

With Barbara Whiting and Joe Di Santis. Three men disguised as police officers are in search of a spy. A young lady traveling cross-country picks up a hitch-hiker and all suspicions rest on the new passenger. This same script was previously dramatized on May 12, 1950 on *Escape*.

December 9, 1956
#677 "An Occurrence at Owl Creek Bridge"

With Victor Jory and Julie Bennett. A Confederate spy attempts to blow up a bridge in hopes of aiding the war cause. He is captured and sentenced to death by hanging from the very same bridge. With

Suspense

luck, the rope will break and he'll survive the plunge into the water. This same script was previously dramatized on December 10, 1947 on *Escape*.

December 16, 1956
#678 "Eyewitness"

With Howard Duff and John Dehner. A reporter for a local newspaper enters a State Penitentiary where the inmates have taken control of the prison. As a hostage, he is allowed a phone call to the editor to deliver an eyewitness account.

December 23, 1956
#679 "Back for Christmas"

With Herbert Marshall and Irene Tedrow. Same story and script from December 23, 1943.

December 30, 1956

Pre-empted

January 6, 1957
#680 "A Shipment of Mute Fate"

Jack Kelly plays a passenger on an ocean liner who retires to his cabin and finds a deadly bushmaster snake in the center of the room. This same script was previously dramatized on October 15, 1947 on *Escape*.

January 13, 1957
#681 "Russian New Year"

With Helmut Dantine. Two men plot the assassination of the Czar by planting explosives in the church where the New Year's celebration will commence. A young lady prays to God that the assassins see the light before they complete their task.

January 20, 1957
#682 "Second Class Passenger"

With Sterling Holloway, Hans Conried and William Conrad. An American tourist is caught up in an espionage caper that is too complicated to follow. Before the evening is through, he will have assistance from a beautiful woman and risk his life for a cause he knows nothing about. This same script was previously dramatized on January 7, 1948 on *Escape*.

January 27, 1957
#683 "Freedom This Way"
With Hans Conried and Jack Kruschen. A Hungarian immigrant tells his sad story to the immigration office, and how he longs for the freedom of the United States of America.

February 3, 1957
#684 "Frankie and Johnny"
With Margaret Whiting and Daws Butler. Same story and script from May 5, 1952.

February 10, 1957
#685 "Door of Gold"
With Myron McCormick and Shirley Mitchell. An archeologist and his wife find themselves trapped in a "lost" Incan temple. Dodging the traps inside they seek an escape route before the oxygen is all used up.

February 17, 1957
#686 "Murder and Aunt Delia"
With Glenn Ford and Lillian Buyeff. Same story and script from November 10, 1949.

February 24, 1957
#687 "227 Minutes of Hate"
With Charles McGraw and Shirley Mitchell. A man steals a plane at the local airport and makes plans to crash it into a radio tower to exact revenge on another man. The police are powerless on the ground and race against time to stop the airplane.

March 3, 1957
#688 "Present Tense"
With Vincent Price and Peg LaCentra. An accused murderer escapes police custody when the train escorting him to prison wrecks. When he returns home, he finds the man, he supposedly killed, alive

and well in his wife's arms. After committing a murder, he finds himself stuck in a time wrap revisiting the same events again and again. This same script was previously dramatized on January 31, 1950 on *Escape*.

March 10, 1957
#689 "The Paralta Map"

With Raymond Burr and Junius Matthews. Two men discover the whereabouts of the Paralta map, which reveals the location of a valuable treasure buried away in unexplored territory. Up until this episode, the music for *Suspense* was original compositions, usually with the musical staff from CBS. Beginning with this episode, the series began using stock music from the CBS library. Many episodes of the past were regarded as superb for their combinations of top-notch acting, sound effects and music. Many people, including the author of this book, felt that part of the high quality was hampered with the use of stock music.

March 17, 1957
#690 "The Outer Limit"

With Frank Lovejoy and Barney Phillips. Same story and script from February 15, 1954. Having been recorded before March 10, this episode marks the final broadcast to feature original music composed specifically for *Suspense*. This same script was previously dramatized on February 7, 1950 on *Escape*.

March 24, 1957
#691 "Shooting Star"

With June Lockhart. Same story and script from November 25, 1954.

March 31, 1957
#692 "A Good Neighbor"

With Jeff Chandler and Virginia Gregg. Andrew Bent, a jewel thief, makes his hideout in the mountains where his neighbor, a kindly old woman, proves to be too much of a maid and landlady, and the cause of his demise.

April 7, 1957
#693 "The Vanishing Lady"

With Vanessa Brown and John Dehner. Based on the short story by Alexander Woollcott. A young lady and her mother check into a hotel and shortly after, her mother disappears. The hotel staff claims she checked in by herself but she knows they are lying. Why else would multiple people insist her mother never existed? This same script was previously dramatized on February 1, 1948 on *Escape*.

April 14, 1957
#694 "Thou Shalt Not Commit"

With Victor Jory. A tall, dark and handsome stranger whisks a married woman off her feet, offering a boarding pass off a private island where her husband prefers to stay.

April 21, 1957
#695 "Chicken Feed"

With Lloyd Bridges. Same story and script from September 8, 1949.

April 28, 1957
#696 "Escape to Death"

With Francis Lederer and Dick Beals. A Communist doctor is sent across the border to apprehend and kill a woman with important information that cannot fall into the hands of the United Nations.

May 5, 1957
#697 "Celebration"

With Joy Lafleur and Irene Tedrow. Same story and script from September 23, 1948. Joy Lafleur (1914-1957) only did two movies in her career, *Whispering City* in 1947 and *Sins of the Fathers* in 1948. How she got the job of acting in a radio broadcast almost ten years after her brief Hollywood career ended remains a mystery.

May 12, 1957
#698 "Tarawa Was Tough"

With John Lund and John Dehner. U.S. Army troops stationed overseas listen to the promises of Tokyo Rose over the radio and suspect their worst fears. Their next mission is to take Tarawa in the Gilbert Islands.

May 19, 1957
#699 "Death and Miss Turner"
With Agnes Moorehead. Same story and script from November 17, 1952.

May 26, 1957
#700 "The Big Day"
Husband and wife John McIntire and Jeanette Nolan star in this humorous tale about a crazy old mechanic determined to prove that the Stanley Steamer is still the fastest engine on the road today.

June 2, 1957
#701 "Crossing Paris"
With Hans Conried and John Dehner. A meat smuggler requires an assistant to help with the trade and when his usual doesn't show up for work, he accepts a substitute with a drinking problem. This same script was previously dramatized on August 25, 1950 on *Escape*.

June 9, 1957
#702 "The Green and Gold String"
Vincent Price plays Dr. Alcazar, a con artist who poses as a mystic so he can steal money from his customers' purses. When he sees a photo of a recent customer in the obituaries, he contacts the family with his knowledge in an attempt to con the mourning relatives.

June 16, 1957
#703 "Trial By Jury"
With Nancy Kelly, Shirley Mitchell and Kenny Delmar. Same story and script from March 24, 1947.

June 23, 1957
#704 "A Load of Dynamite"
With Bartlett Robinson and Barney Phillips. An evil brother, jealous of what his kid brother accomplished in life, attempts to take it all away with a few tons of dynamite and a single rifle bullet.

June 30, 1957
#705 "The Yellow Wallpaper"
   With Agnes Moorehead and Ann Hunter. Same story and script from July 29, 1948.

July 7, 1957
#706 "Alibi"
   With Everett Sloane and Ted de Corsia. A businessman hires a professional assassin to take care of his business partner, and sets up an alibi to keep his good name from being tarnished. Moments before the scheduled "hit," his alibi is nowhere to be seen.

July 14, 1957
#707 "Flood on the Goodwins"
   With Herbert Marshall and Hans Conried. Two Englishmen during the war must face off against a German responsible for the recent deaths on the river. This same script was previously dramatized on November 1, 1949 on *Escape*.

July 21, 1957
#708 "America's Boyfriend"
   With Mercedes McCambridge and Richard Crenna. Mrs. Keats's husband is accused of a crime he did not commit so she sets out to prove his innocence. The only person who was witness to the crime was her two-year-old daughter.

July 28, 1957
#709 "Murder on Mike"
   With Raymond Burr and Alan Reed. Same story and script from December 3, 1951.

August 4, 1957
#710 "Fleshpeddler"
   With DeForest Kelley, Dick Beals and Howard McNear. A persistent talent agent learns the horrible secret of the ventriloquist act known as "Wilson and Oliver."

Suspense

August 11, 1957
#711 "Pigeon in the Cage"
With Lloyd Bridges. Same story and script from May 25, 1953.

August 18, 1957
#712 "Peanut Brittle"
With Skip Homeier and John Dehner. Life behind prison bars isn't easy, especially for a new inmate who is learning the ropes about paying his dues for survival.

August 25, 1957
#713 "Leiningen vs. the Ants"
With William Conrad and Ben Wright. A plantation owner in the thick of Brazil is given advance warning to prepare for the horde of flesh-eating ants that will soon trek through the jungle. Instead of evacuating like everyone else, he remains defiant to the bitter end. It has been rumored and put into print that this episode was originally scheduled for broadcast on August 22, 1956. Internal evidence and common sense dictates that is not so. This episode was recorded days before this broadcast and was never considered for an August 1956 broadcast. This same script was previously dramatized on August 4, 1949 on *Escape*.

September 1, 1957
#714 "Man From Tomorrow"
With Frank Lovejoy and Joan Banks. A jet pilot is hired by a few scientists to experiment with the future evolution of mankind. This same script was previously dramatized on August 23, 1953 on *Escape*.

September 8, 1957
#715 "Old Army Buddy"
With Victor Jory and Paul Frees. Fred turns to an old Army buddy for emotional support, when his wife stubbornly asks for a divorce.

September 15, 1957
#716 "Night on Red Mountain"
With Richard Crenna. When a phone call from the past promises murder, one man has to get his wife and son away from the house before it's too late.

September 22, 1957
#717 "Shadow on the Wall"

Jackie Kelk plays the role of Henry, who kills his brother Roger and hides the body behind the fireplace. As the days pass, the shadow of Roger continues to haunt Henry's conscience. With Jeanette Nolan and John Hoyt in supporting roles. Jackie Kelk played Henry Aldrich on *The Aldrich Family*, so the first name of "Henry" was used as an in-joke for this episode.

September 29, 1957
#718 "Vamp Till Dead"

With Vanessa Brown and Jeanette Nolan. Same story and script from January 11, 1951. This episode was originally scheduled for broadcast on August 25, 1957.

October 6, 1957
#719 "Misfire"

With Jack Carson, Barney Phillips and John Dehner. Written by sound man Tom Hanley, this science-fiction *noir* involves a failed Atomic Bomb test known as "Project Jack Hammer" that confuses the scientists until the cause of the failure is discovered.

October 13, 1957
#720 "The Well-Dressed Corpse"

With Margaret Whiting and John Dehner. Same story and script from January 18, 1951.

October 20, 1957
#721 "Sorry, Wrong Number"

With Agnes Moorehead and Jeanette Nolan. Same story and script from February 24, 1944. This was the seventh and final time Agnes Moorehead would play the lead for this series.

October 27, 1957
#722 "The Country of the Blind"

With Raymond Burr and Ben Wright. An old man tells a tale too chilling to be described in minute detail. It seems he found a hidden valley in the deepest jungles of Brazil where all of the men are blind,

Suspense

and act like zombies in an effort to pluck out his eyes! This script was previously dramatized on November 26, 1947 and June 27, 1948 on *Escape*.

November 3, 1957
#723 "Firing Run"
With Ruth Hussey and Daws Butler. While flying an airplane with newly-developed missiles, a father discovers to his horror that his young children are on board a drone plane set for target.

November 10, 1957
#724 "The Pit and the Pendulum"
With Vincent Price and John Hoyt. Same story and script from January 12, 1943. Vincent Price would later star in the big-screen version of this same story, directed by Roger Corman in 1961.

November 17, 1957
#725 "The City That Was"
With Francis X. Bushman and Jack Kruschen. A Hollywood actor witnesses a close friend attempt murder, and fail. Wishing for the inspiration of a new role, he commits the murder by finishing the job.

November 24, 1957
#726 "The Star of Thessaly"
Hired as a bodyguard, guest star Ray Noble is paid to guard an old man (played by Abraham Sofaer) and his precious jewel worth a fortune. The bodyguard learns there is more at stake than the jewel when someone attempts to kill him and the old man's daughter. Noble's own musical composition, "Goodnight, Sweetheart," was featured in this drama.

December 1, 1957
#727 "Jet Stream"
With Frank Lovejoy and Harry Bartell. An Air National Guard pilot in New York City cleverly murders his wife in California by flying a private plane through a jet stream, thus picking up enough momentum to succeed in fooling the police with an alibi.

December 8, 1957
#728 "Speed Trap"
   With Everett Sloane and William Conrad. Same story and script from April 19, 1955.

December 15, 1957
#729 "An Occurrence at Owl Creek Bridge"
   With Joseph Cotten and William Conrad. Same story and script from December 9, 1956.

December 22, 1957
#730 "Dog Star"
   With Evelyn Rudie and Dick Beals. A cute holiday story about a satellite that crashes near Julie's house, and she receives the Christmas gift she has always wanted, a small dog. But the scientists at N.A.S.A. want the lab animal more than she does. This episode was broadcast a month and a half after the launch of *Sputnik II*, featuring a two-year-old female dog named Laika.

December 29, 1957
#731 "Never Steal a Butcher's Wife"
   With William Conrad and Cathy Lewis. Same story and script from February 9, 1950.

January 5, 1958
#732 "A Week Ago Wednesday"
   With Hillary Brooke and Dee J. Thompson. Same story and script from November 29, 1945.

January 12, 1958
#733 "The Island"
   With John Lund and Lillian Buyeff. Two war vets follow the path of least resistance when a beautiful woman crosses their paths, and their premonition. This same script was previously dramatized on July 11, 1951 on *Escape*.

Suspense

January 19, 1958
#734 "The Crowded Void"
 With Bartlett Robinson and John Dehner. An expectant father is ordered by air traffic command to keep a passenger airliner in the air a little longer till the storm passes, while his wife down on the ground is delivering.

January 26, 1958
#735 "Nineteen Deacon Street"
 With Jerome Thor, Ted de Corsia and Paula Winslowe. Same story and script from November 22, 1945.

February 2, 1958
#736 "The Silver Frame"
 With Charles McGraw and Tracy Roberts. After being released from prison for a crime he was innocent, an ex-con seeks what he believes is the perfect murder for the District Attorney who prosecuted him.

February 9, 1958
#737 "The Long Shot"
 With Herbert Marshall and Florence Walcott. Same story and script from January 31, 1946.

February 16, 1958
#738 "One Chef Well Done"
 French character actor Maurice Marsac stars in this tale about two French chefs who vie for the position of the "best cook in the kitchen" by outdoing the other with tasty dishes.

February 23, 1958
#739 "Five Buck Trip"
 With Karl Swenson and Jerome Thor. Tommy visits his brother on death row and after waking from a blow to the head, finds himself in his brother's clothes. A victim of the ol' switcheroo, Tommy must convince the guards and the warden that they are about to execute the wrong man.

March 2, 1958
#740 "Never Follow a Banjo Act"
   With Margaret Whiting and Eddie Marr. Same story and script from February 1, 1954.

March 9, 1958
#741 "The Chain"
   With Agnes Moorehead and Jay Novello. Same story and script from April 27, 1950.

March 16, 1958
#742 "Game Hunt"
   With Everett Sloane and Lawrence Dobkin. Same story and script from April 3, 1956.

March 23, 1958
#743 "Affair at Loveland Pass"
   With Jim Ameche and Vanessa Brown. A man and a woman find themselves strangely connected on a dark and stormy night and the radio reports a killer evading the police. This script was written by producer and director William N. Robson.

March 30, 1958
#744 "The Sisters"
   With Frances Farmer and Cathy Lewis. Same story and script from February 3, 1944.

April 6, 1958
#745 "Just One Happy Little Family"
   With Ray Noble, Shirley Mitchell and Lee Patrick. After her wedding night, a new bride discovers her husband butchered his previous wives in cold blood. The husband, however, discovers that his wife poisoned her previous husbands.

April 13, 1958
#746 "Win, Place, or Die"
   With Frank Lovejoy and Joan Banks. Joe embezzles money from his

employer and when the act is discovered, he resorts to murder to cover up the first crime.

April 20, 1958
#747 "Alibi Me"
   With Stan Freberg. Same story and script from January 4, 1951.

April 27, 1958
#748 "Winner Lose All"
   With John Lund and Rita Lynn. Bobby makes an agreement with the owner of a gambling house to win a large sum of money and then divide the profits with the owner. The crooked scheme goes well till Bobby skips town with the loot.

May 4, 1958
#749 "Sundown"
   Jackie Kelk plays a young man, who falls victim to a horse thief and, as he grows up in the Wild West, he builds up hatred in his heart. When he feels he's experienced enough, he goes looking for the horse thief to gun him down in a fair duel. This same script was previously dramatized on June 23, 1950 on *Escape*.

May 11, 1958
#750 "Subway Stop"
   With Skip Homeier and Tommy Cook. After being beaten up by a group of young punks, a wounded businessman finds himself begging for help from people in a subway, and mistaken for a homeless bum instead.

May 18, 1958
#751 "Zero Hour"
   With Evelyn Rudy and Lillian Buyeff. Same story and script from April 5, 1955.

May 25, 1958
#752 "Like Man, Somebody Dig Me"
   Elliott Reid plays "Tennis Shoes," a cool cat who lives the beatnik life

without any care in the world. When he's accused of a murder and strung up to be hung, he discovers that the real world tolerates only so much.

June 1, 1958
#753 "Rave Notice"
   With Vincent Price and Jack Kruschen. Same story and script from October 12, 1950.

June 8, 1958
#754 "The Invisible Ape"
   With Larry Parks and Lawrence Dobkin. A scientist makes himself invisible so he can have an edge on the authorities who are on pursuit of an invisible lab specimen. After he finds the ape and returns it to the cage, does he learn the side effects of the invisibility?

June 15, 1958
#755 "Strange for a Killer"
   With Dan O'Herlihy, Joan Banks and Ted de Corsia. Same story and script from March 15, 1951.

June 22, 1958
#756 "The Last Kilometer"
   With Marsha Hunt and Ann Hunter. On a cross-country automobile race, Rene picks up a female hitch-hiker for kicks and she soon discovers he has an ulterior motive for having a woman on board.

June 29, 1958
#757 "Rain Tonight"
   With John McIntire and Tommy Cook. An inmate on death row attempts to escape by disguising himself as the prison's Man of God. This script was written by a former prisoner who spent five years in San Quentin.

July 6, 1958
#758 "Rub Down and Out"
   With Lloyd Bridges and Tracy Roberts. Same story and script from May 24, 1951.

July 13, 1958
#759 "The Long Night"
   With Frank Lovejoy and Barney Phillips. Same story and script from November 18, 1956.

July 20, 1958
#760 "It's All in Your Mind"
   With Barry Kroeger and Shirley Mitchell. A scientist named Howard develops an experimental method of telekinesis and uses his friend Jack as a guinea pig.

July 27, 1958
#761 "The Steel River Prison Break"
   With Bartlett Robinson and Barney Phillips. Same story and script from September 3, 1951.

August 3, 1958
#762 "The Voice of Company A"
   With Everett Sloane and Barney Phillips. A lieutenant in the Army is ordered by the Government to launch a "screamer satellite" that will jam all radio signals around the world for decades with a threat of war. After a visit from a ghost of the past, the lieutenant alters the message so everyone around the world hears a biblical passage.

August 10, 1958
#763 "The Diary of Sophronia Winters"
   With Mercedes McCambridge and Karl Swenson. Same story and script from April 27, 1943.

August 17, 1958
#764 "The Bridge"
   With Virginia Gregg and Bill Quinn. A driver of an automobile loses control of the vehicle and finds himself balancing on the edge of a bridge, on the verge of plunging toward death, with two other passengers. This script received a re-write from producer and director William N. Robson after it was submitted for broadcast.

August 24, 1958
#765 "Remember Me?"
   With Jackie Cooper and Sandra Gould. Same story and script from April 7, 1952.

August 31, 1958
#766 "The Whole Town's Sleeping"
   With Agnes Moorehead and William Conrad. Same story and script from June 14, 1955.

September 7, 1958
#767 "The Wait"
   With Maria Palmer and Karl Swenson. A nightmarish view of the future, when the military and the people overthrow their government. Chaos roams the streets. The future of civilization rests on the hunting of humans for sport.

September 14, 1958
#768 "Command"
   With Richard Anderson and Bill Quinn. A soldier serving in the U.S. Calvary disobeys a direct order and finds himself a captive of the Apaches. Based on the short story by James Warner Bellah. This same script was previously dramatized on December 6, 1949 on *Escape*.

September 21, 1958
#769 "No Hiding Place"
   With Jim Ameche, Lawrence Dobkin and Shirley Mitchell. The normal, average American family builds a bomb shelter and the local press places a bet that they couldn't spend the weekend together without tearing each other apart. They accept the bet with horrifying results.

September 28, 1958
#770 "Affair at Eden"
   With Frank Lovejoy. An American gains the courage to save a young lady who has been kidnapped by the Arabs for the purpose of a wedding against her will.

October 4, 1958
#771 "The Man Who Won the War"
   With Herbert Marshall and Abraham Sofaer. An Englishman accomplishes the feat of a lifetime when he holds back the invading Germans single-handedly along the Belgian line. He is court-martialed for failure to explain how he accomplished his task. Based on the short story by Robert Henry Buckner. This same script was previously dramatized on February 28, 1950 on *Escape*.

October 11, 1958
#772 "The Treasure Chest of Don Jose"
   With Raymond Burr and Tommy Cook. Same story and script from February 4, 1952. This story was originally scheduled for the broadcast of September 7, 1958.

October 18, 1958
#773 "Three Skeleton Key"
   With Vincent Price, Lawrence Dobkin and Ben Wright. Same story and script from November 11, 1956.

October 25, 1958
#774 "Headshrinker"
   With Helmut Dantine and Nina Foch. A patient finds herself the victim of a psychologist's experiment and when the tables are turned on the doctor, she discovers the true horrors of the human brain. This script was written by producer and director William N. Robson.

November 1, 1958
#775 "The Dealings of Mr. Markham"
   With Pamela and James Mason. Same story and script from May 11, 1943.

November 8, 1958
#776 "Two for the Road"
   With Charles McGraw and William Conrad. Two television actors play the role of criminals on a television program and soon find themselves the victim of their own success when they are later picked up by the police on suspicion of murder and robbery.

November 15, 1958
#777 "My Dear Niece"
   With Lee Patrick and Berry Kroeger. Same story and script from January 24, 1946.

Sunday — 5:30 p.m. to 5:55 p.m. (E.S.T.)

November 23, 1958
#778 "A Statement of Fact"
   With Cathy Lewis and John Dehner. This radio script was originally dramatized on May 14, 1953 on *On Stage*.

November 30, 1958
#779 "Misfire"
   With William Conrad and John Dehner. Same story and script from October 6, 1957.

December 7, 1958
#780 "Tom Dooley"
   With Robert Horton and Hilda Hart. Same story and script from March 30, 1953. The folk music for this episode was a recording of the Kingston Trio's number one hit of the same name.

December 14, 1958
#781 "For Old Time's Sake"
   With John Lund and Bill Quinn. An ex-con is released after having served time for robbing a bank. After getting a second chance for a new life being employed at another financial institution, he finds himself on the other side of the counter when an old friend walks in and robs the bank.

December 21, 1958
#782 "Out for Christmas"
   Raymond Burr plays the role of Joe Watson, released on parole in time for the holidays. Purchasing a Santa Claus suit and arming himself with a loaded weapon, he pays a visit to his ex-girlfriend and the man who sent him up.

Suspense

December 28, 1958
#783 "The Thirty-Second of December"
With Frank Lovejoy and Joan Banks. A gambler in need of money finds himself in possession with wristwatch that transports him into the future and the past.

January 4, 1959
#784 "Don't Call Me Mother"
Agnes Moorehead plays a scornful mother who murders her son's new girlfriend and discards the body. When her son discovers what his mother did, he turns her in to the police.

January 11, 1959
#785 "Night on Red Mountain"
With Richard Crenna and Doris Singleton. Same story and script from September 15, 1957.

January 18, 1959
#786 "Ride Down Calhone"
With William Bishop, Joe DeSantis and Bill Quinn. Driving down one of the steepest roads in the state, two men driving a large rig finds themselves on the verge of death when the truck's brakes give out on them, and they make their best attempt at survival as they keep control of the runaway vehicle.

January 25, 1959
#787 "Four of a Kind"
With Elliott Reid, Joan Tompkins and Alan Reed. Same story and script from September 16, 1948. This episode was originally scheduled for the broadcast of December 28, 1958.

February 1, 1959
#788 "Return to Dust"
With Dick Beals, Lawrence Dobkin and Paula Winslowe. A scientist dictates to his colleagues the horrible mistake he made in the lab, causing him to shrink in size with each passing minute. A wonderful one-man performance by Dick Beals, who changes his voice throughout the drama without the need of any technical assistance.

The sound effect of the giant bird eating the shrinking scientist was simulated by breaking a tooth pick or a stick of wood. The scriptwriter, George Bamber, won a national award for this script. Dick Beals recalled, "That was such a challenge to keep getting the voice smaller and smaller and smaller as we went through the show. I had to make it smaller. It was such a difficult thing to do. They did isolate me. They put me in a closed booth where I could see the orchestra and the two people on the show and the director. It wasn't that tough. You do it all the time when you do cartoons and commercials, and it's just a matter of pleasing the director and we just kept doing it, and he liked what I did, and so we went on home." During my interview with author and historian Martin Grams Jr., he revealed to me that this was one of the best episodes of the series, and often the least considered by *Suspense* connoisseurs.

February 8, 1959
#789 "Death Notice"
With Victor Jory and Barney Phillips. When Charlie learns from his doctor that he is dying, he makes amends by dumping his girlfriend and spends his remaining time with his wife and son.

February 15, 1959
#790 "The Signalman"
With Ellen Drew and Ben Wright. Same story and script from March 23, 1953.

February 22, 1959
#791 "Star Over Hong Kong"
Marie Wilson plays an American actress who arrives in Hong Kong for business and finds herself a kidnap victim by her own admirers!

March 1, 1959
#792 "The Waxwork"
With Herbert Marshall. Same story and script from March 20, 1947.

March 8, 1959
#793 "Mad Man from Manhattan"
With Myron McCormick and Doris Singleton. Same story and script from January 19, 1950.

March 15, 1959
#794 "Death in Box 234"
   With Frank Lovejoy and Edgar Stehli. A bank teller embezzles money when a pet store owner asks him to make an unusually large deposit. This was one of the few episodes of the series to star Frank Lovejoy and not feature his real-life wife Joan Banks in the cast. The reason for this may be simple: there was no female in the entire cast.

March 22, 1959
#795 "Script by Mark Brady"
   With Marie Windsor and Vic Perrin. A mystery writer wants to plot a perfect murder and uses his unfaithful wife as the guinea pig in his experiment. This was the second of two episodes of *Suspense* to feature actress Marie Windsor in the cast.

March 29, 1959
#796 "John Barbey and Son"
   With John McIntire and Jack Kruschen. Same story and script from February 22, 1945.

April 5, 1959
   Pre-empted

April 12, 1959
#797 "Too Hot to Live"
   With Van Heflin and Berry Kroeger. Same story and script from October 26, 1950.

April 19, 1959
#798 "See How He Runs"
   With Jim Backus and Gail Bonney. A blind man, who sells newspapers, witnesses the sound of a murder and when the police ask him to identity the murderer, the witness keeps silent. Knowing the killer will come back for him, the blind man sets a trap.

April 26, 1959
#799 "Deep, Deep is My Love"
   With Lloyd Bridges. A deep sea diver meets a mermaid during an

expedition and falls in love with the specter. His wife, unsure of how to cope with his ramblings, tries her best to remind him of their marriage. At the time this *Suspense* episode was broadcast, Lloyd Bridges was also the star of television's *Sea Hunt* playing a deep sea diver-for-fire.

May 3, 1959
#800 "The Amateur"
Jackie Cooper plays a young man who witnesses a hit-and-run killing and rather than turn the physical evidence over to the police, he hands the evidence to a crime lord in town, responsible for the murder. Actor Tommy Cook plays a role in this episode.

May 10, 1959
#801 "On a Country Road"
With real-life husband and wife, Howard Duff and Ida Lupino. Same story and script from November 16, 1950.

May 17, 1959
#802 "A Friend of Daddy's"
With Frank Lovejoy, Dick Beals and Bill Quinn. A Korean War buddy visits a friend from the war and makes himself at home for a short while. When he takes to the housewife, the old friend must brave himself for a battle worse than he faced in the Korean War.

May 24, 1959
#803 "Spoils for Victor"
With Robert Horton and Georgia Ellis. Same story and script from May 23, 1946.

May 31, 1959
#804 "The Man Who Would Be King"
With Dan O'Herlihy and Ben Wright. Two Englishmen find themselves treated like Gods by the natives in India. When one of the men decides to take advantage of their newfound royalty by claiming a wife, the natives get restless. This same script was previously dramatized on July 7, 1947 on *Escape*.

June 7, 1959
#805 "The Pit and the Pendulum"
   With Raymond Burr. Same story and script from January 12, 1943. Even though this same story and script was broadcast on *Suspense* three times previous, and as recently as two years before under the same direction of William N. Robson, Americans of Spanish Ancestry felt the drama reflected unfairly on them and wrote a letter of protest to the producer, who apologized publicly.

June 14, 1959
#806 "Drive-In"
   With Barbara Whiting and Gail Lucas. Same story and script from January 11, 1945.

June 21, 1959
#807 "Ivy is a Lovely Name for a Girl"
   With Frank Lovejoy and Joan Banks. Mr. and Mrs. Peterson find themselves a victim of a blowout while speeding on the freeway. Not a good time since Mrs. Peterson's water broke and she's about to give birth in the backseat.

June 28, 1959
#808 "Analytical Hour"
   With Jack Carson and John Hoyt. A psychologist is shocked when his patient claims he's cured of a year-long headache, almost overnight, because he killed his pestering wife.

July 5, 1959
#809 "Blood is Thicker"
   With Everett Sloane and Bill Quinn. Two men battle to the death during a boat race, and the prize is a beautiful woman. This episode was based on a true story, written by Sam Pierce, an official news correspondent and charter member of the crew of one of the schooners.

July 12, 1959
#810 "Eyewitness"
   With John Lund and Joe DeSantis. Same story and script from December 16, 1956.

July 19, 1959
#811 "An Occurrence at Owl Creek Bridge"
 With Vincent Price and Barney Phillips. Same story and script from December 9, 1956.

July 26, 1959
#812 "Night Man"
 With Marsha Hunt. Same story and script from October 26, 1944.

August 2, 1959
#813 "Red Cloud Mesa"
 With Joseph Cotten and Howard McNear. Same story and script from October 30, 1956.

August 9, 1959
#814 "Everything Will be Different"
 With Lawrence Dobkin and Virginia Gregg. Herb listens to a confession from his girlfriend, and learns that her previous husband died under mysterious circumstances. She blames his death as a result of her own doing.

August 16, 1959
#815 "Like Man, Somebody Dig Me"
 With Dennis Day and Paul Frees. Same story and script from May 25, 1958.

August 23, 1959
#816 "Headshrinker"
 With Agnes Moorehead and Lawrence Dobkin. Same story and script from October 25, 1958. This is the final episode to originate from Hollywood, and the final episode produced and directed by William N. Robson. Robson would write at least three more radio scripts for *Suspense* between this episode and the final broadcast of the series.

August 30, 1959
#817 "A Matter of Execution"
 With Santos Ortega and Ginger Jones. A young boy is entrusted with important evidence that will save a man from the electric chair.

When he tries to hand the evidence over to the police, they dismiss the lad as childish ramblings. Beginning with this episode, the series began originating from New York instead of Hollywood. Paul Roberts takes over the producing and directing chores from William N. Robson.

September 6, 1959
#818 "After the Movies"
With Kevin McCarthy. Same as story and script from December 7, 1950. Stuart Metz joins George Walsh in sharing the announcing duties for *Suspense* beginning with this episode.

September 13, 1959
#819 "Death and the Escort"
With Elspeth Eric and Joseph Julian. When a witness agrees to testify against a racketeer, the District Attorney sends an armed security officer to protect the witness. But has the security officer already been bribed by the racketeer?

September 20, 1959
#820 "The Beetle and Mr. Bottle"
With Mason Adams and John Gibson. Same story and script from August 23, 1955.

September 27, 1959
Pre-empted

October 4, 1959
#821 "Room 203"
With Bernard Grant and Ralph Bell. Newlyweds on their honeymoon witness a murder from their hotel window and when the police investigate their story, they find no evidence of a murder. This episode was originally scheduled for broadcast on September 27, 1959.

October 11, 1959
#822 "Infanticide"
With Santos Ortega and Ralph Bell. A young boy with medical problems is found dead under incriminating circumstances and his father is not the only suspect in the case.

October 18, 1959
#823 "The Crisis of Dirk Diamond"
  With Bernard Grant, Ian Martin and Luis Van Rooten. A comic strip artist finds himself being harassed by the same villain he created in his doodles. This episode was an adaptation of a television episode of *The Web*, by Sam Locke.

October 25, 1959
#824 "The Easy Victim"
  With Paul McGrath and Elspeth Eric. Mr. Ames is forced to marry a woman he doesn't care for, and then plots her murder so he can collect the life insurance money.

November 1, 1959
#825 "Re-Entry"
  With Mason Adams and Margaret Draper. An astronaut is launched into space in an experimental shuttle and finds himself in another world that mirrors a heavenly Earth.

November 8, 1959
#826 "The Last Trip"
  With Bob Dryden and Eugene Francis. An unsuspecting husband carries a locked briefcase containing a time bomb set to explode.

November 15, 1959
#827 "The Companion"
  With Virginia Payne and Rita Lloyd. A young lady stays home alone with her mother, during a dark and stormy evening. To feel safer, she phones for a temporary nurse to stay with them until the storm passes, not suspecting the nurse is a robber in disguise.

November 22, 1959
#828 "The Thimble"
  With Whitfield Connor and Paul McGrath. When a wealthy old woman dies under mysterious circumstances, the family doctor prevents an autopsy from being conducted. The deceased has a daughter, not of sound mind, who demands the doctor be arrested for her mother's murder.

November 29, 1959
#829 "Leiningen vs. The Ants"
With Luis Van Rooten. Same story and script from August 25, 1957.

December 6, 1959
#830 "Dynamite Run"
With Mason Adams and Bob Dryden. Ben is a truck driver who, in need of money to support his family, accepts a job of carrying the largest shipment of dynamite in the State to help with the nearby forest fires. When a killer on the run from the law stows away in the front seat, Ben tries to explain how one gunshot can bury their bodies in a large explosion.

December 13, 1959
#831 "The Country of the Blind"
With Jackson Beck and Bernard Grant. Same story and script from October 27, 1957.

December 20, 1959
#832 "A Korean Christmas Carol"
With Bill Lipton and Santos Ortega. A touching Christmas message is dramatized through a young man spending his first holiday season away from his family, while serving on the war front.

December 27, 1959
#833 "Moonlight Sail"
With Guy Repp and Frank Thomas, Jr. A charter boat captain is accused of attempted murder and sets sail to rescue the damsel in distress to clear his good name.

January 3, 1960
#834 "Zero Hour"
With John Gibson and Ginger Jones. Same story and script from April 5, 1955.

January 10, 1960
#835 "The Long Night"
With Bill Adams. Same story and script from November 18, 1956.

January 17, 1960
#836 "The Time, The Place, and The Death"
　　With Eric Dressler, Maurice Tarplin and Bryna Raeburn. Henry believes a prophesy from a gypsy fortune teller and begins making plans for his death. When his unfaithful wife learns what he is doing, she and her boyfriend ensure that Henry's death goes off without a hitch.

January 24, 1960
#837 "Turnabout"
　　With Larry Haines and Raymond Edward Johnson. A District Attorney is forced at gunpoint by a killer to blame a murder on an innocent janitor. But is the killer legit in his claim of innocence?

January 31, 1960
#838 "End of the Road"
　　With Bernard Grant. A model is beaten and bruised by her husband so she seeks a divorce. A week later he apologizes for his actions and she makes the mistake of letting him in the house again.

February 7, 1960
#839 "The Mystery of the Marie Roget"
　　With Jackson Beck and Robert Dryden. Same story and script from December 14, 1953.

February 14, 1960
#840 "Sorry, Wrong Number"
　　With Agnes Moorehead. This dramatization is not a repeat performance. It is a replay of a recording of the October 20, 1957 broadcast.

February 21, 1960
#841 "The Crank Letter"
　　With Larry Haines and Les Damon. A doctor receives death threats through the mail, and the local police confirm the threat when they too received the same threats by phone.

February 28, 1960
#842 "Lt. Langer's Last Collection"
　　With Ian Martin and Frank Thomas Jr. A cop blackmails a store

owner and falls victim to a heart attack in the streets. Seeking assistance from pedestrians, he discovers how much of an influence he left for the citizens on his beat.

March 6, 1960
#843 "Sleep is for Children"
With Elspeth Eric and Mason Adams. Mrs. Gordon spends a frightening evening at home with her daughter when she discovers that the family friend, spending the night in their house, is the Woodlake Strangler the police have been looking for. The title of this script was originally "Sleeping is for Children."

March 13, 1960
#844 "The Revolution"
With Rosemary Rice and Santos Ortega. American tourists snap a photo of a foreign dictator and face the wrath of the country's law when they are arrested and sentenced to execution.

March 20, 1960
#845 "Talk About Caruso"
With Mason Adams and Robert Dryden. A boxer-turned-stage performer owes his former boxing manager when he hits the high life. This script was written by Milton Geiger, who scripted for other radio programs such as *Inner Sanctum Mystery* and *Murder at Midnight*.

March 27, 1960
#846 "Coffin for Mr. Cash"
With Leon Janney and Mandel Kramer. Using a milk wagon and a coffin, two criminals rob three million in currency from the mob. This radio script was originally dramatized under a different title on *The Mysterious Traveler*.

April 3, 1960
#847 "A Shipment of Mute Fate"
With Bernard Grant and Inga Swenson. Same story and script form January 6, 1957.

April 10, 1960
#848 "Two Horse Parlay"

With Larry Haines. Johnny's aunt has been paying for his piano lessons for the past years and she wants him to come home and perform for her. How can he tell his wealthy aunt that he's been using the money as a means of paying off his gambling debts?

April 17, 1960
#849 "Tonight at 5:55"

With Robert Readick and John Gibson. The United States and a foreign country have been head-to-head with political disagreements and the Government finally gave the other country an ultimatum. Surrender or face nuclear annihilation. They have till 5:55 to give their response, coincidentally the same time this *Suspense* broadcast ends (broadcast 5:30 to 5:55 p.m. E.S.T.). The audience is left to decide the fate of the two countries.

April 24, 1960
#850 "One More Shot"

With William Redfield and Frank Thomas Jr. A newspaper editor dons a disguise and infiltrates a biker gang to uncover the motive of an employee's murder. This episode was scripted by former producer and director William N. Robson.

May 1, 1960
#851 "Bitter Grapes"

With Phil Meader and Edgar Stehli. A vengeful housewife makes a recording for her husband, explaining why she poisoned his food. Learning that an error was made, she races against time to get the record back before her husband plays it.

May 8, 1960
#852 "The Legend of Robbie"

With George Matthews. Robbie steals money from his employer and makes it appear as if an accident was the cause. When his partner wants to tell the truth to the employer, Robbie is forced to kill his partner.

Suspense

May 15, 1960
#853 "Dead Man's Story"
   With Kevin McCarthy. A New York detective is escorting his prisoner back to the city when their boat capsizes and begins sinking. Trapped inside the slowly sinking vessel, the men have to find a way out before it's too late. This script was previously dramatized on *The Mysterious Traveler*.

May 22, 1960
#854 "Out the Window"
   With Santos Ortega and Roger DeKoven. A police commissioner is forced to kill two criminals who break into his office, and taking advantage of the opportunity, kills his wife and girlfriend at the same time, throwing the blame on the hired killers.

May 29, 1960
#855 "Perfect Plan"
   With George Petrie. Henry meets a stranger on the bus, telling him his wife has been held hostage and he has two hours to pay $50,000 or lose her life. When he gets in the office, he phones his house and hears a stranger answer the phone.

June 5, 1960
#856 "Two Came Back"
   With Robert Readick and Connie Lembke. With natives and headhunters following pursuit, English explorers try to escape the jungles of New Guinea with half a million in gold. Based on the short story by Jules Archer. This same script was previously dramatized on August 4, 1950 on *Escape*.

June 12, 1960
#857 "Elementals"
   With Phil Meader and Santos Ortega. Mr. Slate bets a married couple that they couldn't go without food for 14 days and afterwards, not tear each other apart for a single loaf of bread. Based on the short story by Steven Vincent Benet, this radio script was previously dramatized on February 14, 1949 on *Radio City Playhouse* and on October 11, 1953 on

Escape. Benet once recalled, "It seems to me one of the very few decent short stories I've ever written."

June 19, 1960
#858 "Sixty Grand Missing"
With Bernard Grant and Ralph Bell. A detective turns in a false report in order to keep the cash confiscated from a criminal investigation. This script was previously dramatized on *The Mysterious Traveler*.

June 26, 1960
#859 "Daisy Chain"
With Joan Lorring and Bret Morrison. Sharon dates a young man who may or may not be the strangler loose in the streets of London, and questions his past when she gets the opportunity to meet her mother.

July 3, 1960
#860 "Bon Voyage"
With Robert Readick and Joseph Julian. After embezzling $200,000 from his employers, a nervous employee races back to the office to cover up a clue he left at the scene of the crime. In doing so, he bumps into a robber who has plans of his own.

July 10, 1960
#861 "Report from a Dead Planet"
With Bernard Grant and John Larkin. A spaceship lands on a planet that was once inhabited with a civilization much like our own. The astronauts gather the evidence to take back home, hoping to find a cure that will prevent the same from happening to their own planet.

July 17, 1960
#862 "Memorial Bridge"
With Robert Dryden and Larry Dobkin. A construction supervisor murders his wife and discards her body in the freshly-poured concrete. In memory of his late wife, he names the bridge after her. This script was written by former producer and director William N. Robson.

July 24, 1960
#863 "Cold Canvas"
   With William Redfield and Guy Repp. A new employee working for an insurance company scores the largest deal for the company, and his cheers turn to sorrow when his client mysteriously dies days later in an auto accident. Was this premeditated murder?

July 31, 1960
#864 "End Game"
   With Santos Ortega. A crooked sheriff blackmails a killer into keeping him at his house so he can play a game of chess with the victim.

August 7, 1960
#865 "The Big Dive"
   With Leon Janney, Rosemary Rice and Ralph Bell. Danny King, a professional diver for a traveling carnival, plans to take the biggest dive in history, without a swimming pool on the ground to catch his fall.

August 14, 1960
#866 "Night Ferry to Paris"
   With William Redfield and Robert Dryden. A stranger asks a woman to help carry his luggage on board a train, only to find herself caught in the middle of an espionage ring.

August 21, 1960
#867 "Truck Stop"
   With Mandel Kramer, Larry Haines and Robert Readick. Two men make plans to rob an armored truck, and in doing so, note every detail of the truck's delivery.

August 28, 1960
#868 "The Girl in the Powder Blue Jag"
   With Rita Lloyd and Robert Dryden. A married couple nurses an elderly woman who is very wealthy. They plan to speed up her demise so they can inherit the fortune sooner.

September 4, 1960
#869 "A Rest for Emily"
With Abbey Lewis and Bill Smith. A farmer murders his wife and then buries the body under the barn.

September 11, 1960
#870 "Rakovsky's Rubbles"
With Santos Ortega, William Redfield and Robert Readick. Ivan robs his employer and hides the money before the police arrest him. After serving twenty years for robbery, Ivan is released to retrieve the money, only to discover his old flame has the same interest.

September 18, 1960
#871 "A Statement of Fact"
With Mason Adams and Lawson Zerbe. Same story and script from November 28, 1958.

September 25, 1960
#872 "Time on My Hands"
With Santos Ortega, Ted Osborne and Robert Dryden. Two time travelers go back to 1908, in hopes of preventing Adolf Hitler's rise to power, only to discover a twist in time travel. This episode was originally dramatized on *The Mysterious Traveler*. Certain radio stations chose to broadcast something else during this time slot, so only certain areas across the country heard this broadcast.

October 2, 1960
#873 "Ivy is a Lovely Name for a Girl"
With Phil Meader and Johnny Spencer. Same story and script from June 21, 1959.

October 9, 1960
#874 "Witness for Death"
With William Redfield and Frank Thomas, Jr. A witness to a murder case is forced to choose between prudery and revealing the facts behind the murder his best friend committed.

Suspense

October 16, 1960
#875 "Inferno"
 With Mandel Kramer. A young couple must apply their brains over brawn to survive in the middle of the desert, when two prospectors steal their car.

October 23, 1960
#876 "Night Man"
 With Ginger Jones. Same story and script from October 26, 1944.

October 30, 1960
#877 "The City That Was"
 With Bernard Grant and House Jameson. Same story and script from November 17, 1957.

November 6, 1960
#878 "The Green Lorelei"
 With John Gibson and Robert Readick. A pulp fiction writer discovers the beautiful woman living in the apartment above him is a beautiful Lorelei in disguise. Can he evade his landlady in time to meet the woman of his dreams?

November 13, 1960
#879 "The Man Who Murders People"
 With Maurice Tarplin and George Petrie. On board a train, a woman meets two men who may or may not be the killers plaguing the front pages of the local newspapers. Tarplin plays one of the passengers on the train. For nine years he played the host, a passenger on a train, on *The Mysterious Traveler*.

November 20, 1960
#880 "Night on Red Mountain"
 With Mandel Kramer and Lawson Zerbe. Same story and script from September 15, 1957.

November 27, 1960
#881 "Home is Where You Find It"
 With Mandel Kramer and William Redfield. A young man meets a

kind soul named Tex, who offers to give him food and shelter in exchange for a few services.

Sunday — 6:35 p.m. to 7:00 p.m. (E.S.T.)

June 25, 1961
#882 "Call Me at Half Past"

With Elspeth Eric, Lawson Zerbe and Bernard Grant. Mr. Simmons lost his daughter years ago and his wife, who could not accept reality, went mental. Now that she escaped the looney house, she's searching for her husband, ready to make him pay for his past crimes. This is the first episode of the series to be directed by Bruno Zirato, Jr. Stuart Metz is the lone *Suspense* announcer, since George Walsh left the series beginning with this episode.

July 2, 1961
#883 "Night of the Storm"

With Rosemary Rice and Lawson Zerbe. A desperate wife uses any means possible to save her husband from death row. Finding the only witness who will clear her husband's name, the wife learns that the witness is willing to take her secret to the grave before talking to the police.

July 9, 1961
#884 "Epitaph"

With Paul McGrath and Joan Lorring. Lucinda marries her brother-in-law after the death of her sister, only to discover the truth. Was it an accident or was it murder?

July 16, 1961
#885 "The Man Who Knew How to Hate"

Joan Lorring plays a wife who falls in love with another man, and together they plot the murder of her husband. Also stars Robert Dryden and Leon Janney.

July 23, 1961
#886 "Stranger With My Face"

With Bernard Grant and Lawson Zerbe. In a rip-off of Cornell Woolrich's *The Black Curtain*, but with a twist, a man is hit by an automobile and wakes four years in the future to discover his identity and face have changed. Did he commit a murder during the four missing years of his life?

July 30, 1961
#887 "You Can Die Laughing"
With Larry Haines, Ian Martin and Gertrude Warner. This script was originally written for *The Mysterious Traveler*. When Betty's husband discovers his wife has been cheating on her, he fires the young man under his employment to get even. Angry, the two kill the wealthy husband and then bury the body in the cellar of a haunted house.

August 6, 1961
#888 "Bells"
With Rosemary Rice and Lawson Zerbe. A young couple move into a house supposedly haunted. Every so often the sound of bells rings out, such as the doorbell and phone, when no one is calling on them. Could it be angels from heaven trying to communicate?

August 13, 1961
Pre-empted

August 20, 1961
#889 "Murder is a Matter of Opinion"
With Maurice Tarplin and Lawson Zerbe. Two boys in law school plan a fake murder to prove that an innocent man can go to the chair for a crime he did not commit. This script was previously dramatized on *Radio City Playhouse* on May 23, 1949.

August 27, 1961
#890 "Sold to Satan"
With Robert Dryden and Ian Martin. Harry is blackmailed by a woman holding incriminating photos and he asks a friend to help him get the pictures back.

September 3, 1961
#891 "The Juvenile Rebellion"
With Court Benson. A school teacher learns by accident that one of

her pupils is really a mutant with telekinesis powers. She also learns that there are at least a million other children with gifted powers across the world and a takeover will begin in a few days.

September 10, 1961
Pre-empted for Bob Hite's "Battle of the Batters."

September 17, 1961
#892 "The Green Idol"
With Abby Lewis, Mercer McCloud and Guy Repp. A vacation in Meca, Arabia turns into a disaster when American tourists purchase a small green statue in the marketplace. They soon learn a curse lies on the owners of the statue when the green little man comes to life and attempts to strangle them.

September 24, 1961
#893 "The Man in the Fog"
With Robert Dryden and Guy Repp. In a rip-off of *The Lodger*, an old man with strange behavior is suspected of being the "monster" on the loose, slashing women to death on the foggy nights of London, England.

October 1, 1961
#894 "No Hiding Place"
With Leon Janney and Court Benson. Same story and script from September 21, 1958.

October 8, 1961
#895 "Dreams"
Raymond Edward Johnson plays Robert, a man who is haunted by evening dreams he mistakes as premonitions. His wife and friends think the premonitions are just coincidences after the dreams come true but Robert things otherwise.

October 15, 1961
#896 "Seeds of Disaster"
With Bernard Grant, Guy Repp and Robert Dryden. When a young couple discover that the necklace they brought back from a recent

vacation is made of poisonous seeds, they race back home to save the life of their young daughter, who, like any child, has a habit of putting things in her mouth.

October 22, 1961
#897 "Witness to Murder"
   With Robert Dryden, Leon Janney and Guy Repp. A female passenger on board a luxury liner is starting to lose her mental capacity. She went insane on board the same boat years before, and her husband suspects she is about to suffer the same symptoms.

October 29, 1961
#898 "Death of an Old Flame"
   With Larry Haines and Ralph Bell. A piano player meets up with an old flame of his, who convinces him to help her steal some furs from a warehouse. Soon after the job is done, her new boyfriend shows up on the scene and sets fire to the building, with the intention of leaving the piano player inside to take the blame.

November 5, 1961
#899 " 'Til Death Do Us Part"
   With Bill Lipton. A vengeful husband gives his wife a lethal dose of medicine, using stolen prescription pads from a doctor's office. She should have died since day one but weeks later she's still moving about. This script was previously dramatized on August 2, 1951 on *Hollywood Star Playhouse*.

November 12, 1961
#900 "The Imposters"
   With Arline Blackburn and Bill Lipton. A butler and maid look so much like their employers that they kill the older couple to assume their identities, and their wallets.

November 19, 1961
#901 "The Black Door"
   An archaeologist and his guide, played by Robert Readick and Ralph Camargo, discover a lost ancient city of ruins where the human-like statues with dog heads come to life. A very creepy episode and one

of the scariest of the series. This script was previously dramatized on the March 18, 1952 broadcast of *The Mysterious Traveler*.

November 26, 1961
#902 "Man Trap"
With Joseph Julian, Lawson Zerbe and Ralph Bell. When a road construction worker kills a man by accident with dynamite, the police and the widow suspect he committed murder. He even starts to doubt his sanity when the ghostly figure of the dead man returns to haunt him.

December 3, 1961
#903 "The Luck of the Tiger Eye"
With Raymond Edward Johnson and Leon Janney. By order of her late uncle's will, a young lady, played by Joan Lorring, and her fiancé, have to spend the night in her uncle's creepy old mansion to inherit the uncle's fortune. After they steal a valuable ring from the dead man's hand, they learn what the curse of the Tiger's Eye is all about.

December 10, 1961
#904 "And So to Sleep My Love"
With William Redfield and Bryna Rayburn. A husband attempts to dispose of his wife by driving her crazy with a hidden record player and an overdose of sleeping pills. Abby Lewis supplies the voice of the woman screaming on the recording.

December 17, 1961
#905 "Yuletide Miracle"
Originally dramatized on *Inner Sanctum Mystery* on December 26, 1949, with Frank Sinatra in the lead. Larry Haines plays the role of Chris, and ex-con who is asked by a dying young man to deliver important Christmas packages. To aid him in his quest is Sir Benjamin, an invisible Christmas ghost.

December 24, 1961
Pre-empted for a Christmas Special, with Bing Crosby entitled "Sing Along With Bing."

December 31, 1961
#906 "The Old Man"
   With Guy Repp and Lawson Zerbe. On New Year's Eve, old man 1961 will not make room for baby 1962. It seems he has a grudge against the youth of today.

January 7, 1962
#907 "Breakthrough"
   With Robert Dryden and Guy Repp. A family attempts to cross the border before the Iron Curtain is completed. One son, returning to fetch his stubborn mother, is too late as he finds the wall completed a little early.

January 14, 1962
#908 "Feathers"
   With Lawson Zerbe and Ian Martin. Feathers shoots his business partner in the back when he discovers he was being backstabbed. The dying man swears his ghost will haunt Feathers till the day he dies.

January 21, 1962
#909 "2462"
   With Lawson Zerbe, Robert Dryden and Rosemary Rice. In a nightmarish vision of the future, where writing poems is considered "producing non-productive literature," Frank Smith, also known as number 108303715, is arrested and sentenced to death for his writing.

January 28, 1962
#910 "Please Believe Me"
   With Robert Readick and Joan Lorring. A cheating wife and a husband who married for money decide to eliminate the other. Who will succeed first?

February 4, 1962
#911 "Friday"
   With William Redfield and Lawson Zerbe. The Captain of a sailing vessel named *Friday* decides to prove to the sailors on port that deporting on a Friday is not cause for superstition.

February 11, 1962
#912 "The Man Who Went Back to Save Lincoln"
　　With Ian Martin and Ralph Bell. A brilliant scientist creates a time machine and travels back to 1865, where he plans to prevent the assassination of Abraham Lincoln. This script was previously dramatized on *The Mysterious Traveler* on February 7, 1950. Lincoln's birthday was February 12, the day after this broadcast.

February 18, 1962
#913 "The Old Boyfriend"
　　With Elspeth Eric, Joseph Julian and Lawson Zerbe. Maggie meets up with an ex-boyfriend from her high school days who happens to be on the run from the police. He kidnaps Maggie's daughter and holds her hostage.

February 25, 1962
#914 "Date Night"
　　With Rosemary Rice, Guy Repp and Lawson Zerbe. Young Kathy is out on her first date and her father is home worried, dreaming of the many ways her boyfriend could be taking advantage of her daughter. This episode was scripted by William N. Robson, a former producer and director and writer of *Suspense*.

March 4, 1962
#915 "Doom Machine"
　　With Bernard Grant, Leon Janney and Cliff Carpenter. In the year 2500, Dr. Ferris creates an artificial brain and commands it to create a power source generated from the sun's rays.

March 11, 1962
#916 "Heads, You Lose"
　　With Raymond Edward Johnson and Santos Ortega. A private detective is hired to find Joshua Franklin, a man who disappeared a few years ago.

March 18, 1962
#917 "Perchance to Dream"
　　With Paul McGrath and Guy Repp. When a woman's husband is

Suspense

released from the hospital from a nervous breakdown, she soon discovers that he sees her as the spitting image of a woman he killed in an accident. This script was previous dramatized on *Starring Boris Karloff* on October 19, 1949.

March 25, 1962
#918 "Memory of a Murder"

With Ralph Bell and Lawson Zerbe. A young man is hired to work for a theater where a jealous stage magician has a reputation for disposing of young men who fall for the wiles of his beautiful assistant. This script, written by John Roberts, was previously dramatized on *Tales of Fatima* and *Inner Sanctum Mystery*.

April 1, 1962
#919 "You Died Last Night"

With Santos Ortega and Robert Readick. In a rip-off of *The Day the Earth Stood Still* (1951), a Martian tells an Earthling that our species is too dangerous, having reached the atomic age, and must be destroyed before they become a threat to the Martians' existence. This script was previously dramatized on *The Mysterious Traveler*.

April 8, 1962
#920 "Let There Be Light"

With Ivor Francis and Teri Keane. A blind man finds himself a party in a deadly game of cat and mouse when diamond thieves force their way into his territory.

April 15, 1962
#921 "Brother John"

With William Redfield and Paul McGrath. Charlie wakes to find his brother dead. After finding out who the murderers are, instead of turning them in to the police, he blackmails them.

April 22, 1962
#922 "The Curse of Kamoshek"

With Ian Martin and Raymond Edward Johnson. Donald inherits his uncle Egyptian artifacts, including an Egyptian bone that supposedly has a curse on it.

April 29, 1962
#923 "Blackbeard's Ace"
With Robert Dryden and John Thomas. A married couple spends a week in their aunt's house, only to discover pirate ghosts roaming the hallways.

May 6, 1962
#924 "The Second Door"
With Robert Dryden, Robert Readick and Paul McGrath. A scientist creates a doorway that allows people to walk through and take them anywhere.

May 13, 1962
#925 "Hide and Seek"
With Jackson Beck and Larry Haines. Dandy gambles a debt of $1,000 and when he cannot pay up, he is forced to play a game of cat and mouse through the city streets with gunmen.

May 20, 1962
#926 "Dagger of the Mind"
With Leon Janney and Guy Repp. Vicki discovers the root of her nightmares when her husband brings home a female business associate over for dinner.

May 27, 1962
#927 "That Real Crazy Infinity"
With Jack Grimes and Robert Readick. Two young musicians acquire a scientist's invention that plucks sounds from the past, and use this gimmick to cash in by "discovering" what was once considered "lost" recordings. This was the final episode directed by Bruno Zirato, Jr.

June 3, 1962
#928 "Stand-In For Murder"
With Jack Grimes and Larry Haines. Jimmy kills his wife Lora during an argument, so he turns to his girlfriend Kay for assistance. Kay dresses and acts the role of his wife to avoid suspicion of a murder. This was the first episode directed by Fred Hendrickson, a former studio technician, who would direct the remainder of the episodes for the *Suspense* series.

June 10, 1962
#929 "Formula for Death"
With Robert Readick, Guy Repp and Lawson Zerbe. A professor develops the formula of the century and every nation of the world wants ownership. Before he can turn it over to the United States Government, the professor is killed in an auto accident. But the scientist used his formula to help deliver the secret through the dead body of an enemy agent.

June 17, 1962
#930 "The Lunatic Hour"
With Les Damon, Rosemary Rice and Donald Buka. Ten years ago, Tom made an error, causing the wreck of Train 1155. Now the ghost of Gully Reeves, the train engineer who died in the crash, comes back to haunt Tom. This script was previously dramatized on *Inner Sanctum Mystery*.

June 24, 1962
#931 "With Murder in Mind"
With Jack Kruschen, William Redfield and Gilbert Mack. Anton is a mentalist who really can read minds, but limits his talents to petty nightclub performances.

July 1, 1962
#932 "Black Death"
With Mary Jane Higby and Leon Janney. A young couple takes shelter from a storm and stumble on the abode of a scientist who invented a disintegrating machine.

July 8, 1962
#933 "The Sin Eater"
With Jim Boles and Guy Repp. Two American tourists discover the ritual of a sin eater, and the tradition that carries on to the children of the family.

July 15, 1962
#934 "Snow on 66"
With William Mason. Charlie and his wife are being harassed on the

highway by a madman who flashes his headlights and honks his horn. The police cannot do anything until they catch him in the act.

July 22, 1962
#935 "The Next Murder"

With Joseph Julian and Lawson Zerbe. Two men from the same hometown discover they each have a past that was never reported in the newspapers.

July 29, 1962
#936 "Weekend at Gleebes"

With Raymond Edward Johnson. Young Wallace runs away from home and is mistaken for a young English Lord and moves in to a grand estate in England. His mother, back in America, pleads for him to return home.

August 5, 1962
#937 "Run Faster"

With Bill Lipton, Guy Repp and Robert Readick. An air-traffic controller has to make a decision that will affect his life; talk an inexperienced pilot on to the ground safely, or run home and save his wife from a strangler holding her hostage. This episode was originally scheduled for the broadcast of July 29, 1962.

August 12, 1962
#938 "The Silver Shoe"

With Rita Lloyd and Gertrude Warner. A sailor meets up with a beautiful woman who might actually be the same woman of his past that was put into a mental institution. This script was written by radio actor Robert Readick.

August 19, 1962
#939 "Pages from a Diary"

With Henry Backus and Jim Backus. John suffers from a multiple personality disorder and uses the diary he wrote as a means to snap out of it. Both Henry and Jim Backus, real-life radio actors and brothers, play the same role with different personalities.

Suspense

August 26, 1962
#940 "The Lost Ship"
With Bill Adams and Jean Gillespie. A couple of thieves steal $50,000 and attempt to make a run for it, only to be stranded in the middle of the desert where an old man laughs at the old Spanish ship rumored to be buried under the sand.

September 2, 1962
#941 "The Death of Alexander Jordon"
With Paul McGrath and Edgar Stehli. Uncle Alex dies and leaves the children his entire estate and fortune, provided they spend a week on the estate. But throughout the weekend, a bell attached to Uncle Alex's crypt continues to ring. This script was previously dramatized on the short-lived 1944 radio series *Creeps by Night*.

September 9, 1962
#942 "A Strange Day in May"
With William Mason and Maurice Tarplin. Thomas Manning is a professional astronaut who is blasted into space in hopes of finding the whereabouts of two previously-missing space men. When he returns to Earth, he finds it a little different. Maurice Tarplin played the role of himself, a radio reporter.

September 16, 1962
#943 "Golden Years"
With Elspeth Eric, Bret Morrison, Mary Jane Higby and Rosemary Rice. Buddy's girlfriend races against time to prevent him from killing his stepfather.

September 23, 1962
#944 "At the Point of a Needle"
With Robert Readick. George decides to eliminate his nagging wife when they move into their summer beach house for a week.

September 30, 1962
#945 "Devilstone"
With Gilbert Mack. Timothy Martin inherits a haunted castle where a ghost is rumored to roam the hallways.

HISTORY: THE TELEVISION SERIES

IN MARCH OF 1949, UNDER the sponsorship of Auto-Lite, the *Suspense* radio program made the transition to television. For four seasons the series offered similar tales featured on the radio series, often the same stories. The television production was broadcast "live" and originated from New York where many New York stock actors played roles, and Hollywood actors making brief appearances on the East Coast for stage productions was guests on the television series.

Elliott Lewis, the producer and director of the radio series, verified this in an interview commenting: "They are both sponsored by the same firm, Auto-Lite, and sometimes TV *Suspense* does stories we've used on radio, but they are entirely separate productions."

The television version of this popular show attempted to create the atmosphere of its radio predecessor by using the same opening announcement — "And now, a tale well calculated to keep you in.... SUSPENSE!" — accompanied by the same chilling theme heard on the radio counterpart. Being dramatized on the stage however, limited the producers, directors and technicians with what they could present and how they presented it.

The first broadcast, entitled "Revenge," was given a very negative review by *New York Times* radio and television columnist Jack Gould. He candidly stated that the program had more "corn than chill" and that the drab story about a man who stabs his wife while she is posing for a photograph gave actors "little opportunity for anything more than the most stereotyped portrayals."

In a dramatization of "Dr. Jekyll and Mr. Hyde," guest Ralph Bell played two roles. The drama was reproduced again a year or two later with Basil Rathbone in the role. Ralph Bell explained how the process of limited production did not stop any creativity when explaining how they did the transformation scene. "You only saw Dr. Jekyll at the beginning of the program," Bell explained. "And then he took the elixir, as it were, as I recall. And then there was a dissolve and we saw the effect of the elixir and not his face. And of course it became rather grotesque. And then what happened was you saw it from the perspective of the camera moving all the time, and I was in tow of it with a voice over, following it around. And the only time that you ever saw Mr. Hyde was toward the climax of the show."

Another highlight of the series was the Christmas episode of 1950, with Wally Cox in an adaptation of Damon Runyon's "Dancing Dan's Christmas." Jack Palance starred in "Cagliostro and the Chess Player" on December 15, 1953 as an eighteenth-century magician. Grace Kelly made one of her few television appearances on the July 1, 1952 broadcast of *Suspense* in "Fifty Beautiful Girls." The true story of Representative Douglas Stringfellow of Utah and his mission to cross into Germany and capture the country's leading atomic scientist was dramatized on the June 22, 1954 offering titled "String." The real Stringfellow appeared as a guest on the television series *This is Your Life* a week afterwards. On May 26, 1953, Basil Rathbone played the role of Sherlock Holmes in "The Adventure of the Black Baronet," supposedly a pilot for a television series with Rathbone in the starring role.

The only story not dramatized on television's *Suspense* which still puzzles this author is "Sorry, Wrong Number." It was dramatized on *Climax!* on November 4, 1954 with Shelley Winters in the lead, but never dramatized on TV's *Suspense*.

TV GUIDE REPRINT

From May 21, 1954

SUSPENSE — Within Limits

AFTER YEARS OF WHOLESALE BLOODLETTING, *Suspense* has apparently decided to apply a tourniquet. Producer Martin Manulis, who took over after the show had shed gallons of gore, has revamped the program's point of view.

"The public is becoming surfeited with outlandish crime," theorizes Manulis. "B movies and early television thrived on gangland stories, but now the viewer has to make some sort of personal identification with what he's watching or there's no impact. We've moved away from horror and unnecessary violence because there's been a reaction against it. In general, an audience won't accept in a living room what it will in a movie house. So we've had to adjust."

Adjusting has proved to be a pretty wise idea. The show's rating is up. So is fan mail. So is the Manulis morale, at these signs of public approval of what is unquestionably a more moral approach to TV programming. Not that violence is out altogether. Carnage, when called for, is used — but as tastefully as Manulis can manage. "There'll be no more hoods or professional gangsters," reports the producer. "We now deal exclusively with crime melodrama, involving recognizable people. In many cases we've found ourselves doing documentaries, rather than criminal suspense stories."

Though *Suspense* was a successful show long before he came into the picture, Manulis has no trouble justifying his position. "Any show reflects the people who work on it," he explains. "Other shows, like *Martin Kane* and *Man Against Crime*, must stick with detective stories.

But we considered *Suspense* primarily a dramatic show and so we didn't hesitate to expand it beyond routine crime stuff. We now try to do stories based on real crimes. We've also used stories by Dickens, Zola and Balzac. Our writers have found that trying to stress reality of behavior almost automatically results in less violence."

Suspense was almost caught in its own (excuse the expression!) web when it went all out to present the "real life story" of a Canadian with an incredible war record. They intended to televise author Quentin Reynolds' version of this story, "The Man Who Wouldn't Talk." Shortly after they bought the rights, the story was found to be not only incredible, but untrue. *Suspense* converted liability into asset by having Reynolds on the show to explain how it was discovered "The Man Who Wouldn't Talk" had done nothing else but.

If the truth were known, Manulis would like, every so often, to smuggle in a story that isn't really a suspense story at all. Occasionally he surrenders to the temptation. A Broadway director before taking on TV chores, Manulis once had the job of "directing" Tallulah Bankhead in her hugely successful revival of "Private Lives," an experience which would seem ideal preparation for the wacky world of television. Actually, however, he credits Tallulah with furnishing fresh and valuable slants on the drama business.

Right now Manulis is striving to get some special point of view for each *Suspense* plot, so the stories will steer clear of hackneyed whodunit formulas. If the public starts crying for more blood, he'll reluctantly loosen the granny knot on that tourniquet. Through some of the old chop-licking crowd have given up the show as too well-mannered. Manulis doesn't recommend *Suspense* for the kiddies. It's still pretty scary at times.

Episode Guide: The Television Series

March 1, 1949
#1 "Revenge"
    With Eddie Albert and Margo.

March 15, 1949
#2 "Suspicion"
    With Sylvia Field and Ernest Truex.

March 29, 1949
#3 "Cabin B-13"
    With Charles Korvin and Eleanor Lynn.

April 5, 1949
#4 "The Man Upstairs"
    With Mildred Natwick.

April 12, 1949
#5 "After Dinner Story"
    With Otto Kruger.

April 19, 1949
#6 "The Creeper"
    With Nina Foch and Anthony Ross.

April 26, 1949
#7 "A Night at an Inn"
    With Boris Karloff and Jack Manning.

May 3, 1949
#8 "Dead Ernest"
   With Tod Andrews and Josh Shelley.

May 10, 1949
#9 "Post Mortem"
   With Sidney Blackmer and Peggy Conklin.

May 17, 1949
#10 "The Monkey's Paw"
   With Mildred Natwick and Boris Karloff.

May 24, 1949
#11 "Murder Through the Looking Glass"
   With William Prince and Ruth Madison.

May 31, 1949
#12 "The Door's on the Thirteenth Floor"
   With Robert Sterling and Louisa Horton.

June 7, 1949
#13 "The Yellow Scarf"
   With Boris Karloff.

June 14, 1949
#14 "Help Wanted"
   With Otto Kruger.

June 21, 1949
#15 "Stolen Empire"
   With Audrey Christie and Kenneth Lynch.

June 28, 1949
#16 "The Hands of Mr. Ottermole"
   With Ralph Bell.

September 6, 1949
#17 "The Lunch Box"
   With John McGovern and Edgar Stehli.

September 13, 1949
#18 "Collector's Item"
   With Lon McCallister.

September 20, 1949
#19 "Dr. Jekyll and Mr. Hyde"
   With Ralph Bell.

September 27, 1949
#20 "The Comic Strip Killer"
   With Lilli Palmer and Rex Harrison.

October 4, 1949
#21 "Doctor Violet"
   With Hume Cronyn and Evelyn Varden.

October 11, 1949
#22 "The Cask of Amontilado"
   With Bela Lugosi.

October 18, 1949
#23 "The Serpent Ring"
   With Donald Buka and Royal Dano.

October 25, 1949
#24 "The Murderer"
   With Jeffrey Lynn.

November 1, 1949
#25 "Black Passage"
   With Stella Adler and William Prince.

November 8, 1949
#26 "Suspicion"
   With Charlton Heston and Edgar Stehli.

November 15, 1949
#27 "The Thin Edge of Violence"
   With George Reeves.

November 22, 1949
#28 "The Third One"
   With Theodore Newton.

November 29, 1949
#29 "A Man in the House"
   With Alan Baxter and Boyd Crawford.

December 6, 1949
#30 "The Scar"
   With Edgar Stehli.

December 13, 1949
#31 "The Gray Helmet"
   With Jack Lemmon.

December 20, 1949
#32 "The Seeker and the Sought"
   With Grace Valentine and Eileen Heckart.

December 27, 1949
#33 "The Case of the Lady Sannox"
   With Berry Kroeger and Henry Brandon.

January 3, 1950
#34 "Morning Boat to Africa"
   With Nina Foch.

January 10, 1950
#35 "The Bomber Command"
   With George Reeves and Susan Douglas.

January 17, 1950
#36 "Summer Storm"
   With E.G. Marshall and Jackie Diamond.

January 24, 1950
#37 "The Horizontal Man"
   With Mildred Natwick.

January 31, 1950
#38 "The Distant Island"
   With Patricia Kirkland.

February 7, 1950
#39 "Escape This Night"
   With Donald Buka and Robert Harris.

February 14, 1950
#40 "The Suicide Club"
   With Donald Buka and Ralph Clanton.

February 21, 1950
#41 "Roman Holiday"
   With Leslie Nielsen.

February 28, 1950
#42 "The Man Who Talked in His Sleep"
   With Don Briggs and Edith Atwater.

March 7, 1950
#43 "The Ledge"
   With E.G. Marshall and Dick Foran.

March 14, 1950
#44 "The Parcel"
   With Ann Thomas and Conrad Janis.

March 21, 1950
#45 "The Old Man's Badge"
   With Barry Nelson and Steven Hill.

March 28, 1950
#46 "Second Class Passenger"
   With Leslie Nielsen and Monica Boyer.

April 4, 1950
#47 "One Thousand Dollars For Your Money"
   With Betty Garde and Paul Stewart.

April 11, 1950
#48 "Steely, Steely Eyes"
   With Betty Garde.

April 18, 1950
#49 "Murder at the Mardi Gras"
   With Hume Cronyn and Tom Drake.

April 25, 1950
#50 "The Gentleman From America"
   With Barry Nelson.

May 2, 1950
#51 "Death of a Dummy"
   With Conrad Janis.

May 9, 1950
#52 "Red Wine"
   With Tom Drake and Hume Cronyn.

May 16, 1950
#53 "One and One's a Lonesome"
   With Robert Emhardt and Nina Foch.

May 23, 1950
#54 "Photo Finish"
   Ralph Clanton and Eileen Heckart.

May 30, 1950
#55 "Listen, Listen"
   With Mildred Natwick.

June 6, 1950
#56 "Black Bronze"
   With Franchot Tone.

June 20, 1950
#57 "I'm No Hero"
   With Hume Cronyn.

Suspense

June 27, 1950
#58 "Wisteria Cottage"
   With Conrad Janis and Marjorie Gateson.

August 29, 1950
#59 "Poison"
   With Arnold Moss.

September 5, 1950
#60 "A Pocketful of Murder"
   With Steven Hill and Barry Nelson.

September 12, 1950
#61 "Edge of Panic"
   With Louisa Horton and Patrick McVey.

September 19, 1950
#62 "Dark Shadows"
   With William Redfield and Robert Harris.

September 26, 1950
#63 "Six of One"
   With Edith Atwell.

October 3, 1950
#64 "The Monkey's Paw"
   With Mildred Natwick.

October 10, 1960
#65 "Criminal's Mark"
   With Richard Kiley and Joseph Wiseman.

October 17, 1950
#66 "The Man Who Would Be King"
   With Francis L. Sullivan.

October 24, 1950
#67 "Breakdown"
   With Don Briggs and Ellen Violett.

October 31, 1950
#68 "Halloween Hold-Up"
  With Conrad Janis.

November 7, 1950
#69 "Nightmare"
  With Richard Kiley and Berry Kroeger.

November 14, 1950
#70 "The Brush-Off"
  With Mary Sinclair and Leslie Nielsen.

November 21, 1950
#71 "The Death Cards"
  With Francis L. Sullivan.

November 28, 1950
#72 "The Hands of Mr. Ottermole"
  With Robert Emhardt and Lawrence Fletcher.

December 5, 1950
#73 "The Guy From Nowhere"
  With Barry Nelson and Lawrence Fletcher.

December 12, 1950
#74 "The Mallet"
  With Walter Slezak and Victor Beecroft.

December 19, 1950
#75 "Dancing Dan's Christmas"
  With Wally Cox.

December 26, 1950
#76 "The Tip"
  With Stanley Ridges and Felicia Montealegre.

January 2, 1951
#77 "Death in the River"
  Cast unknown.

Suspense

January 9, 1951
#78 "Tough Cop"
    With Katherine Bard and Barry Nelson.

January 16, 1951
#79 "The Fool's Heart"
    With Henry Hull.

January 23, 1951
#80 "Dead Fall"
    With Barry Nelson.

January 30, 1951
#81 "The Rose Garden"
    With Mildred Natwick and Estelle Winwood.

February 6, 1951
#82 "Night Break"
    With E.G. Marshall and Jane Seymour.

February 13, 1951
#83 "Double Entry"
    With Robert Emhardt and Virginia Gilmore.

February 20, 1951
#84 "The Victim"
    With Eileen Heckart and Stanley Ridges.

February 27, 1951
#85 "Margin for Safety"
    With Denholm Elliott.

March 6, 1951
#86 "Dr. Jekyll and Mr. Hyde"
    With Basil Rathbone.

March 13, 1951
#87 "On a Country Road"
    With Mildred Natwick, Mary Sinclair and John Forsythe.

March 20, 1951
#88 "Telephone Call"
  With Robert Emhardt and Russell Collins.

March 27, 1951
#89 "The Three of Silence"
  With Betty Garde and Walter Slezak.

April 3, 1951
#90 "Go Home, Dead Man"
  With Jackie Cooper.

April 10, 1951
#91 "The Foggy Night Visitor"
  With Cloris Leachman and Leslie Nielsen.

April 17, 1951
#92 "The Juice Man"
  With Cloris Leachman.

April 24, 1951
#93 "The Meeting"
  With Jackie Cooper, Mildred Natwick and Wally Cox.

May 1, 1951
#94 "No Friend Like an Old Friend"
  With Judith Evelyn and Tom Helmore.

May 8, 1951
#95 "Murder in the Ring"
  With Don Briggs, Audrey Christie and Hiram Sherman.

May 15, 1951
#96 "Too Hot to Live"
  With Olive Deering and Billie Redfield.

May 22, 1951
#97 "Escape This Night"
  With Judith Evelyn and Theo Goetz.

May 29, 1951
#98 "Vamp Till Dead"
   With Mary Sinclair.

June 5, 1951
#99 "The Call"
   With Lawrence Fletcher, William Redfield and Cloris Leachman.

June 12, 1951
#100 "De Mortuis"
   With Clive Deering and Walter Slezak.

June 19, 1951
#101 "A Killing in Abilene"
   With William Prince.

June 26, 1951
#102 "The Greatest Crime"
   With Walter Slezak.

July 3, 1951
#103 "Blood on the Trumpet"
   With John Forsythe and Cloris Leachman.

July 10, 1951
#104 "Tent on the Beach"
   With Paul Langton and Eileen Heckart.

July 17, 1951
#105 "Wisteria Cottage"
   With William Redfield and Marjorie Gateson.

July 24, 1951
#106 "The Incident at Story Point"
   With Donald Buka and Rusty Lane.

July 31, 1951
#107 "A Vision of Death"
   With Henry Hull and Jerome Cowan.

August 7, 1951
#108 "Killers of the City"
　With Conrad Janis.

August 14, 1951
#109 "Death Sabre"
　With Felicia Montealegre and Leslie Nielsen.

August 21, 1951
#110 "This is Your Confession" Part One
　With Eva Gabor, William Bishop and Sidney Blackmer.

August 28, 1951
#111 "This is Your Confession" Part Two
　With Eva Gabor, William Bishop and Sidney Blackmer.

September 4, 1951
#112 "This Way Out"
　With Richard Coogan and Jean Parker.

September 11, 1951
#113 "Strange for a Killer"
　With John Forsythe and Anthony Ross.

September 18, 1951
#114 "Merryman's Murder"
　With Red Buttons and Joe E. Louis.

September 25, 1951
#115 "Doctor Anonymous"
　With Walter Slezak and Josephine Brown.

October 2, 1951
#116 "Santa Fe Flight"
　With Charlton Heston and Margaret Phillips.

October 9, 1951
#117 "High Street"
　With Mildred Natwick and Mary Sinclair.

October 16, 1951
#118 "The Fifth Dummy"
　With Francis L. Sullivan.

October 23, 1951
#119 "The Train from Czechoslovakia"
　With Richard Kiley and Maria Riva.

October 30, 1951
#120 "Court Day"
　With Richard Coogan and Parker Fennally.

November 6, 1951
#121 "Moonfleet" Part One
　With John Baragrey, Jack Diamond and Edgar Stehli.

November 13, 1951
#122 "Moonfleet" Part Two
　With John Baragrey, Jack Diamond and Edgar Stehli.

November 20, 1951
#123 "Frisco Payoff"
　With Paul Langton and Anthony Ross.

November 27, 1951
#124 "Mikki"
　With Joan Chandler and Brandon Peters.

December 4, 1951
#125 "The Man With No Face"
　With Judith Evelyn and Henry Jones.

December 11, 1951
#126 "Meditation in Mexico"
　Cast unknown.

December 18, 1951
#127 "Pier 17"
　Cast unknown.

December 25, 1951
#128 "The Lonely Place"
 With Judith Evelyn and Boris Karloff.

January 1, 1952
#129 "Routine Patrol"
 Cast unknown.

January 8, 1952
#130 "Flare Week"
 With Eileen Heckart and Conrad Janis.

January 15, 1952
#131 "The Spider"
 With Olive Deering and Arnold Moss.

January 22, 1952
#132 "The Red Signal"
 With Thomas Helmore and Beatrice Straight.

January 29, 1952
#133 "Death Drum"
 With Maria Riva.

February 5, 1952
#134 "Betrayal in Vienna"
 With Claude Dauphin and Irja Jensen.

February 12, 1952
#135 "North of Shanghai"
 With Thomas Mitchell and Dorothy Peterson.

February 19, 1952
#136 "Summer Night"
 With Parker Fennelly and Carmen Mathews.

February 26, 1952
#137 "Night Drive"
 With Robert H. Harris and Neva Patterson.

March 4, 1952
#138 "Day of Infamy"
  With Signe Hasso.

March 11, 1952
#139 "Four Hours to Kill"
  With Joseph Buloff and Robert Keith, Jr. [Brian Keith].

March 18, 1952
#140 "The Mystery of Edwin Drood" Part One
  With John Baragrey.

March 25, 1952
#141 "The Mystery of Edwin Drood" Part Two
  With John Baragrey.

April 8, 1952
#142 "Black Panther"
  With Chester Morris.

April 15, 1952
#143 "Night of Evil"
  With Skip Homeier and Henry Hull.

April 22, 1952
#144 "Alibi Me"
  With Don Hanmer.

April 29, 1952
#145 "The Letter"
  With Arnold Moss and Mary Sinclair.

May 6, 1952
#146 "The Mandarin Murders"
  With Cloris Leachman and William Redfield.

May 13, 1952
#147 "Fingers of Fear"
  With Lawrence Fletcher and Robert Keith Jr. [Brian Keith].

May 20, 1952
#148 "Hunted Down"
   With John Baragrey.

May 27, 1952
#149 "The Debt"
   With Conrad Janis and Robert Keith Jr. [Brian Keith].

June 3, 1952
#150 "A Murder of Necessity"
   With John Forsythe.

June 10, 1952
#151 "House of Masks"
   With Geraldine Fitzgerald and William Redfield.

June 17, 1952
#152 "Phantom of the Riviera"
   With Olive Deering and John Baragrey.

June 24, 1952
#153 "Night of Reckoning"
   With John Baragrey.

July 1, 1952
#154 "Fifty Beautiful Girls"
   With Grace Kelly and Robert Keith Jr. [Brian Keith].

July 15, 1952
#155 "For the Love of Randi"
   With Rita Lynn and Darren McGavin.

July 29, 1952
#156 "The Crooked Frame"
   With Neva Patterson and Richard Kiley.

August 5, 1952
#157 "Death Cargo"
   With Anthony Ross and Robert Keith Jr. [Brian Keith].

August 12, 1952
#158 "Remember Me?"
   With Martin Brooks and Cloris Leachman.

August 19, 1952
#159 "Her Last Adventure"
   With Lloyd Bridges and Arlene Francis.

August 26, 1952
#160 "Woman in Love"
   With Arnold Moss.

September 2, 1952
#161 "The Old Lady of Bayeux"
   With Nicole Stephan.

September 9, 1952
#162 "Call From a Killer"
   With Anne Jackson.

September 16, 1952
#163 "The Return of Dr. Bourdette"
   With John Baragrey and William Price.

September 23, 1952
#164 "Stand Up for Death"
   With Mary Sinclair and Robert Keith Jr. [Brian Keith].

September 30, 1952
#165 "The Beach of Falesa"
   With John Forsythe.

October 7, 1952
#166 "The Man in the Mirror"
   With Constance Ford.

October 14, 1952
#167 "Blue Panther"
   With Phyllis Brooks.

October 21, 1952
#168 "The Man Who Had Seven Hours"
   With Robert Sterling.

October 28, 1952
#169 "All Hallow's Eve"
   With Franchot Tone.

November 11, 1952
#170 "The Moving Target"
   With Jamie Smith and Irja Jensen.

November 18, 1952
#171 "Monsieur Vidocq"
   With Jacques Aubuchon and Luis Van Rooten.

November 25, 1952
#172 "The Whispering Killer"
   With George Mathews, Richard Webb and Nina Foch.

December 2, 1952
#173 "A Time of Innocence"
   With Patricia Hitchcock and Thomas Mitchell.

December 9, 1952
#174 "The Girl Who Saw Tomorrow"
   With Lois Wheeler and Eugene Ruyman.

December 16, 1952
#175 "The Tortured Hand"
   With Peter Lorre.

December 23, 1952
#176 "The Deadly Lamb"
   With Patricia Breslin and Dick Haymes.

December 30, 1952
#177 "The Invisible Killer"
   With Jackie Cooper, Anne Sargent and John Dall.

Suspense

January 6, 1953
#178 "Little Camorra"
  With William Prince and Mary Sinclair.

January 13, 1953
#179 "Mr. Matches"
  With Warren Stevens and Henry Jones.

January 20, 1953
#180 "Vacancy for Death"
  With Joan Blondell.

January 27, 1953
#181 "Career"
  With Fay Bainter.

February 3, 1953
#182 "Mutiny Below"
  With Murray Hamilton and Eddie Albert.

February 10, 1953
#183 "A Study in Stone"
  With Joan Westmore and Roger Dann.

February 17, 1953
#184 "The Quarry"
  With Robert Middleton and Jeffrey Lynn.

February 24, 1953
#185 "They Haven't Killed Me Yet"
  With Harry Lowe and Shizu Moriya.

March 3, 1953
#186 "The Kiss-Off"
  With Jack Palance and Virginia Baker.

March 10, 1953
#187 "The Legend of Lizzie Borden"
  Cast unknown.

March 17, 1953
#188 "The Black Prophet"
   With Boris Karloff.

March 24, 1953
#189 "Portrait of Constance"
   With Ann Rutherford.

March 31, 1953
#190 "Death in the Cave"
   With Zachary Scott and David Clarke.

April 14, 1953
#191 "Kiss Me Again, Stranger"
   With Maria Riva and Richard Waring.

April 21, 1953
#192 "The Duel"
   With Roger Dann and Eva Gabor.

April 28, 1953
#193 "F.O.B. Vienna"
   With Mike Kellin, Jayne Meadows and Walter Matthau.

May 5, 1953
#194 "The Suitor"
   With Mildred Natwick.

May 12, 1953
#195 "Death of an Editor"
   With Anthony Ross and Mario Gallo.

May 19, 1953
#196 "Come Into My Parlor"
   With John Carradine.

May 26, 1953
#197 "The Adventure of the Black Baronet"
   With Basil Rathbone and Martyn Green.

June 2, 1953
#198 "The Queen's Ring"
   With Mildred Dunnock and Scott Forbes.

June 9, 1953
#199 "The Man Who Cried Wolf"
   With David Stewart and Marion Winters.

June 16, 1953
#200 "See No Evil"
   With Betty Jane Watson and John Conte.

June 23, 1953
#201 "The Signalman"
   With Boris Karloff and Alan Webb.

June 30, 1953
#202 "The Fury of Senorita Gomez"
   With Nina Foch and Harold Gordon.

July 7, 1953
#203 "The Mascot"
   With Margaret Hayes and Mike Wallace.

July 14, 1953
#204 "The Dutch Schultz Story"
   With Harry Bellaver and Rod Steiger.

July 21, 1953
#205 "Pigeon in the Cage"
   With John Howard and Jacqueline Susann.

July 28, 1953
#206 "The Dance"
   With John Baragrey and Katherine Bard.

August 4, 1953
#207 "Vial of Death"
   With Claude Dauphin.

August 11, 1953
#208 "Point Blank"
    With Chester Morris.

August 18, 1953
#209 "Nightmare at Ground Zero"
    With O.Z. Whitehead and Louise Larabee.

August 25, 1953
#210 "Death in the Pasig"
    With Sir Cedric Hardwicke.

September 1, 1953
#211 "Paradise Junction"
    With Tod Andrews and Dorothy Donahue.

September 8, 1953
#212 "Reign of Terror"
    With Miro Slava, Rosa Stradner and Leonard Barry.

September 15, 1953
#213 "The Runaway"
    With Peggy Ann Garner.

September 22, 1953
#214 "The Riddle of the Mayerling"
    With Viveca Lindfors and Christopher Plummer.

September 29, 1953
#215 "The Sisters"
    With Judith Evelyn and Martha Scott.

October 6, 1953
#216 "Death at Skirkerud Pond"
    With Quentin Reynolds.

October 13, 1953
#217 "The Accounting"
    With Everett Sloane.

October 20, 1953
#218 "The Valley of the Kings"
   With Jack Livesey and Herbert Bergoff.

October 27, 1953
#219 "The Others"
   With Geraldine Fitzgerald and Hugh Reilly.

November 3, 1953
#220 "The Interruption"
   With Sir Cedric Hardwicke and Evelyn Varden.

November 10, 1953
#221 "Needle in the Haystack"
   With Edwin Cooper and Lee Marvin.

November 17, 1953
#222 "The Newcomer"
   With Zachary Scott.

November 24, 1953
#223 "My Short Walk to Freedom"
   With Joseph Anthony and John Baragrey.

December 1, 1953
#224 "Laugh It Off"
   With Dick Haymes.

December 8, 1953
#225 "The Day Never Came"
   With John Baragrey.

December 15, 1953
#226 "Cagliostro and the Chess Player"
   With Jack Palance and Dana Wynter.

December 22, 1953
#227 "The Gift of Fear"
   With Bud Flannagan and Paul Hartman.

December 29, 1953
#228 "Mr. Nobody"
   With Art Carney and Constance Bennett.

January 5, 1954
#229 "Diamonds in the Sky"
   With Annabella, Eddie Carr and Jackson Young.

January 12, 1954
#230 "The Scrap Iron Curtain"
   With Bart Burns.

January 19, 1954
#231 "The Haunted"
   With John Archer, Augusta Dabney and Helmut Dantine.

January 26, 1954
#232 "An Affair With a Ghost"
   With Darren McGavin and Felicia Montealegre.

February 2, 1954
#233 "The Man Who Wouldn't Talk"
   With Peter Capell and Harry Townes.

February 9, 1954
#234 "The Moonstone"
   With Phyllis Kirk and Noel Leslie.

February 16, 1954
#235 "The Execution"
   With Joseph Anthony and Katherine Bard.

February 23, 1954
#236 "Death on the Screen"
   With Don Hammer and Paul Langton.

March 2, 1954
#237 "I Do Solemnly Swear"
   With Royal Dano and Nancy Kelly.

March 9, 1954
#238 "Before the Act"
   With Jo Van Fleet and Jeffrey Lynn.

March 16, 1954
#239 "The Fourth Degree"
   With Joseph Wiseman.

March 23, 1954
#240 "The Tenth Reunion"
   With Patricia Barry and Margaret Hayes.

March 30, 1954
#241 "Torment"
   With Louise Rainer and Martin Kosleck.

April 13, 1954
#242 "Operation: Barracuda"
   With Otto Preminger and Dana Wynter.

April 20, 1954
#243 "The Open Transom"
   With Art Carney and Kay Medford.

April 27, 1954
#244 "The Terror Begins"
   With Everett Sloane and Stefan Schnabel.

May 4, 1954
#245 "Smoke"
   With Kenny Delmar, E.G. Marshall and Pat Hingle.

May 11, 1954
#246 "Operation Nightmare"
   With Anne Burr and Douglas Rodgers.

May 18, 1954
#247 "Breakout"
   With Anthony Ross.

March 25, 1954
#248 "Fingerprints"
   With John Emery.

June 1, 1954
#249 "Race Against Murder"
   Cast unknown.

June 8, 1954
#250 "North Side"
   With Edward Binns.

June 15, 1954
#251 "The Pistol Shot"
   With Hurd Hatfield and Dana Wynter.

June 22, 1954
#252 "String"
   With Jack Lord and Harry Townes.

June 29, 1954
#253 "The Hunted"
   With Ward Bond and Steve Parker.

July 6, 1954
#254 "The Girl in Car Thirty-Two"
   With Edith Adams and Gene Barry.

July 13, 1954
#255 "Conversation at an Inn"
   With Mildred Natwick, Jacques Aubuchon and Maria Riva.

July 20, 1954
#256 "Once a Killer"
   With Martin Brooks and Michael Strong.

July 27, 1954
#257 "Main Feature: Death"
   With Nina Foch.

August 3, 1954
#258 "The Last Stand"
    With Pat Hingle and Joan Lorring.

August 10, 1954
#259 "The Iron Cop"
    With J. Pat O'Malley and Ray Walston.

August 17, 1954
#260 "Barn Burning"
    With E.G. Marshall and Beatrice Straight.

KRAFT SUSPENSE THEATRE: AN EPISODE GUIDE

DIRECTORS INCLUDED IDA LUPINO, Robert Altman and Sydney Pollack.

Sponsor: Kraft Foods

This series is still copyrighted property of Universal Studios.

Fine crafted episodes with great stories, also known as the last great anthology from the "Golden Age of Television." Many of the episodes were actually pilots for other television programs and while most did not venture further than the pilot, others proved a success. "Rapture at Two-Forty" was the pilot for the later series, *Run for Your Life*. This series was most recently aired on The Sci-Fi Channel as a late-night filler, and was edited down with each episode missing as much as seven minutes to make room for more commercials. There are episodes in circulation among collectors with their original Kraft commercials, but are seen in black and white instead of color.

NBC, Thursday 10:00 — 11:00 p.m., E.S.T.

October 10, 1963
#1 "The Case Against Paul Ryker" Part One
   With Peter Graves, Lee Marvin, Vera Miles, Lloyd Nolan, Bradford Dillman and Charles Aidman.

October 17, 1963
#2 "The Case Against Paul Ryker" Part Two
   With Peter Graves, Lee Marvin, Vera Miles, Lloyd Nolan, Bradford Dillman and Charles Aidman.

October 24, 1963
#3 "The End of the World, Baby"
   With Peter Lorre, Gig Young, Nina Foch and Katherine Crawford. *Suspense* radio performers Ben Wright and Lou Krugman play supporting roles for this television production.

October 31, 1963
#4 "A Hero for Our Times"
   With John Ireland, Sandra Church and Lloyd Bridges.

November 7, 1963
#5 "Are There Any More Out There Like You?"
   With Robert Ryan and Adam Rourke.

November 14, 1963
#6 "One Step Down"
   With Leslie Nielsen, Ida Lupino, Jack Weston and Gena Rowlands.

December 5, 1963
#7 "The Machine That Played God"
   With Anne Francis, Josephine Hutchinson and Gary Merrill.

December 12, 1963
#8 "The Long, Lost Life of Edward Smalley"
   With Philip Abbott, Richard Crenna and James Whitmore.

December 19, 1963
#9 "The Hunt"
   With Mickey Rooney, Bruce Dern and James Caan.

December 26, 1963
#10 "The Name of the Game"
   With Pat Hingle and Jack Kelly.

January 2, 1964
#11 "The Deep End"
   With Clu Gulager, Aldo Ray and Tina Louise.

January 9, 1964
#12 "A Truce to Terror"
   With John Gavin, Michael Ansara and Steve Forrest.

January 16, 1964
#13 "Who is Jennifer?"
   With Dan Duryea, David Brian and Gloria Swanson.

January 30, 1964
#14 "Leviathan Five"
   With Robert Webber and Vince Williams.

February 6, 1964
#15 "My Enemy, This Town"
   With Scott Marlowe, Barbara Nichols, Phil Carey and Diane McBain.

February 20, 1964
#16 "The Action of the Tiger"
   With Telly Savalas and Stephen McNally.

February 27, 1964
#17 "Doesn't Anyone Know Who I Am?"
   With Barney Phillips, Cornel Wilde and Martha Hyer.
   A serious case of amnesia is the subject of this episode.

March 12, 1964
#18 "The Threatening Eye"
   With Jack Klugman, Phyllis Thaxter and Pat O'Brien.

March 19, 1964
#19 "A Cause of Anger"
   With Brian Keith, Anthony Caruso and Nancy Malone.

March 26, 1964
#20 "Knight's Gambit"
   With Murray Matheson and Chester Morris.

April 2, 1964
#21 "Once Upon a Savage Knight"
   With Carroll O'Connor and Andrew Duggan.

April 16, 1964
#22 "Portrait of an Unknown Man"
   With Clint Walker, Robert Duvall and Mala Powers.

April 23, 1964
#23 "Their Own Executioners"
   With Dean Stockwell, Guy Stockwell and Herschel Bernardi.

April 30, 1964
#24 "The Sweet Taste of Vengeance"
   With John Forsythe and Diana Hyland.

May 7, 1964
#25 "Charlie, He Couldn't Kill a Fly"
   With Keenan Wynn, Richard Kiley and Beverly Garland.

May 14, 1964
#26 "The Watchman"
   With Telly Savalas, Jack Warden and Victoria Shaw.

May 28, 1964
#27 "The Robrioz Ring"
   With Robert Loggia, Julie Adams and Julie Harris.

June 4, 1964
#28 "A Cruel and Unusual Night"
   With Ronald Reagan, Scott Marlowe and Anne Helm.

October 1, 1964
#29 "The World I Want"
   With Albert Dekker, Leonard Nimoy, Patricia Hyland and Jo Van Fleet.

October 8, 1964
#30 "Operation Grief"
　With Claude Akins, Robert Goulet and Peter Helm.

October 22, 1964
#31 "A Lion Amongst Men"
　With James Whitmore and Tommy Sands.

November 5, 1964
#32 "That He Should Weep For Her"
　With Milton Berle and Alejandro Rey.

November 12, 1964
#33 "The Kamchatka Incident"
　With John Forsythe and Leslie Parrish

November 19, 1964
#34 "The Jack is High"
　With Henry Jones, Larry Storch and Edd Byrnes.

November 26, 1964
#35 "Graffiti"
　With Louis Jourdan and John Marley.

December 3, 1964
#36 "One Tiger to a Hill"
　With Barry Nelson, James Gregory and Warren Stevens.

December 10, 1964
#37 "Three Persons"
　With Vincent Gardenia, John Gavin and Ralph Meeker.

December 24, 1964
#38 "The Gun"
　With Eddie Albert and Dina Merrill.

December 31, 1964
#39 "The Wine-Dark Sea"
　With Roddy McDowall and John Larkin.

January 14, 1965
#40 "In Darkness, Waiting" Part One
   With Hugh O'Brian, Barbara Rush and Neil Hamilton.

January 21, 1965
#41 "In Darkness, Waiting" Part Two
   With Hugh O'Brian, Barbara Rush and Neil Hamilton.

February 11, 1965
#42 "That Time in Havana"
   With Dana Wynter, Victor Jory and Steve Forrest.

February 18, 1965
#43 "Four Into Zero"
   With Jack Kelly, Robert Conrad and Martha Hyer.

February 25, 1965
#44 "Streetcar, Do You Read Me?"
   With Martin Milner, Richard Long and Nancy Malone.

March 11, 1965
#45 "The Last Clear Chance"
   With Barry Sullivan and Glenn Corbett.

March 18, 1965
#46 "Won't It Ever Be Morning?"
   With Ben Cooper, Carl Benton Reid and John Anderson.

March 25, 1965
#47 "Nobody Will Ever Know"
   With Pippa Scott and Tom Tryon.

April 1, 1965
#48 "The Green Felt Jungle"
   With Leslie Nielsen, Richard Conte, Macdonald Carey and Michael Pate.

April 15, 1965
#49 "Rapture at Two-Forty"

With Michael Rennie, Ben Gazzara, Katherine Crawford and Antoinette Bower.

April 22, 1965
#50 "Jungle of Fear"
With Robert Fuller, Ann Blyth, Richard Anderson, Robert Fuller and Robert Loggia.

April 29, 1965
#51 "Kill No More"
With Lew Ayres, Julie Adams, Leonard Nimoy and Robert Webber.

May 6, 1965
#52 "The Long Ravine"
With Broderick Crawford, Andrew Prine and Jack Lord.
This episode was scripted by *Suspense* radio producer and director Anthony Ellis.

May 13, 1965
#53 "The Easter Breach"
With Katherine Crawford and Richard Beymer.

May 20, 1965
#54 "The Safe House"
With Steven Hill, Dane Clark and Frances Lederer.

May 27, 1965
#55 "Twixt the Cup and the Lip"
With Larry Blyden, Ethel Merman and Charles McGraw.

June 10, 1965
#56 "The Trains of Silence"
With Tippi Hedren, Lloyd Bochner, Warren Stevens and Jeffery Hunter.

June 17, 1965
#57 "Kill Me on July 20th"
With Jack Kelly and Kathryn Hays.

June 24, 1965
#58 "The Rise and Fall of Eddie Carew"
   With Dean Jones and Sheilah Wells.

July 1, 1965
#59 "Peter Breck, Gary Lockwood and Shelly Hermy.
   Aired only in syndication

#60 "Shadow of a Man"
   With Broderick Crawford. Possibly the unaired pilot for the series.

THE BEST OF SUSPENSE

IN THE FALL OF 2003, Radio Spirits, Inc., a MediaBay, Inc. company (listed on NASDAQ/NMS [Symbol: MBAY]) in Cedar Knolls, New Jersey, commercially released a 20 Compact Disc set in an attractive bookshelf album as "The Best of Suspense: Radio's Outstanding Theater of Thrills." The collection contained what were essentially the Top 40 episodes of the series, selected by editor Anthony Tollin.

Anthony Tollin co-authored *The Shadow Scrapbook* and was a scriptwriter of Radio Spirits' *When Radio Was* syndicated series. He served as historical consultant on the Sci-Fi Channel special *Martian Mania: The True Story of the War of the Worlds*, and has produced and directed dozens of radio seminars during the past 20 years, including reunions of *The Shadow* and *Suspense* casts. As an authority on broadcasting history, Tollin has been interviewed by the *New York Times*, CBS, NBC, CNN, the Associated Press, *Entertainment Tonight* and the History Channel.

Anthony Tollin wrote a 32-page booklet for the album, describing in detail the episodes that accompanied the collection. Much of the material in the booklet was reprinted from *Suspense: Twenty Years of Thrills and Chills* book by Martin Grams Jr. Some of the trivia labeled as "Suspense Lore" in the booklet did not have much to do with the radio program. On page 5, for example, Anthony Tollin catalogued the episode "Dime a Dance," listing Lucille Ball as the guest. For the "Suspense Lore," the following was printed: *Though best-known as a comedienne, Lucille Ball starred on-screen in many noir thrillers, including* The Big Street, The Dark Corner *and* Lured. *As head of Desilu Studios, Ball approved the development of* Star Trek *and* Mission: Impossible.

According to the back page of the booklet, William Nadel, Martin Grams Jr., Derek Tague, Gary Yoggy and Donald Ramlow helped assist the decision making in choosing the 40 best episodes of the series.

In a personal correspondence by e-mail with Martin Grams Jr., I was informed that this set was a notch above the rest. "Most of the 40 episodes in that set are what I would have considered the best episodes of the series, but one episode I recommended that never made it to the set was 'Return to Dust' with Dick Beals from 1958. I still feel that packs a punch when the final line and sound cue are delivered. There are a couple episodes that I would question why they made it in the set, but for the most part, buying that set and getting a copy of 'Return to Dust' would give anyone who has never heard the program a good example of how radio dramas still entertain."

The 40 episodes chosen as the best of the series are:

"The Hitch-Hiker" September 2, 1942 Orson Welles
"Cabin B-13" November 9, 1943 Philip Dorn and Margo
"Back for Christmas" December 23, 1943 Peter Lorre
"Dime a Dance" January 13, 1944 Lucille Ball
"Sorry, Wrong Number" February 24, 1944 Agnes Moorehead
"The Dark Tower" May 4, 1944 Orson Welles
"Donovan's Brain" Part One May 18, 1944 Orson Welles
"Donovan's Brain" Part Two May 25, 1944 Orson Welles
"The Walls Came Tumbling Down" June 29, 1944 Keenan Wynn
"The Most Dangerous Game" February 1, 1945 Joseph Cotten
"Crime Without Passion" May 2, 1946 Joseph Cotten
"Dead Ernest" August 8, 1946 Wally Maher
"You'll Never See Me Again" September 5, 1946 Robert Young
"Hunting Trip" September 12, 1946 Vincent Price and Lloyd Nolan
"The House in Cypress Canyon" December 5, 1946 Robert Taylor
"The Thing in the Window" December 19, 1946 Joseph Cotten
"Back Seat Driver" February 3, 1949 Jim and Marian Jordan
"The Trap" June 16, 1949 Agnes Moorehead
"Ghost Hunt" June 2, 1949 Ralph Edwards
"Search for Isabel" November 3, 1949 Red Skelton
"The Red-Headed Woman" November 17, 1949 Lucille Ball and Desi Arnaz
"Mission Completed" December 1, 1949 James Stewart
"The Bullet" December 29, 1949 Ida Lupino

Suspense

"On a Country Road" November 16, 1950 Cary Grant
"The Treasure Chest of Don Jose" February 4, 1952 J. Carrol Naish
"The Wreck of the Old '97" March 17, 1952 Frank Lovejoy
"The Moonstone" Part One November 16, 1953 Peter Lawford
"The Moonstone" Part Two November 23, 1953 Peter Lawford
"The Earth is Made of Glass" June 15, 1954 Joseph Kearns
"The Last Letter of Dr. Bronson" November 4, 1954 John Dehner
"The Screaming Woman" March 1, 1955
"Zero Hour" April 5, 1955
"Kaleidoscope" July 12, 1955 William Conrad
"The Cave" December 20, 1955 Dick Beals
"The Waxwork" May 1, 1956 William Conrad
"Three Skeleton Key" November 11, 1956 Vincent Price
"Present Tense" March 3, 1957 Vincent Price
"Leiningen vs. the Ants" August 25, 1957 William Conrad
"The Black Door" November 19, 1961 Robert Readick
"The Second Door" May 6, 1962 Robert Readick

THE MYSTERY MAGAZINE

THERE WERE TWO SEPARATE MYSTERY magazines that were printed, based on the *Suspense* radio program. Both were officially approved through CBS, the parent owner of the program. Each printing lasted four issues, or one year. The first magazine was edited by Leslie Charteris, the same author who created the fictional character "The Saint" for novel, novella and short story formats. Charteris wrote an introduction for the first issue. He also wrote a feature titled *Hold Your Breath* for each issue, allowing the readers a la Ellery Queen-style, to solve the mystery before the solution was explained. All of the stories featured within the pages were adaptations of radio scripts performed on *Suspense*. For example, *A Sense of Smell* was an adaptation of the radio broadcast "The Bluebeard of Belloc." Printed in Los Angeles, California.

The second magazine was produced under arrangement with the program's sponsor, Auto-Lite. The short stories featured in this magazine were originals, not adaptations of the radio episodes. John Dickson Carr, who originally wrote scripts for *Suspense*, had one of his short stories featured in the premiere issue. The title was *Honeymoon Terror*, which was a short story adapted from the November 1943 broadcast of "Cabin B-13." Some of the short stories were reprints of previously-published stories from older magazines. Freelance writer Theodore Irwin was the editor for this magazine. Ray Bradbury's *The Screaming Woman* in issue four was later adapted into a *Suspense* radio drama.

Issue #1, November 1946
This Will Kill You, by Cleve Cartmill
Portrait Without a Face, by Eugene King
Fury and Sound, by Roby Wentz
Hold Your Breath, by Leslie Charteris

The Palmer Method, by Michael Corbin
The Bet, by Valerie Kurtz
The Defense Rests, by Mark O'Steele
No More Alice, by Findaly Harrigan

Issue #2, December 1946
Eve, by Roby Wentz
Sneak Preview, by Mark O'Steele
Hold Your Breath, by Leslie Charteris
The King's Birthday, by Robert Black
Thieves Fall Out, by Cleve Cartmill
This Was a Hero, by Lang Miller
Marry for Murder, by Carmen Morrison
Ride to Nowhere, by Findaly Harrigan

Issue #3, February 1947
Double Entry, by Ruby Wentz
Fool Proof, by George MacGuire
The Ten Grand, by Cleve Cartmill
The Pasteboard Box, by Fred K. Hamm
Hold Your Breath, by Leslie Charteris
The Black Shawl, by H.J. Jonas
Of Maestro and Man, by Mark O'Steele
A World of Darkness, by Barj Karolian

Issue #4, March 1947
A Sense of Smell, by Ruby Wentz
Short Order, by B.D. Rockford
The Last Letter of Dr. Bronson, by Cleve Cartmill
The Strange Case of Mark Boren, by H.P. Lester
Murder Off Key, by Stanley Sprague
Death at Miss Plimm's, by Finn Harrigan
Life Ends at Midnight, by Eugene King
Hold Your Breath, by Leslie Charteris

SECOND SERIES

Issue #1, Spring 1951
The Deathless One, by John Chapman and Oliver Saari
Voice in the Night, by William Hope Hodgson (reprinted from *Blue Book*, 1907)
A Most Amazing Murder, by A.B. Shiffrin
Obviously Suicide, by S. Fowler Wright
The Eye-Witness Who Wouldn't See, by James A. Kirch (reprinted from *Argosy*, 1949)
Small Assassin, by Ray Bradbury (reprinted from *Dime Mystery Magazine*, Nov. 1946)
The Quick and the Bomb, by William Tenn
She Didn't Bounce, by Peter Phillips
Jeannie with the Light Brown Cure, by Alexander Samalman (reprinted from *Thrilling Wonder Stories*, Feb. 1942)
Ghost of a Chance, by Theodore Sturgeon (reprinted from *Unknown*, June 1943)
Honeymoon Terror, by John Dickson Carr (reprinted from *Ellery Queen's Mystery Magazine*, May 1944)
Faces Turned Against Him, by John Gearson

Issue #2, Summer 1951
Operation Peep, by John Wyndham
Blood Will Tell, by Nathaniel Weyl
The Nightmare Face, by Walter Snow
Survival, by Thomas Gilchrist
Criminal at Large, by Larry Holden
Elusive Witness, by George Simenon
Black Death, by John Krill
Fatal Mistake, by John Basye Price
Penny Wise, Fate Foolish, by Mary Elizabeth Counselman
World Within, by Thomas A. Coffee
Pardon My Terror, by Irving Burstiner
Evil is the Night, by Edith Saylor Abbot
Maiden Beware, by Richard Lewis

A Horseman in the Sky, by Ambrose Bierce
The Perfectly Calm Murder, by F. Hugh Herbert

Issue #3, Fall 1951
The Saboteur, by William Sambrot
My Favorite Corpse, by Dorothy F. Horton
Love Ethereal, by Horace L. Gold
The Thing in the Snow, by Waldo Carlton Wright
Dear Automation, by A.E. Van Vogt (reprinted from *Other Worlds*, Sept. 1950)
Rip Tide, by Russell Branch
Wall of Fear, by William F. Jenkins
You Can't Run Away, by Philip Weck
Not a Leg to Stand On, by Don Mardick
Terror in the Sun, by Talmage Powell
How Can You Be Reading This?, by Charles H. Gesner
The Seventh Man, by Sir Arthur Quiller-Couch (reprinted from *Old Fires and Profitable Ghosts*, Scribner's, 1900)
Pattern for Dying, by Morris Cooper
Dark Vengeance, by Fritz Lieber, Jr.

Issue #4, Winter 1952
Threat of Violence, by R.J. Burrough
The Screaming Woman, by Ray Bradbury
And Never Come Back, by Dorothy Marie Davis
The Third Degree, by Charles Lenart
Ask No Quarter, by Duane Yarnell
Find the Witness, by Ted Stratton
Hot Eyes, by Dean Evans
You Killed Elizabeth, by Brett Halliday
Give Back the Dead, by James Robbins Miller
Murder Town, by Raymond Drennen
The Way Out, by Lorrie McLaughlin

The Comic Books

THE PREMIERE ISSUE OF THE comic books featured an attractive shot of Peter Lorre and Sydney Greenstreet from *The Verdict*, the 1946 Warner Bros. motion picture. The cover of the second issue featured Gale Storm and Dennis O'Keefe from the 1949 Universal-International motion picture, *Abandoned*. All of the other comics featured original artwork representing the comic's contents. There were many people who wrote the stories for these comics, but a few need to receive further credit. Dick Ayers co-created *Ghost Rider*. John Buscema would later create the Conan series. Bill Everett created Sub-Mariner. John Romita co-created Marvel villains/heroes The Punisher, The Kingpin and Satanna. According to author Martin Grams Jr., "Bernard Krigstein was an early inventor in the make-up and panel breakdown of comic books. He left the comic book career when the E.C. [Entertaining Comics] color books folded in 1956, turning to commercial illustration and teaching."

Issue #1, December 8, 1949
The Graveyard Ghouls, by Matt Baker
The Corpse Came Back, by Bob Powell
The Curse of the Coin (text)
The Bride Vanishes
Here Comes the Hangman
Alone With Murder, by John Buscema and Chu Hing

Issue #2, February 1950
I Bet With Death, by Gene Colan
The Clay Pipe (text)
Pursuit
The Hidden Money

The Man Who Lived Again
When Time Stood Still

Issue #3, May 1950
The Man Who Lost His Head, by Joe Maneely and Gene Colon
The Black Pit, by Vernon Hinkle
Mind over Murder
Quiet Destiny (text)
The Creature Who Didn't Exist
The Forbidden Room

Issue #4, August 1950
The Man in Black, by Gene Colan and Vince Alascia
The Closing Door, by Gene Colan
Two Lives Had I, by John Buscema
Escape (text)
The Creature Who Followed, by Vernon Hinkle
The Man Who Refused to Die
The Victim

Issue #5, November 1950
Hangman's House, by Bill Everett
Mark of the Witch, by Russ Heath
The New Whaler
The Eyes that Starred, by Joe Maneely
Return from the Grave, by George Tuska
The Painted Scarf, by Richard Briefer
Even After Death, by Bernard Krigstein
Are You A Detective?: A Murder Act

Issue #6, January 1951
The Sinister Stone, by Russ Heath
I Deal in Murder, by Bill Evertt
The Dark Factory, by George Tuska
The Curse of the Coin (text)
Frame-Up, by Myron Bass
Felix the Great, by Bill Everett
The Waiting Grave, by Pete Morisi

Issue #7, March 1951
Murder
Behind the Mask, by Don Rico
The Web, by Ed Winiarski
Quiet Destiny (text)
Terror in the Tent, by Richard Briefer
The Phantom, by Murphy Anderson
Dracula Lives

Issue #8, May 1951
Don't Open This Door, by Russ Heath
You Take a Pin, by Vernon Hinkel
The Other Head, by Hank Chapman and Gene Colan
The Face of Doom (text)
The Evil Eye, by Pierce Rice and John Tartaglione
The Walking Ghost, by Gene Colan
The Maker of Dolls
The Picture, by Don Rico

Issue #9, July 1951
Back From the Dead, by Bill Lacaza
The Weather Man, by Jim Mooney
Ghost of Hate (text)
Step into My Parlor, by Don Rico
The Little Men, by Dick Rockwell
Norman's Nightmare, by Hank Chapman and Gene Colan

Issue #10, September 1951
Dance of Death, by Russ Heath
Trapped in Time, by Rudy Palais
The Shadow, by Al Hartley
Too Many Murders, by Rocke Mastroserio and Moe Marcus
Tiger Man, by Norman Steinberg

Issue #11, November 1951
In the Dead of Night, by Hank Chapman and Pete Tumlinson
Haunted, by Stan Lee and Joe Maneely

Dog-Watch Death (text)
The Suitcase, by Manny Stallman
Harry's Hate, by Mike Skewsky
Behind the Door, by Norman Steinberg

Issue #12, December 1951
The Dark Road, by Russ Heath
The Trumpet, by Joe Maneely
You're Killing Me, by Norman Steinberg
Draw Me a Picture, by George Tuska
Fingers of Fire
The Old Woman, by Paul Reinman

Issue #13, January 1952
The Strange Man, by Joe Maneely
When Willie Woke Up, by George Kline and Bill Lacava
Speak to Me
The Serpent, by Mike Sekowsky
The Man Who Built the Ark, by Bill Walton

Issue #14, February 1952
Death and Doctor Parker, by Russ Heath
We Meet at Midnight, by Allen Belman
The Last Man, by Mike Sekowsky
The Hide-Out, by George Kline
Out of This World, by Bernard Baily

Issue #15, March 1952
The Machine, by Warner Roth
The Strange Shoes, by Norman Steinberg
The String of Pearls, by Hank Chapman and Ogden Whitney
The Wrong World, by Bill Savage
Death Comes Calling

Issue #16, Spring 1952
Alone in the Dark, by Fred Kida and Stan Lee
My Coffin is Crowded, by Bob Fujitani
The Place, by Pete Tumlinson

The Corpse, by Frank R. Siminsky
Backstage Horror, by Ogden Whitney

Issue #17, April 1952
The Little Black Box, by Joe Maneely
Night of Horror, by Warner Roth
Norman Was Right, by George Roussos
Joe's Friend, by Pete Morisi
The Dungeon, by Hy Rosen
The Murder Club, by Gene Colan
The Thing in the Shadows, by Allen Bellman
Dead Witch, by Dick Ayers and Hank Chapman

Issue #18, May 1952
The Cozy Coffin, by Joe Maneely
The Joke, by Jay Scott Pike
Creep, Hands, Creep, by George Roussos
The Man I'm Gonna Kill, by Hank Chapman and Tony DiPreta
Escape From Death, by Manny Stallman
Stay Away, by Bernard Krigstein
The River, by Manny Stallman

Issue #19, June 1952
Birdface, by George Roussos
The Tough Guy, by Bill Everett
The Day That Never Ends, by Tony DiPreta
The Labyrinth, by Manny Stallman and Tony DiPreta
Second Chance, by Bob Fujitani
The Perfect Mate, by Jim Mooney and Bernard Sachs
The Growing Terror, by Fred Kida

Issue #20, July 1952
The Beast-Man, by Stan Lee
Stranger in the House, by John Romita
The Pain in the Neck, by Allan Bellman
Furnished Room with Corpse, by John Romita
Fairytale, by Goldfarb and Baer

The Brute, by Jerry Sasano
The Oath, by Jim Mooney and Bernard Sachs
The Man with No Face, by Dick Ayers

Issue #21, August 1952
The Ghost of Grimm Towers, by Stan Lee and Tony DiPreta
No Escape, by Don Loprino
The Horrible Hog, by Carl Hubble
The Graveyard Ghoul, by Ed Winiarski
The Secret, by Jack Abel and William Weltman
Terror at Midnight, by Manny Stallman
Up From the Grave, by Goldfarb and Baer

Issue #22, September 1952
The Blood Brothers, by George Roussos
The Gabby Ghost, by Bernard Krigstein
The Strike, by Manny Stallman
Hate, by Ogden Whitney
Too Late, by Stern
Each Night I Drown, by Vernon Hinkle
The Bomb, Fred Kida

Issue #23, October 1952
Molu's Secret, by Stan Lee and Carmine Infantino
Death and Mr. Marko, by Joe Sinnott
Vampire Beware, by Stan Lee and Bill Everett
The Return Trip, by Cal Massey
The Man in Black, by Cy Grudko
The Ugly Man, by Stan Lee and Joe Maneely
Skin-Deep, by Syd Shores

Issue #24, November 1952
Horror Story, by Stan Lee and George Tuska
Back from the Dead, by Stan Lee and Joe Maneely
The Striped Suit, by Jim Mooney
Boiling Point, by Stan Lee and Carmine Infantino

Suspense

Issue #25, December 1952
Men with Fangs, by Joe Sinnott
Where the Werewolf Prowled, by Tony DiPreta
I Died at Midnight, by Jim Mooney
The Man Who Sold his Soul, by John Romita

Issue #26, January 1953
Worse Than Death, by Stan Lee and George Roussos
Beauty and the Beast, by Al Eadeh
Alone with a Ghost, by Vic Dowling
Vampire Killer, by Fred Kida

Issue #27, February 1953
If!, by Fred Kida
Storm Warning, by Stan Lee and Ed Winiarski
Terror in the Tropics, by Sam Zitron
The Man Who Killed Himself
Hall of Mirrors, by Richard Briefer

Issue #28, March 1953
With Intent to Kill, by Stan Lee and Joe Maneely
Two Hands, by Chuck Winter
He Walks With a Ghost, by Al Hartley
You've Got to Kill Me, by Jim Mooney
The Poor Fish, by Stan Lee and Bill Everett

Issue #29, April 1953
The Man Behind the Blinds, by Stan Lee and Fred Kida
By the Light of the Moon, by Ed Robbins
Strong as an Ox, by Stan Lee and Jerry Robinson
The Raving Maniac, by Stan Lee and Joe Maneely
The Man Who Was Going to... DESTROY AMERICA!, by Rob Fujitani

Fury and Sound

(From the "lost" July 26, 1945 episode)

by Roby Wentz

From the CBS Radio Script by Robert E. Lee and Irving Reis.

"Somewhere in the radio business there may be a more stupid, insensitive collection of people, but I doubt it. Roachler has asked for *tender* adlibs — *not* the Fulton fish market. You're butchering -"

The actors, musicians and technicians in the rehearsal studio stood silent under the tirade. The orchestra men stared at their music-stands; the cast kept their eyes on their scripts; the sound effects man inspected his bells and whistles.

Charles Fowler, assistant producer, was less fortunate. His eyes remained fixed on the control booth and hence on the author of the tongue-lashing. Fowler's face was blank of expression. Script in hand, he waited, eyes on the small, ugly man with an abnormally small head, crouched over the rehearsal mike behind the thick glass window. The rasping voice from the talk-back was "in sync" with the movements of the sneering lips.

"Roachler would further like to remind the sound effects man, for the seventh time," the talk-back blared on, "that he wishes the rain effect to sneak in after the bridge music, not crash in. And would the talented assistant producer, Mister Fowler, get word to the musicians that pianissimo means softly?"

Charles Fowler's face was a mask.

"And now, if it won't interfere anyone's more important business, may Roachler proceed with his rehearsal? Thank you. Adlibs, please."

His face unchanging, Fowler nodded at the group of extras. They broke into their brief lines. "Good-bye." "Take time to write, Johnny." "Drop me a postcard from Paris."

One of Fowler's eyebrows went up, and a sugary phrase of "bridge" music seeped from the violins. The sound effects man, eyes on the "mixer" in the booth, caught the signal and poured a stream of fine gravel down his tin trough-rain.

Fowler pointed a finger at a girl in a black dress, and she moved up to the mike. "Dear Daisy," she began, "how can I tell you what my own heart cannot say...?" The sentimental lines crooned on in throaty tones.

With the crack of a pistol shot, a music-stand slipped in its adjustable sleeve. The girl stopped in mid-sentence. So did the musical background. Almost palpably, muscles tensed, faces stiffened. The talk-back activated with a click.

"Roachler has worked with insensitive asses in many places and under many conditions, but he is forced to yield top honors to the radio artists of California!" The shrieking voice verged on a note of hysteria. "How can this girl perform these sensitive thoughts against the opposition of your noise and indifference? How can these fragile dreams, crystallized through nights of creative sweat, compete with your gum-chewing, chair-creaking, walking-talking, thick-skinned detachment? How can..."

Fowler spoke into the studio mike.

"I'm sorry, King. It was my fault. I tried to adjust the stand and give the cues at the same time and..."

"Mister Fowler honorably confesses!" If possible, the voice was more scathing. "Roachler has employed Mister Fowler for three years. His principal function is to run my errands, reflect my thoughts, do the unimportant trivia of producing for radio." The voice dripped contempt. "In the fullest sense, Mister Fowler is an extension of Roachler's brain. But he still has not evolved a satisfactory method of doing his work without kicking the studio down."

Fowler looked at his tormentor. "Look, King—how about holding that up until the cast leaves?"

Suspense

"Well!" The small, ugly man's eyebrows shot up the domed forehead. "Roachler seems at long last to have located a sensitive zone in Mister Fowler! We'll break for dinner, now, and anyone else who feels that Roachler's work, which seems to interest a mere fourteen million listeners, is too dull to warrant their entire attention, can be paid off now."

He turned his back on the mike and disappeared through the control booth door. The tension broke in the studio. People spoke freely. Music stands clattered; scripts crackled. The personnel of "ROACHLER PRESENTS" straggled out to dinner.

Fowler did not move. Taking a pencil from his pocket, he began jotting notes on the margin of his script as the studio emptied around him.

"How did my performance sound, Charles?"

Fowler raised his eyes. The girl whose speech his miscue had interrupted stood before him. She was small, with cloudy black hair, a sullen, provocative mouth done in cherry black lipstick and a figure that stopped just short of voluptuousness.

"Okay, I guess." His voice was toneless.

"You guess?"

"All right. I'll tell you. It seemed a little corny to me."

Sparks jumped in the smoldering dark eyes. "It didn't seem corny to King. Naturally, he only gets two thousand a week for running the show."

Fowler reached for his coat, shrugged his shoulders into it. "If you want apples polished, don't send 'em to me."

"You're getting more impossible to live with every day!" The girl's sulky anger took dame. Fowler's gaze seemed to search her face before he answered.

"Let's not start another of those cycles, dear. So Roachler thinks you're the greatest actress in the world. So he's the guy you have to sell. So he's sold. So you're all set."

"Jealous... Charley?"

"No. Why?"

Her laughter bubbled. "You are! In five years of being married to you, Charley, I thought I'd seen every facet of your fine art of being disagreeable, but jealousy's a new one."

"Fine. Let it go at that."

"Oh, no. If you're going to be jealous, Charley. I'll give it something to feed on. Would it make you any more jealous to know that I'm on my way to dinner with King to discuss my performance?" She watched to see if the barb took effect.

"Tell him hell for me."

She laughed again. "Oh, I will, darling." Her full lips twisted. "King tells me he's found a marvelous new place for dinner. It's very private. 'Bye."

She was gone. Fowler sat down in a canvas chair. He put one hand to his forehead. For a moment, only. But the fingers trembled a little as he reached for a cigarette. With the match lit, he remembered studio rules, blew it out, made a half-movement of irritation.

"Aren't you going to eat, Charley?"

Fowler started slightly. "Eh...?"

"Aren't you going to eat tonight?"

Fowler turned to see Van Meter, the sound effects technician, regarding him with a friendly smile. He carried a lunch pail in his hand.

Fowler tried to smile back. "I — wasn't hungry, Van. Gotta mark up these scripts, anyway."

"Hell, you can't live without eating." Van Meter, a gangling redhead with a crop of freckles on his skinny forearms, sat down and opened the lunch box. There were neat stacks of sandwiches wrapped in waxed paper, an orange, chocolate topped cupcakes. "Here, I'll split with you. Ham on rye — how's that? Barbecued, too. Fixed this ham myself. Better than the ham we cook up here at work." He shot a sly look at Fowler. Fowler grinned crookedly.

"Got a barbecue pit on my own backyard in Glendale," Van Meter went on. "I can do a lot of things besides ring bells and pour sand into a bucket, Charley."

Fowler stripped the waxy paper from around a sandwich, bit into it; the pink, flaking ham, with taste overtones of barbecue sauce, was delicious.

Chewing, he leaned back in the canvas chair. "Jeez, Van — it's good, at that. Don't you eat out on the job, here?"

"Why wouldn't I? My wife's the best cook in the world. I couldn't get out of the house without a lunch. Packs it for me the first thing every morning. Have some coffee. Reach yourself one of those Dixie cups."

They chatted about people and things, not about their work. Fowler took another sandwich. He found himself laughing a little at something Van had said. Over the second cup of coffee they were silent a moment, and Fowler laughed again — a short bark.

"What's the joke?"

"No joke," said Fowler. "It just struck me, Van. You're a happy man."

"Me? We-ell, maybe so, at that. Never thought about it just that way."

"Your wife loves you, you've got your house in Glendale and your backyard and your barbecue pit. You're independent. When your time's up here, you pick your lunch box and get the hell out, home to your wife and your yard. Independent."

Van Meter grinned. "You ought to write scripts, Charley. Quite a speech, that."

"Didn't mean it to be. It just happened to strike me, all at once, how different it is with me, all at once, how different it is with me. Me and my pet genius."

"Yeah," the sound man nodded, "That must be rugged, Charley."

"It was only the time I spent with him here in the studio," and Fowler. "But when we finally call it a day here, that's just the beginning. We go home and it keeps right on."

"You live with him?"

Fowler grimaced wryly. "Yeah. When we come out here from New York to launch this new show, he took a house in Benedict Canyon, away back in the hills, and insisted Merle and I move in with him."

"Merle?"

"My wife."

Van exclaimed. "The gal in the cast?"

"Sure."

Van whistled. "No disrespect, old boy. You're doin' all right."

"Thanks."

"So you live with him?"

"Well, he insisted on it, practically. 'For the good of the show.' So we could 'talk things over at night.' Cozy."

Van exhaled slowly. "Yeah. Very cozy. You know," he went on, in a light tone, "it's funny about these wonder-boys."

"How do you mean?"

"Well, in my capacity of plain and fancy maker of noises, I've seen a steady parade of these boy geniuses come and go. In the early stages they go in for Indian bracelets, sweatshirts, beards. That's the first manifestation. Later they develop another characteristic, an acute sensitivity to sounds. After awhile they even hear things that aren't there. Like that rain effect of mine this afternoon."

"What about it?"

"Well, after Roachler bawled me out for the fifth time about the effect being too loud, I just let one bridge go by and *I didn't even run the sand down the trough*. He still yelled that it was too loud!"

Fowler's eyes puckered thoughtfully. "That sounds impossible."

"Not to a connoisseur in geniuses like me. It's a standard stage in the evolution of the wonder boy species. They grow more and more hysterical from there on. Then, just about the time a psychopathic hospital starts warming up four guys with white coats and a canvas T-shirt for a new customer — what happens? Why, the movies discover the genius. So they pay a thousand dollars a week more for his particularly brand of paranoia than he can make in radio, only in a quieter, setting."

Fowler nodded. "They have been after him on a movie deal."

Van stood up and brushed crumbs off his trouser legs. "They better step on it. This time it's gonna be a close race between the talent scouts and the four white coats." He stuffed papers into the lunch box and snapped it shut. "Yup, he's got the occupational disease of radio geniuses. Newspapermen get the shakes, movie producers got ulcers, bank presidents jump out of windows. But the wonder boys of the kilocycles get open nerves in their ear drums."

"Let's take a smoke." They went outside and Fowler offered his pack of cigarettes. They lit up and Fowler exhaled and said, "Yeah ... Sometimes I think it's happening to me."

"Could be, if you stay in the racket long enough. Stands to reason — radio is sound, nothing else. The more sensitive your ears are, the better radio man you'll be — up to a point, anyway."

"I read somewhere," Fowler said musingly, "that if everyone's hearing was increased ten percent, we'd all go nuts."

Van laughed triumphantly. "You took it right out of my mouth, Charley. There's a whole vast world of fantastic, unimaginable sound roaring away just below the threshold of our hearing. Take the studio for example. They say it's soundproof. Throw away your smoke and we'll go back in for a minute, and I'll show you something."

The doors behind them.

"Listen," Van said. "Hear anything?"

After a moment of silence, Fowler shook his head. "Nothing."

"Now see what happens."

From his pocket, Van produced a tiny black thing with long wires and a plug dangling from it. Swiftly, a quiet smile on his face, he unplugged a floor-mike and plugged in the tiny gadget.

"That's a contact mike, isn't it?" Fowler said curiously.

"Right. But this is something a little special. It's the most sensitive thing in the line of an 'electrical ear' that science knows about. You might call it a 'sound microscope.' "

"It's certainly little enough."

"Small but potent. Look, I'll press it against the wall of the studio. Like so." He suited the action to the word. "Charley," he called, "will you turn up the volume on that amplifier?"

Fowler gave the knob a tentative twist — and flinched, as the studio became a bedlam of noise — street traffic, trolley-bells, klaxons, squealing brakes mingled with boomy, bass voice-sounds from somewhere, clumping footsteps, hissing air.

"Hey!" shouted Van, "Not so loud! I told you it was sensitive!"

Fowler spun the knob and the sound dwindled to a murmur. "My God!" he said in a drained voice.

"See what I mean?" the technician said, grinning. "Can you imagine what would happen to the geniuses if the movies didn't rescue 'em?"

"Even a genius hasn't got a microphone in his ears," said Fowler slowly.

"Hasn't he?" Van dropped his treasure in his pocket. "Guys like Roachler live in a world of sound. Mr. R. gets two grand a week to sit in that glass fish bowl and just listen. Weighing sounds. His ears are his stock in trade. The nerve endings in the ear drums get more and more sensitive. When he hearing becomes as acute as this contact mike's — he won't be able to stand it. Then, in come the white coats."

"Where do you get one of those things?" asked Fowler casually.

"This contact mike?"

"Yes."

"Built it myself. Look at it." He tossed it to Fowler. The assistant producer turned it over in his hands.

"That's the works," said Van.

"Yeah," commented Fowler. "Pretty neat."

The doors swung open and a trio of trumpet-players walked in, talking loudly.

Fowler handed the microphone to the sound effects man. "Thanks for showing it to me," he said casually. "Thanks very much."

"Farewell, my love..." Merle's voice, dripping corn, sighed into the mike. "Good night across the latitudes and longitudes of space and time. Farewell across the hours and the days, the mountain peaks and the plains between the darkness and the sun. You are with me here because love is here."

The orchestra came up with a triumphant chord that was half-drowned in a sea of terrific applause from the studio audience. The announcer stepped to his microphone. "You have just heard another original by Roachler to the series 'ROACHLER PRESENTS.' It was produced, written and directed by Mr. Roachler, who also suggested the musical theme. Next week Roachler, acclaimed as the most imaginative dramatist in radio, will — but let radio's foremost producer tell you about it himself. Ladies and gentlemen, Kingsley Roachler!" He swung a finger at Roachler. The little man, his gnome like appearance accentuated by the thick glasses, came to the mike.

"Roachler speaking," he said crisply. "Next week Roachler fans will hear a vivid contrast to tonight's romantic theme. It is a drama fought with social significance entitled 'Farewell to Apes.' What would happen if an ape..." He sketched in the idea. "Until next week, then," he finished, "Roachler says good night. Roachler will be pleased if you return to hear another 'ROACHLER PRESENTS!'"

The music danced into a gay march as the crowd pushed for the exits and curtains swung across the proscenium. Roachler sauntered over to Fowler, standing in the wings.

"It was one of the most impressive shows of the series, in my opinion — don't you think so, Charley?"

"You should know," Fowler said shortly.

Roachler caught Merle's eye and smiled at her, and Fowler caught the exchange of looks.

"It would have been a more polished production," the virtuoso went on, carelessly, "if you hadn't botched up the music cues. In three places they were distinctly sluggish. I've told you a thousand times, *watch me*."

"Save it," said Fowler.

"- and pay attention," Roachler continued. Then he stopped short. "*What did you say, Charley?*"

"I said, 'save it,'" answered Fowler. "I could tell you something else to do with it, too. I'm through."

"Through what...?"

"Through being your whipping boy. Better find yourself another one just as dumb as I am."

Roachler rallied quickly.

"Charley! I can't believe it! You didn't say it. No, I've erased it from my mind."

"Scribble it right back again, then," Fowler said brutally. "I'm finished."

Roachler saw people halt, curious faces watching. He pulled Fowler into an ante-room, shut the door. "You don't know what you're saying. The realist in me says 'It's possible.' Anything is possible in this vast distortion called life. But the artist in me is shocked, Charley."

Fowler stood stony-faced.

"You and Merle have been like brother and sister to me," Roachler purred smoothly, laying a hand on Fowler's arm. The thick spectacles concentrated his gaze on Fowler's hard features. "I've labored to groom you to be a great producer, too, Charley — brought Merle to the verge of a great acting career."

"If it hadn't been for Merle, I'd have walked out a year ago."

"Charley! I bleed! I can understand when those dolts, actors, technicians, fiddlers, misunderstand my sensitivity, these little moods brought on by the seeing creative fire! But you, an artist in your own right—"

The door opened and Merle came into the room. "What's all the glaring about?" She stared from one to the other. She was still in the gown she had worn for the broadcast, a lithe, provocative thing in black, shaped to her figure, slid high along one well-turned leg.

"Charley wants to quit the show," said Roachler.

She laughed. "Don't mind him," said Charles Fowler's wife scornfully. "He's tired. He'll forget it in the morning. Coming, King?"

"Charley -" began Kingsley Roachler.

"Skip it," said Fowler. He walked past them out of the room, out of the studio, to the parking lot where his car stood, got in, and started the engine.

"You shouldn't ought to gun her that way, starting up cold, Mr. Fowler," said the attendant. "Scores the cylinders." He stared after the convertible as it roared across the lot and lurched into the street, through a red light.

"What do you s'pose is eatin' him, Bill?" he asked his co-worker.

"Ah, these radio guys are all nuts," opined Bill.

The hands of the clock besides the bed stood at four A.M. as the key turned in the lock in the front door. Fowler lay on the bed in his clothes, eyes wide open. He heard the door open and close, softly Roachler's voice said something, and Merle laughed — an intimate, caressing sound, with a sensual undertone. Roachler was talking again. They both laughed softly. Followed a period of complete silence lasting for several minutes, and then Fowler heard footsteps climbing the stairs, heard good-nights spoken, and Merle's step approaching the bedroom door. The light clicked on.

"Oh... You're still awake."

"Do you know what time it is?" asked Fowler from the bed.

Her quick glance took in the situation. "Objection...?"

"Oh, no. No objection. I'm just your husband. I was just thinking how tired you get around ten-thirty when I suggest you and I going out alone."

"Do I always have to go out with you?"

"Come on to bed."

She flung aside the black dress and whirled on him. "Don't tell me that to do!" She shook her cloud of dark hair angrily. "I'm buzzed to the years with you, Charley. I might as well admit it. Let's wash it up right now, like adults."

"It's just me, of course."

"Just you."

"Roachler doesn't have a thing to do with it."

"Of course not. The point is, Charley, we don't get along anymore. Why not stop trying?"

"All right... Let's," said Fowler tonelessly.

She smiled. "That's the way to talk, Charley. Be sensible. Look. We'll finish this series of shows and I'll run up to Reno and get a divorce. No upsets or hard feelings. Just good friends."

"Okay," Fowler got up and started to undress.

Fowler almost collided with Van Meter in the studio hallway before he recognized him. "Why, hello, Van!" He seemed about to hurry on. "Say!" He snapped his fingers. "Glad I met you. You know that gimmick you showed me the other day — that contact mike? I'd like to borrow it a few days. I want to work out some sound effects for next week's show."

"Why, sure." Van Meter fished in his pocket. "Got it with me. Here."

"Swell." Fowler slipped it into his *own* jacket. "I may need it for a couple of weeks, Van."

The sound men waved a hand. "Keep it as long as you like. All you have to do is hook it up to a record player."

"Thanks a lot, Van!"

The doctor in the Vine Street office building shook a waggish head at Fowler. "You radio fellows!" he said. "How do you expect to sleep when you're so tense all the time? Well, this ought to do the business. Take two envelopes of those powders just before retiring, and you'll sleep. Oh, by the way..."

Fowler paused on his way out. "Yes, doctor..."

"Watch the dose. Too much can be dangerous."

"How much?"

"Anything over three of 'em. You'll only need two."

It was after eleven when he left himself into the apartment that evening. Merle was alone, chain-smoking.

"Where's King?"

"He went to bed." She ground out her cigarette. "I'm jumpy."

"We both need sleep," Fowler said. "Let's get to bed ourselves." His voice was casual. "I've been having trouble sleeping lately. Saw a doctor today and got some sleeping powders. What say we both give ourselves a break?"

"Sure. Fix me a slug."

In the bathroom, Fowler dissolved three of the powders in a glass of water. He filled another glass with plain water.

When he turned off the tap, it continued to drip in to the washbowl. He went into the bedroom and handed a glass to Merle. "Drink up."

"Here's to sleep." They drained their glasses.

In bed, a few minutes later, she spoke sleepily, "Charley..."

"What?"

"Will you turn off that water tap — the one that's dripping?"

"It leaks. You can't make it stop."

"Oh, well... The devil with it."

Fowler lay beside her until her breathing grew slow and regular. Occasionally she snored a little. He raised himself on one elbow, shook her slightly.

"Merle?" he said, in a normal voice. There was no answer.

Fowler got up, and went into the bathroom.

Kingsley Roachler woke up, eyes wide open and staring. He gazed around at the familiar, dusky room. He jumped from bed and ran to the open window. Outside, the brush-covered canyon hillside lay silent in the dim starlight.

He was turning back toward the bed when the sound struck again... An incredible, metallic note, like the plucking of a cosmic fiddle-string over the crash of a supernatural gong, menacing, apocalyptic.

He uttered an involuntary cry and clapped his hands to his ears. The vast sound came at him again, and it seemed that the house walls swelled with it. With an inarticulate scream, Roachler ran out of the room and down the hallway. He wrenched at a door, threw it open.

"Charley! Merle!"

"What's trouble, King?" Fowler's voice was drugged and sleepy.

"That — that sound! Like a faucet dripping magnified a million times!"

"Don't know..." Fowler seemed struggling to wake up. Maybe a tap leaking somewhere."

"No... like a bomb exploding. Listen!"

"I can't hear a thing, King."

There was no more sound — only the muted, normal night noises of the hills. Roachler passed a hand over his eyes. "It's gone. Why — you could hear it all over the place!"

"You must have been dreaming. It didn't wake either Merle or myself." Fowler lay down again. "Try to go to sleep, King."

"But I know I heard something. Don't try to tell me -"

"I'm tired, King. Good night."

Roachler stood a moment in uncertainty. "Yeah... I — I guess it was a dream. You're sure you didn't..."

"Oh, hell, King. You're getting jumpy. Go to bed."

"Yeah, I dreamed it, I guess. Good-night, Charley."

Van Meter came up to Fowler during a break, next day. "Notice anything about the maestro this afternoon?" he asked.

Fowler looked at him. "Shouldn't I?" he queried.

The sound man raised his eyebrows. "My gosh, I should think anyone would. He's actually been polite to a couple of people. Seems — oh, I don't know; he seems worried about something."

"Probably having an off-day. How's the little home getting along, Van?"

"Swell. Lotta work though. I'm putting up insect-screens, tonight after work. What with hot weather, the mosquitoes are getting bad."

"Insects," said Fowler.

"What?"

"Oh... I said yes, the insects are bad."

He watched Roachler leave the studio after work. The producer brushed off the usual post-rehearsal conferences with network executives, advertising men and his staff, and disappeared.

Fowler found him sitting up in bed, penciling a script, when he arrived at the Benedict Canyon house that night. The little man had swathed his oversize head in a huge towel; the thick folds enclosed his ears, accentuating his naturally grotesque appearance.

"What?" he said loudly, almost in the manner of a deaf person. "I can't hear you."

"If you'd take off that damned towel you could," shouted Fowler. "All I asked was, how are you?"

"What do you mean?" countered Roachler.

"You look bad," said Fowler.

"I'm all right," said Roachler. "My ears hurt a little, is all. Damn odd."

"Well, good-night," shouted Fowler.

"Good-night."

After a time Roachler laid the script aside, took off the towel, switched out the light, and tried to sleep, but sleep refused to come. He was twitching in a fitful doze when something broke the night silence in the room. Roachler stopped twitching and lay still. The sound was a faint, ominous whining, a steady, high-pitched hum that set nerves on edge like the sounds of a band-saw on a pine knoll.

Roachler sat bolt upright in bed. As he did so, the high, singing whine grew into a scream, rising and falling, the sound of a squadron of diving fighter-planes. Behind the screaming, dull, vibrating blow suggested heavy bodies striking against thin, metallic surfaces. The terrifying manifestation was inside the room, outside the room, throughout the house.

Kingsley Roachler uttered a high, agonized shriek, as though in pain. His hands went to his ears.

The sound ceased.

Quivering, the little man sank back among the pillows, his hands still on his ears. He moaned softly. Finally he was quiet.

Like a blast from a choir of demonic clarinets, the sound was with him again, shaking the walls, rattling a teacup on the bedside table.

Kingsley Roachler leaped from bed, sobbing ran out the door and down the hall. He rushed into Fowler's room.

"Charley! Charley!"

"What's the matter, King?" Fowler's voice was sleepy and a little irritated.

The sound was gone.

"Will you come into my room?" Roachler's voice vibrated like a saw blade as he fought to keep it calm.

"Okay, keep your shirt on." Fowler got into a robe and slippers and followed Roachler down the hall. "What is it — another brainstorm for the show?"

"It's the same thing I had trouble with last night. You heard it, of course."

"Are you hearing noises again?"

Roachler was almost pleading. "Don't tell me you slept through that!"

"Don't shoot at me!"

"Please, Charley. I — I must be getting a little jumpy, I didn't mean to shout. Listen, Charley — didn't you hear a buzzing, whining sound, something like a mosquito buzzing against a screen, only louder. Enormously louder! It shook the walls!"

"You'd better switch your brand, King." Fowler lit a cigarette.

"You're deaf! Merle — she must have heard it."

"She's sleeping like a baby."

Roachler stood irresolutely a moment. "Charley," he said, "get dressed and get out the car. I'm going to see a doctor."

"You think that's smart?"

"Why not...?"

"Well, what do you think a doctor will say when you try to convince him that you heard a mosquito buzzing so it shook the walls of your room? Or that a dripping water-faucet sounds like exploding bombs to you?"

"What do you mean?"

"Well..." Fowler shrugged. "I've often wondered what would happen to a man if his hearing became too sensitive... If he heard too much. He could never find rest or quiet. Eventually, I suppose, he'd blow his top."

"I — I do have very sensitive hearing."

"Sure." Fowler laughed lightly. "So sensitive that you're hearing things that aren't there. I wonder how long you'd have a sponsor if they knew the shape you're in."

"I'm in perfect shape!" There was a high note of alarm in Roachler's voice.

"Glad to hear it."

"I've been working too hard, that's all. I just need a little rest."

"Well..." Fowler was resigned. "I'll get the car out and drive you to the hospital."

"No! No!" Roachler seized his arm. Fowler stood looking down at the little man. "I'll be all right, Charley. Go on back to bed."

Fowler shrugged again. "Whatever you say. But I'm getting a little tired of being waked up every night about your 'noises.' Good night."

"Charley!" Roachler's voice as carefully restrained, but the undertone of terror in it was clearly audible. He stood in Fowler's doorway, the following night. The clock hands stood at two A.M.

"What is it, King?"

"I — I've got a terrific idea for next week's show, Charley. Come into my room and see if it tweaks you."

"Okay." Fowler followed him through the doorway. "Go ahead — shoot."

Roachler sat down. "Well, there's this French girl. She's escaped from the Nazi's, and -" The man's hands shook as he tried to light a cigarette. Fowler took no notice. "Charley, how far are we from Sunset Boulevard?"

"Sunset? Oh, about a mile and a half, I guess."

"We couldn't hear traffic — automobiles gunning their motors, brakes squealing horns — that distance, could we?"

Fowler stared at him and Roachler colored under the look.

"I couldn't," said Fowler, after a pause.

"Yeah. Well, this gal's a painter and she falls in love with a — y'know, Charley, I get these ideas in the middle of the night, and I like to talk 'em out before I forget 'em. I'll tell you — why don't you bunk in here with me for awhile?"

After a pause, Fowler said flatly, "Seems sort of silly."

"Please, Charley!" His voice almost broke. "Roachler needs you, Charley." And when Fowler regarded him coldly, he added humbly, "*I* need you, Charley."

"I'll bed down here, if you want it that way," said Fowler shortly.

"Quiet!" rasped the voice. "Roachler insists on complete quiet! Will you please stop your insufferable scuffling and scraping and babbling until called upon to utter your required sounds?"

Charles Fowler, in shirt-sleeves, script in hand, let his arms fall to his sides. He kept his gaze on the gnome-headed figure in the control booth.

Roachler's face was suffused with heavy red. Through the thick glass, the prominent veins on his forehead were clearly visible.

"Right back in the groove!" murmured Van Meter.

"Roachler heard that remark!"

The silence was complete.

"The man who made that statement is hereby discharged!" The producer's voice vibrated like a tuning fork.

"But, King, you can't fire Van," said Fowler. "He isn't working for you. The studio pays him."

"Roachler cannot tolerate insubordination!" The little man screamed it. "May I remind you that Roachler is directing? I can replace anyone, do you understand, any -"

His throat seemed to constrict. Strangled gaspings issued from his mouth. His face went waxy pale and he slumped forward. The watchers in the studio saw his head strike the microphone, knock it over.

Fowler was the first into the control booth.

"What's the matter, King?"

The horrible strangling ceased. Kingsley Roachler set his hands against the edge of the control-board and pushed himself upright.

"I — it's this noise... I've got to get away from it. I'm a little dizzy, is all... Be all right after a bit..."

Merle stepped to his side. "There's a cot in my dressing room."

Fowler pushed her aside. "Dressing room, hell. The place for him is at home! Leave everything to me." He glanced around, a slight smile on his lips. "Somebody call an ambulance. We'll go on with the rehearsal. The show's going right ahead!"

"I've got to hand it to you, Charley; you didn't louse up the broadcast after all."

They were at home after the show. Merle began pulling off her long black gloves.

"Thanks." Fowler was tight-lipped.

"Say..." Merle eyed him curiously. "You're white as a sheet yourself, Charley. Anything wrong?"

"Damn it, no! Why should there be?"

"Well, after all! I was only asking. How's King?"

Fowler sat down. "Resting."

"What does the doctor say?"

"He doesn't want a doctor."

"That's insane!" Merle stepped to the telephone. "I'm going to call a doctor." She was picking up the phone when Fowler crossed the room in two strides and snatched the instrument from her.

"He doesn't want a doctor! Is that clear?"

She stared at him. "Charley, are you all right...?"

Fowler smiled. "Just a little on edge, what with everything, I guess. Well — how about our usual sleeping powder, to make it all pass away smoothly? Hm?"

The girl shook her head. "I don't think so. I've been waking up sort of fogged..."

"You will take the sleeping powder!"

He was standing before her, features taut, eyes burning. She recoiled a step. "Charley...!"

"I've got to get rest, tonight! How can I, if you're going to be twisting and tossing?"

"I'm not taking any, is that clear? Say, what's this all about, anyway?" He eyes narrowed. "This sleeping powder business was *your* idea from the first. Why are you so anxious to have me take it?"

Fowler was in the bathroom. He came out with a glass of water. "Drink it!" he gritted, thrusting it at her.

The girl's eyes widened at sight of the look on his face. In a movement of sudden panic, she struck the tumbler out of his hand; it crashed to the floor.

"How do I know what's in it...?" She tried to get past him. "Kingsley! King... Help -"

Fowler's short-arm punch stopped her in the middle of a step. Her body stiffened in grotesque rigidity for a split second. Fowler's second blow caught her in that position and hurled her against the glass-topped dressing table. She slumped against its frilly "skirt."

Fowler ripped her blouse open, jammed the little black thing into her pink-net bra. The small, black wires trailed from her breast across the floor...

He stepped to the cabinet in the corner and worked swiftly for a moment.

At first the throbbing was something suggested, rather than heard — a deep, distant thudding in a queer, double meter — thump-ta-THUMP, thump-ta-THUMP, thump-ta-THUMP... It swelled, increased in volume, marched closer... thump-ta-THUMP!... thump-ta-THUMP!... thump-ta-THUMP!... like the reason wrecking throbbing of an inhuman juju drum that broke through the walls, ear drums, sense itself.

"*Charley...!*"

The scream was an animal cry of distilled, fine-drawn agony. It rang through the house. Almost before it sounded, Fowler was in Kingsley Roachler's room.

"What is it, King? What's wrong?"

The little figure of the genius of radio lay full length on the bedroom carpet. His hands, white-knuckled, clutched his ears.

"Stop it, Charley, for God's sake, stop it!"

The inhuman drum beats rattled the furniture.

"Stop what, King?"

"That throbbing! It's driving me insane!" He was grasping between sobs. "My head, Charley — oh my head...!" It's a heart beat, Charley. It's my own heart — beating, pounding. Can't you hear it, Charley? Say that you — hear it — Charley..."

THUMP-ta-THUMP! THUMP-ta-THUMP! THUMP-ta-THUMP!

With one high, shrill cry, Kingley Roachler leaped to his feet and rushed from the room.

"Quiet — quiet — quiet...!" His despairing cry trailed back from the hallway, from the stairway. A door was wrenched open downstairs.

The horrible sonic hammer pounded on. Fowler continued to smile. He stood in the middle of Kingsley Roachler's bedroom without moving.

From below came a single, shattering detonation.

Only then did Charles Fowler move. Stepping to the telephone at Roachler's bedside, he spun the dial.

"Police," he said, and waited. "Police? This is Charles Fowler speaking, 3141 Benedict Canyon Lane. Kingsley Roachler has just committed suicide... Yes, the same Roachler. Shot himself. Yes, I'll be here. What sound? I don't know."

He hung up and walked over to a wall cabinet. He opened the polished wood doors, reached inside, and came out with a decanter, into a small glass with the initials KR on it, he splashed whiskey, drank it off, poured more whiskey, drank again.

THUMP-ta-*THUMP*, THUMP-ta-*THUMP*... Charles Fowler started to pour another drink.

THUMP-ta-*THUMP*, THUMP-ta... The pounding stopped.

The decanter remained poised above the glass. Charles Fowler stood silent in the silent house; very gently, he set down the decanter. Very deliberately, he walked down the hallway.

Merle lay crumpled where she had fallen, against the dressing table. Her dark eyes were wide open; she seemed to be staring at him.

"Merle!" shouted Fowler.

Her eyes stared on, unwaveringly. Fowler fell on his knees alongside his wife and shook her. "Merle! Merle!" There was no change in either the expression or direction of the dark eyes' gaze. He jammed his ear against her heart. When he straightened the look on his face was dazed, incredulous.

"Merle..."

Far down the canyon, he heard the siren rising and falling, rising and falling in the steep gorge. Beneath it sounded the threatening drone of the racing motor. Charles Fowler's head sank against the dead girl's breast. His shoulders shook. In front of the house, brakes squealed, and the siren moaned into silence. Footsteps drummed on the graveled path. The sharp blows of the knocker reverberated through the big house.

"Open up, in there!"

Fowler walked slowly into the bathroom. From the medicine chest he took six small envelopes, opened then one by one and poured the powder in them into a tumbler. Then he filled the tumbler with water and drank the mixture in it, turned, and walked from the bathroom to the head of the stairs leading to the floor.

"Coming!" he called.

Radio Script for the "Lost" Episode of "The Keenest Edge"

Suspense

PRESENTED BY ROMA WINES

"THE KEENEST EDGE"
STARRING
MR. RICHARD GREENE

5:00 – 5:30 P.M. PST
9:00 – 9:30 P.M. PST

THURSDAY, FEBRUARY 28, 1946

BRADLEY:	Now... Roma Wines... R-O-M-A... Made in California for enjoyment throughout the world... Roma Wines present... (KNIFE CHORD)
NARR:	SUSPENSE!
MUSIC:	(KNIFE CHORD... HOLD UNDER)
NARR:	Tonight Roma Wines brings you Mr. Richard Greene as star of "The Keenest Edge"... A suspense play... Produced, edited and directed for Roma Wines by

	William Spier.
MUSIC:	(UP TO CUT OFF)
BRADLEY:	"Suspense"... radio's outstanding Theatre of Thrills... Is presented for your enjoyment by Roma Wines... That's R-O-M-A... Roma Wines, those excellent California Wines that can add so much pleasantness to the way you live... to your happiness in entertaining guests... To your enjoyment of everyday meals... Yes... right now a glassful would be very pleasant... As Roma Wines bring you Richard Greene in a remarkable tale of...
MUSIC:	(KNIFE CHORD)
NARR:	SUSPENSE!
MUSIC:	(SWELL UP CHORD)
JACK:	I knew there was something to be afraid of the minute I saw the place. Some people have a sort of sixth sense about things like that, you know. Anyway, I do. But I needed work and I needed a place to stay.
SOUND:	(BLAST OF A TRUCK HORN, AND THE TRUCK ITSELF, AS IT ROARS PAST ALONG THE HIGHWAY. LITTLE OFF AND UNDER.
JACK:	(CONT'D) And I'd been walking ever since daylight, out along the highway from town. It was just a little roadside place, with a sign that said Café and Barbecue, spelt B-A-R and then a capitol B and a Q, like they do out west here — nothing special about it. Maybe it was seeing the girl in there that made me afraid. That might have been it. But I didn't think about it then. I'd seen in the window where it said "Cook's Helper Wanted." So
SOUND:	(THREE OF FOUR STEPS ON GRAVEL
JACK:	(CONT'D) I walked across the gravel driveway and up to the screen door.
SOUND:	(FLIMSY SCREEN DOOR OPENING AND

SLAMMING UNDER

JACK: (CONT'D) and went in. There was nobody inside but the girl. She was a pretty girl, too. But she wouldn't look at me. Not even when she spoke…

MILDRED: Something for you?

JACK: Uh — I see it says there in the window you want a cook's helper.

MILDRED: Oh. I thought you wanted a cup of coffee or something.

JACK: No. I just want job.

MILDRED: Oh.

JACK: Is the job still open?

MILDRED: I guess so. But I couldn't tell you anything about it, myself.

JACK: Don't you run the place?

MILDRED: Oh no. My uncle does that. I just work here.

JACK: Well, where's your uncle?

MILDRED: Out back, I guess.

JACK: Could I see him?

MILDRED: I don't know. He's busy… I couldn't take you out there just now…

JACK: Why not?

MILDRED: I have to mind the counter.

JACK: If you'll show me the way, I'll go myself.

MILDRED: Oh no! Maybe I could call him though…

JACK: All right.

SOUND: (THREE OR FOUR STEPS ACROSS FLOOR)

MILDRED: (CALLING) Uncle Ed…

ED: (OFF) Yeah?

MILDRED:	There's a man here to see you.
ED:	What's he want?
MILDRED:	It's about the job.
ED:	Oh. All right. Send him on back.
MILDRED:	(COMING ON) He says you can go on back. He's in the kitchen.
JACK:	I went on back, like she told me. It was a pretty big kitchen for such a little place, and a couple of good-sized chill-boxes beyond that. Her uncle was big too, like a cop or a judge.
SOUND:	(THE CLEAR GRATING WHISTLE OF A STEEL KNIFE BEING DRAWN CAREFULLY AND DELIBERATELY)
JACK:	(CONT'D) He was standing at a meat block sharpening a set of knives. Not kitchen knives, but good ones, the kind a butcher uses. And you could see he liked what he was doing. He didn't look at me either. And for a minute, I just stood there.
SOUND:	(REGISTER KNIFE SOUND BRIEFLY)
ED:	You know a good bonin' knife when you see it, son?
JACK:	That looks like a good one.
ED:	You're doggone right it's a good one! Trouble with most people is they don't know how to take care of a knife. Nor handle it neither. You know how to sharpen a knife? Lemme see you sharpen this one.
JACK:	Well.
SOUND:	(THE KNIFE SOUND HAS GONE OUT. THEN ONE BRIEF SCRAPE AS JACK TRIES IT.)
ED:	No! Gimme that knife! Don't _never_ push a knife across the grain of a stone like that! Never! You'll ruin it! Looka here now — I can shave the hairs off my arm with this knife — see that?

JACK: Uh huh.

ED: That's the way I knife's gotta be if it's gonna be any good to you.

JACK: Do you do a lot of butchering?

ED: What do you mean, do I do a lot of butchering?

JACK: Those are butcher knives, aren't they?

ED: You <u>gotta</u> have sharp knives around a kitchen. You oughta know that if you ever worked around a kitchen. <u>Did</u> you ever work in a kitchen before?

JACK: Sure. Some.

ED: Well, you leave them knives alone. If I want you to use them knives, when the time comes, I'll tell you.

JACK: Do you mean I can have the job?

ED: Are you single? Not tangled up with any women, are you?

JACK: Oh no. I should say not.

ED: All right. I'll show you around.

JACK: Thanks Mister.

ED: Harkins. Ed Harkins. I just want to show you the ropes here so there won't be no chance of there bein' no trouble.

JACK: Oh I won't give you any trouble, Mr. Harkins.

ED: I don't mean that. <u>I'll</u> see to that. But did you ever stop to think that a kitchen is one of the most dangerous places a man could be?

JACK: Oh. That.

ED: Yes. That. Take your griddle here, for instance. A smoking-hot slab of steel. Suppose you was to get careless some day and fall onto that. Eh? What do you think would happen?

JACK: I hadn't thought about that.

ED:	Well, you better. And there's your French-fryer — three four gallons of boiling grease.
SOUND:	(BUBBLING OF GREASE UNDER)
ED:	(CONT'D) I saw a fellow once tripped over something and went into one of those things. Both arms. Clear up to his elbows. It would have made your blood run cold to hear that fella scream.
JACK:	Did yours, Mr. Harkins?
ED:	Did my what?
JACK:	Did your blood run cold?
ED:	(HE LAUGHS WITHOUT ANSWERING) Know what this is?
JACK:	A meat grinder, isn't it?
ED:	Electric. This here's the switch. I'll show you how it works.
SOUND:	(WHINE OF GRINDER TURNED ON)
ED:	And when you use it, don't never poke the meat in with your hand. Use this here wooden pusher.
JACK:	Uh huh.
ED:	Look in there. Know what would happen if you got your fingers caught in there? Here, gimme your hand, I'll show you.
SOUND:	(GRINDER UP A LITTLE, UNDER)
JACK:	No. No!
ED:	(LAUGHS) What's the matter? You didn't think I was gonna hurt you, did you?
SOUND:	(GRINDER TURNED OFF)
JACK:	No. I didn't think that.
ED:	(LAUGHS) I wouldn't hurt anybody. Say, you aren't going to be drafted, are you?

JACK:	Well, I don't think so … I've …
ED:	Oh. That a discharge button you got there? Been in the Army?
JACK:	Uh huh. The Canadian Army.
ED:	Guess you must have seen a few things yourself then — men killed, blown to pieces, everything else I suppose. Probably killed a few of your own too, huh?
JACK:	When do I go to work, Mr. Harkins?
ED:	(LAUGHS) Don't want to talk about it, huh? I'm glad you been through it though, just the same. I got no use for a man who can't stand to get a little blood on his hands.
MUSIC:	(PUNCTUATES)
JACK:	I went to work, but that old feeling was beginning to come up in me, that something was going to happen. I'm sensitive about things that way. I guess I told you before. I found out her name was Mildred, the girl. She was all right. I didn't really have anything against her, but she acted stranger, in a way you get to recognize after awhile, if you know what it means. And it was only two days later when something came up that brought everything much closer. I was working out in the kitchen that morning with Mr. Harkins …
ED:	(QUICK FADE ON) And then you can bone out them New York steaks like I showed you and cut 'em up. Be careful of that knife now!
JACK:	I can use it all right, Mr. Harkins.
SOUND:	(DOOR OPENS)
MILDRED:	(COMING ON) Uncle Ed.
ED:	Yeah?
MILDRED:	Those two Highway Police are outside.

ED:	At the counter?
MILDRED:	Yes. They said…
ED:	You didn't tell 'em I was here, did you?
MILDRED:	Oh no. I just said I'd see. They said…
ED:	Well, I ain't got time to talk to them now. Tell 'em I ain't here. Say, I've… Hey, Jack. You go out and talk to 'em.
JACK:	All right, Mr. Harkins.
ED:	Mildred acts so scared half the time, nobody ever <u>would</u> believe her. And try to find out what they want, you hear?
JACK:	I'll try, Mr. Harkins.
ED:	(FADING UNDER STEPS) You stay here, Mildred.
SOUND:	**(STEPS. DOOR CLOSES. STEPS BUT IN THE LUNCHROOM**
JACK:	Did you want to see Mr. Harkins about something?
1ST COP:	That's right.
JACK:	Well, he's not here. Maybe if you could tell me.
2ND COP:	You're kind of new around here, aren't you?
JACK:	Yes. I just got out of the Canadian Army.
2ND COP:	Oh. I See.
JACK:	But if you could tell me what you wanted to see Mr. Harkins about…
1ST COP:	You just tell him we want to see him and we'll be back. Okay?
JACK:	Okay.
SOUND:	**(COUPLE OF STEPS AS THEY START TO LEAVE)**
JACK:	(OVER THE STEPS) Say…
1ST COP:	Yeah?

Suspense

JACK: You're trying to find who did those two murders, aren't you?

2ND COP: What murders?

JACK: Those two in town. Those two women. It's all in the papers about the police putting out a three-state alarm. I was reading it today.

2ND COP: (SILENT PAUSE) You just tell Ed we want to see him. And we'll be back.

JACK: All right. I will.

SOUND: <u>(STEPS UNDER JACK'S SPEECH. SCREEN DOOR CREAKING OPEN AND SLAMMING, KITCHEN DOOR OPENING SOFTLY AND CLOSING.)</u>

MILDRED: (COMING ON) Jack — what did they want?

SOUND: <u>(CAR DRIVING AWAY. OFF. UNDER MILDRED'S SPEECH.)</u>

JACK: I don't know, Mildred. But I think maybe it was something about those two murders.

MILDRED: Murders!

JACK: Of those women. Didn't you read about it?

MILDRED: Oh. Those.

JACK: I guess maybe they just wanted to ask your uncle if he'd seen any suspicious men around. You see, they think it was a man because — well, because they were both women who were killed.

MILDRED: It <u>could</u> have been another woman.

JACK: I don't think so, Mildred. Anyway, they figure it was somebody who knew something about — <u>butchering</u>.

MILDRED: Oh.

JACK: Say, Mildred — doesn't your uncle ever take a day off once in awhile?

MILDRED:	Sure, he does. He goes into town every week, pretty regular.
JACK:	When does he go?
MILDRED:	Saturday night, as a rule in the pick-up truck. I think he goes to see some lady.
JACK:	<u>Saturday</u> night.
MILDRED:	Sure. What of it?
JACK:	Why that's tonight.
MILDRED:	(SOTTO) Jack.
JACK:	What, Mildred? What are you whispering for?
MILDRED:	(STILL SOTO) Jack — you're an awful nice boy. And I like you a lot. But — my uncle is awful strict about some things. And if he ever thought… (SHE STOPS)
JACK:	Thought what?
MILDRED:	That — well, you know — that you and I…
JACK:	Why, Mildred, I didn't mean that at all.
MILDRED:	Oh.
JACK:	Maybe you wish I <u>had</u> meant it. Is that it, Mildred?
MILDRED:	Of course not! I just thought you ought to know — well, how Uncle Ed is about those things. That's all. (LITTLE PAUSE) What <u>did</u> you mean about Saturday night — about tonight?
JACK:	Nothing much… I was just thinking I was glad you weren't going to be here alone <u>this</u> Saturday night.
MILDRED:	Why?
JACK:	You don't follow things in the papers much at all, do you?
MILDRED:	What's that got to do with it?
JACK:	Why it was on a Saturday night both times. When those two women were murdered.

Suspense

MUSIC:	(WALLOPS IN, SPREAD TO B.G.)
NARR:	For Suspense, Roma Wines are bringing you as star Richard Greene in "The Keenest Edge" by Robert Richards. Roma Wines presentation tonight in radio's outstanding theatre of thrills — Suspense!
MUSIC:	(RESOLVES WITH THREE CHORD PHRASE)
BRADLEY:	Between the acts of Suspense, this is Truman Bradley for Roma Wines.

(SPONSOR'S PITCH)

NARR:	And now Roma Wines bring back to our Hollywood soundstage, Richard Greene who as Jack in "The Keenest Edge" continues as a narrative well calculated to keep you in...
MUSIC:	(KNIFE CHORD)
NARR:	SUSPENSE!
MUSIC:	(SECOND OVERTURE)
JACK:	That feeling I had was getting stronger all the time now, that something was going to happen. It was just a little roadside Barbecue stand, and all I'd done was take a job there as a cook's helper. But I was afraid. First it was Mr. Harkins and those butchering knives he kept in the kitchen, and the way he grabbed my arm that first day. And then Mildred and the funny way she acted with me, as though she wanted to catch me at something, or make me do something wrong. The two women who'd been murdered in town on two Saturday nights seemed to have something to do with it too; if I could only have figured what it was... It wasn't any of it very clear in my mind though, really. It was all too mixed up. And then it was Saturday night coming on again. We were getting ready for the evening rush, and I was out back helping Mr. Harkins...
ED:	(QUICK FADE IN) Better put that veal back in the

	chill-box until we need it. The left hand one.
JACK:	All right, Mr. Harkins. But I think it's locked.
ED:	Oh. Guess it is. Here are the keys. But the one on the left, you hear? You remember what I told you about the other one.
JACK:	I remembered. He'd told me not to go into it. Ever.
SOUND:	<u>(PADLOCK UNSNAPPING. CHILL-ROOM DOOR OPENING AND THEN CLOSING. PADLOCK SNAPPING SHUT AGAIN, UNDER.)</u>
JACK:	(CONT'D) I opened up the chill-box where the mat was kept, and put the veal away, and closed the box again. And all the time I was thinking about the other door right next to it. The one I wasn't supposed to go in. I felt weak all over; I wanted so much to see what was in there. I just had to. I slipped the key in the lock.
SOUND:	<u>(PADLOCK UNSNAPPING, HEAVY DOOR SLOWLY CREAKING OPEN. UNDER.)</u>
JACK:	(CONT'D) and opened the door and went inside, and pulled the door to after me, all but an inch or so. I didn't dare turn on the light, and for a couple of minutes I just stood there, shaking and trembling from excitement and from trying so hard to think. Then suddenly the door swung open.
SOUND:	<u>(SWISH OF DOOR OPENING)</u>
ED:	(HIS VOICE IS LOW AND VIBRATING WITH ANGER) Get out of there!
JACK:	Yes, Mr. Harkins. I thought I saw a light on in there and…
ED:	Thought you saw a light. You were snooping, that what you were doin'. Get out!
JACK:	Please — don't! You're hurting my arm!
ED:	And if I ever catch you sticking your nose into what's

Suspense

	none of your business again, I'll break every bone in your body!
MILDRED:	(COMING ON) Uncle Ed! What's the matter?
ED:	Lock that door again ...
JACK:	Yes, Mr. Harkins.
SOUND:	(PADLOCK CLICK)
ED:	And remember what I said. (QUICK FADE OFF) Because I ain't foolin'.
JACK:	(OVER FADE) Yes, Mr. Harkins.
MILDRED:	Jack! What happened?
JACK:	I went into the chill-box. He found him there.
MILDRED:	Oh Jack, you shouldn't have done that! He's got a terrible temper — and don't know how he is sometimes! When I heard him, I was afraid.
JACK:	What does he keep in there, Mildred? In that other box?
MILDRED:	I don't know ... Didn't you see?
JACK:	No. Are you sure you don't know?
MILDRED:	I swear I don't! It's just something that — could spoil easy, I guess.
JACK:	Why did you come back here just now, Mildred?
MILDRED:	I told you — when I heard him, I was afraid he might — do something.
JACK:	To me?
MILDRED:	Uh huh.
JACK:	That's funny. You being afraid of me.
MILDRED:	I don't see why it's so funny. He's a terribly strong man and ...
JACK:	I'm pretty strong myself. (PAUSE) You're afraid of him for yourself through, too, aren't you?

MILDRED:	Well, I guess a little ...
JACK:	Why?
MILDRED:	I told you. Because of his temper, and — the way he feels about some things.
JACK:	What kind of things?
MILDRED:	My going out with boys, things like that. Or anything he doesn't think is just right.
JACK:	Is that the only reason you're afraid of him, Mildred?
MILDRED:	Jack, I've told you! Why do you keep asking?
JACK:	Mildred, are you sure it's only just one particular lady he goes to see on Saturday night?
MILDRED:	I don't know. He doesn't tell me what he does. Anyway, what's the difference?
JACK:	Mildred, you know some people don't like women. Some people hate women.
MILDRED:	Well, Uncle Ed doesn't, I know that much!
JACK:	He might just the same though, without you knowing anything about it.
MILDRED:	Why? Why should he? Why should anybody hate women?
JACK:	Some people think they're — the cause of evil.
MILDRED:	Jack, what are you talking about?
JACK:	Is that the reason you're afraid of him, Mildred?
MILDRED:	Oh, don't be silly! You've just got too much imagination! (NERVOUS LITTLE LAUGH) You ought to be a writer or something!
JACK:	I am pretty sensitive, Mildred. Anyway, I'm glad I'm going to be here with you tonight.
MILDRED:	Tonight? Oh, you mean when Uncle Ed goes to town?
JACK:	Uh huh.

Suspense

SOUND:	<u>(THE KNIFE BEING SHARPENED. LITTLE OFF)</u>
JACK:	What's that sound?
MILDRED:	That? (SHE LISTENS A BRIEF MOMENT. THEN, A HINT OF RELIEF IN HER VOICE) Oh, that's just Uncle Ed sharpening his knives again.
JACK:	This is a funny time for him to be sharpening knives.
MILDRED:	Why? What's funny about it?
JACK:	I wonder if when he goes to town — he takes his knives along with him.
SOUND:	<u>REGISTER KNIFE SHARPENING A MOMENT, TAKEN OUT BY</u>
MUSIC:	<u>COMING UP TO PUNCTUATE, THEN SLIDING DOWN, LEAVING</u>
SOUND:	<u>KNIFE SHARPENING, NOW ONSTAGE LEVEL</u>
MILDRED:	(OFF, CALLING) I'm closing up now, Uncle Ed — is that all right? Everybody's gone... Did you hear me? I said I'm closing up.
SOUND:	<u>OFFSTAGE LEVEL. STEPS IN EMPTY LUNCH ROOM. COUPLE PF CHAIRS BEING MOVED INTO PLACE, DOOR BEING LOCKED, STEPS COMING ONSTAGE. ON THE ONSTAGE LEVEL, THE KNIFE SHARPENING CONTINUES.</u>
MILDRED:	(ONSTAGE) Uncle Ed, what are you doing out here in the dark? Anyway, I thought you were going.
JACK:	It's me, Mildred.
SOUND:	<u>(THE SHARPENING STOPS AS HE SPEAKS)</u>
MILDRED:	Oh.
JACK:	Your uncle went to town. Quite awhile ago.
MILDRED:	Well. I was wondering... What's the matter with the lights? I can't see a thing.

JACK:	I can see quite well in the dark.
MILDRED:	Well, I can't and I guess we don't have to keep the light bill down <u>that</u> bad. I'll turn them on.
JACK:	No! Don't...
MILDRED:	Why not, for heaven's sake?
JACK:	Well — all right. Just for a minute.
SOUND:	<u>(CLICK OF LIGHT SWITCH)</u>
MILDRED:	(WITH SOUND) A minute is right — I don't want to stick around here all night. I'm tired.
SOUND:	<u>(KNIFE SHARPENING AGAIN)</u>
MILDRED:	Say, you better not let Uncle Ed catch you fooling with those knives. You know what he said...
JACK:	These aren't his knives, Mildred. They're mine.
MILDRED:	Oh.
JACK:	When do you think he'll be back, Mildred?
MILDRED:	I don't know — it's usually pretty late...
JACK:	It might not be so late this time...
SOUND:	<u>(SHARPENING OUT)</u>
MILDRED:	I guess this is sharp enough now. We'd better pull down the shades, though.
JACK:	Why? Aren't you leaving?
SOUND:	<u>(SHADES BEING PULLED DOWN)</u>
JACK:	After while. But there are some things to do first... And we better lock the outside door, too.
SOUND:	<u>(DOOR BEING LOCKED)</u>
MILDRED:	I always lock up before we go, silly!
JACK:	I know. But we've got some things to do.
MILDRED:	Well what's so much that we've got to do? Tomorrow's Sunday. And we'll just have to serve a few breakfasts.

	And I've already made up the hot-cake batter.
JACK:	I know. But there's some other things. It won't take long.
MILDRED:	Oh, all right! If he told you to do something. How about a cup of coffee?
JACK:	Yes. Let's both have a cup of coffee.
SOUND:	<u>KNIFE SHARPENING AGAIN</u>
MILDRED:	Jack, if you've got something to do why don't you stop playing with that knife and get busy! It's getting late.
JACK:	I want to be awful sure it's sharp enough.
MILDRED:	Well, my goodness. How sharp do you want it? It's like a razor now.
JACK:	Yes. I guess it is <u>pretty</u> sharp.
SOUND:	<u>KNIFE SHARPENING OUT</u>
MILDRED:	Here's your coffee.
JACK:	Thanks, Mildred. You don't know much about me, do you?
MILDRED:	I know you do your work. And you don't pester a girl like some fellows would. That's something.
JACK:	I didn't use to be like that, though. Before I went into the army, I was bad. I was wicked, Mildred!
MILDRED:	<u>You</u> were <u>wicked</u>? (SHE LAUGHS)
JACK:	I mean it, Mildred. I was — an evil person! Don't you see, that's why I <u>had</u> to go into the Army?
MILDRED:	You mean — you'd <u>done</u> something?
JACK:	Uh huh.
MILDRED:	Jack — <u>what did you do</u>?
JACK:	You don't understand, Mildred. What do you think causes all these terrible things to happen to the world, like wars and things? It's because people are wicked, and

	sinful — not just me, but millions of other people, too. Only most of them never even know what they're doing. But I found out. That's why I had to be in the Army. I had to — atone — somehow.
MILDRED:	(NERVOUS LITTLE LAUGH) Why, Jack! You make it sound as though you'd caused the whole war, all by yourself!
JACK:	It took me a long time to figure it out, Mildred. All the things that I'd seen. And had to do. Why they'd happened. For awhile they didn't realize I'd found out. Only one in a million ever do, you know...
MILDRED:	You mean you were a sort of — mental case?
JACK:	That's what they thought. But when they realized I'd found out the real meaning of it all, they let me go.
MILDRED:	What — meaning, Jack?
JACK:	Why some people have to die. Why some people have to be sacrificed — to help the rest of us.
MILDRED:	(SHE'S REALLY GETTING SCARED NOW) Jack, we'd better go now. It's late.
JACK:	Mildred — you've been awfully good to me. Nicer than any girl I've ever known. I don't want to do this, Mildred...
MILDRED:	Do — what?
JACK:	What I'm going to do. But I have to. Don't you see?
MILDRED:	(LAST PATHETIC ATTEMPT TO BE BRAVE AND KID HIM OUT OF IT) You're not going to do anything, Jack.
JACK:	Oh yes I am, Mildred.
SOUND:	(RAPPING ON DOOR, OFF)
JACK:	(QUIETLY) I thought something like this might happen.

Suspense

SOUND:	(RAPPING)
MILDRED:	I'll go!
JACK:	No, you can't. And I'm going to have to take this towel and tie your mouth up, Mildred.
MILDRED:	Jack! No!... (HER CALLS MUFFLED)
SOUND:	SLIGHT SCUFFLE, WHICH QUICKLY SUBSIDES
JACK:	It's no use fighting against me, Mildred. I'm pretty strong, when I have to be... There... I don't like this any more than you do, Mildred, but if I didn't do it, you might spoil everything...
SOUND:	(MEAT GRINDER HUM, AS HE SPEAKS)
JACK:	And I guess I'd better turn on the meat grinder. In case you make any noise while I'm gone.
SOUND:	(RAPPING)
JACK:	I won't be but a minute, Mildred. (CALLING) I'm coming...
SOUND:	(STEPS. DOOR UNLOCKED AND OPENED)
JACK:	Yes? Oh, hello, officer.
1st COP:	We're still looking for Ed Harkins. Is he around?
JACK:	Why no, he's gone into town.
2nd COP:	Working kind of late here, aren't you?
JACK:	Oh, I'm just catching up on a few odds and ends of things for tomorrow — grinding some meat and things like that.
1st COP:	You alone back there?
JACK:	Yes, Mildred's gone to the house.
1st COP:	I see...
JACK:	Mr. Harkins just left a few minutes ago. If you hurry, you might be able to catch up with him.

2ND COP:	Okay, thanks. (QUICK FADE OUT) Let's go, Harry...
SOUND:	(DOOR CLOSED AND DELIBERATELY LOCKED. STEPS, GRINDER, WHICH FADED OFF FOR SCENE WITH COPS, FADES ON AGAIN.)
JACK:	It's all right now, Mildred. They've gone. And I'll untie the towel, if you'll promise to be very quiet.
MILDRED:	(FAINT SOUND THROUGH TOWEL)
JACK:	You will?
MILDRED:	(Affirmative SOUND)
JACK:	All right...
SOUND:	MEAT GRINDER OFF
JACK:	And I'll turn off the meat grinder for awhile.
MILDRED:	(ALMOST A WHISPER, IN ABJECT TERROR) Jack! Not the knife!
JACK:	That's why I wanted to get it specially sharp...For you...
MILDRED:	Jack! Please! Wait!
JACK:	Just close your eyes for a second, Mildred. You won't even know when it happens.
MILDRED:	(A CHOKING SOUND)
SOUND:	(DOOR THROWN OPEN, OFF STEPS COMING ON)
2ND COP:	(COMING ON) All right, where is it?
MILDRED:	(SOBS OF RELIEF)
ED:	In the right hand chill-box.
2ND COP:	Open it up, Harry — here are the keys.
SOUND:	(KEYS, OPENING LOCK AND DOOR UNDER FOLLOWING)

Suspense

ED:	But they're my animals, and I bought 'em and paid for 'em. I got a right to slaughter 'em if I want to, and butcher 'em too!
2ND COP:	Not without that old government stamp, you don't. Not and sell it to the public.
MILDRED:	(BETWEEN SOBS) Oh, Uncle Ed! He was going to kill me!
ED:	What?
MILDRED:	With that knife — in his hand!
2ND COP:	Drop it son!
JACK:	(IN HIS DREAM WORLD) What... What do you say, please?
2ND COP:	Drop that knife!
JACK:	Oh... I couldn't drop it. It would spoil the edge... it would... but I'll put it down... gently... gently...
SOUND:	(KNIFE ON TABLE)
2ND COP:	Now what goes on here?
JACK:	Only by sacrifice can the evil man be unburdened of his sins... You see, I... (HE TRAILS OFF UNCERTAINLY)... (PAUSE)
2ND COP:	Were you trying to kill her?
JACK:	I just remembered it tonight... I didn't want to, though. She was the nicest girl I'd ever known.
MUSIC:	(PUNCTUATES)
JACK:	Maybe I should have gone to them in the first place, and told them how bad I was, before I killed those other two. Maybe they'd have punished me a little, and then I wouldn't have had those awful feelings anymore. But now, I guess they'll punish me — a lot.
MUSIC:	(FINALE)

NARR: SUSPENSE... (<u>KNIFE CHORD</u>)

BRADLEY: Presented by Roma Wines... R-O-M-A... made in California for enjoyment throughout the world... Before we hear again from Richard Greene, the star of "The Keenest Edge" tonight's Suspense play, this is Truman Bradley for Roma Wines.

(SPONSOR'S PITCH)

NARR: Richard Greene appeared through courtesy of Twentieth Century-Fox, producers of "Leave Her to Heaven." Next Thursday, same time, Roma Wines will bring you Mr. Cary Grant as star of (<u>KNIFE CHORD</u>) SUSPENSE... Radio's outstanding theatre of thrills.

<u>MUSIC:</u> <u>(FLARE UP CHORD)</u>

BRADLEY: Produced by William Spier for the Roma Wines Company of Fresno, California.

<u>MUSIC:</u> <u>(FADE UP THEME)</u>

BRADLEY: This is CBS... The Columbia... Broadcasting System.

(OPTIONAL IF CUED IN)

BRADLEY: Suspense is broadcast from coast to coast and to our men and women of the Armed Forces overseas by shortwave, and through the world wide facilities of the Armed Forces Radio Service.

About the Author

Darryl Shelton was raised in New York and grew up outside the city. Amassing a large collection of old-time radio shows over the past decades, he has been researching old-time radio shows for more than ten years. He enjoys cooking and writing magazine articles. He has contributed a number of features for other people's websites. A librarian by occupation, he lives with his wife of twelve years and an eight-year-old daughter. This is his first book.

BearManorMedia
PO BOX 71426 · ALBANY, GEORGIA 31708

THE PHILIP RAPP JOKE FILE
For the first time ever, be privy to the open caverns of mirth that is the profilic Philip Rapp joke file! Rapp, writer for Baby Snooks, Eddie Cantor and creator of the *Bickersons*, wrote and collected jokes for years, drawing from it during his classic radio and TV years. Now we've taken the best quips and put them together for one great and funny book! Illustrated.
ISBN: 1-59393-102-6. $14.95

NOT SO DUMB
THE LIFE AND CAREER OF MARIE WILSON
by Charles Tranberg
Ready for the first biography on blonde, bubbly Marie Wilson? Was she really that vapid? Well — read the book on this *My Friend Irma* star!
ISBN: 1-59393-049-6. $19.95

TWENTY QUESTIONS
by Robert VanDeventer
A novelized memoir of *Twenty Questions,* one of the first weekly panel quiz shows on the radio.
ISBN: 1-59393-077-1. $19.95

INCORRECT ENTERTAINMENT
by Anthony Slide
Cultural Historian Anthony Slide, who has been described by the *Los Angeles Times* as a one-man publishing phenomenon, strikes again with a book guaranteed to contain something OFFENSIVE for everyone. From FASCISM in Hollywood to the latest topical jokes on the *Challenger* disaster & more.
ISBN: 1-59393-093-3. $19.95

FRED MACMURRAY: A BIOGRAPHY
by Charles Tranberg
A biography of Hollywood's most famous dad! Features an introduction by Don Grady of *My Three Sons.* Coming in October!
ISBN: 1-59393-099-2. $24.95.

ANGELIC HEAVEN
A Fan's Guide To Charlie's Angels
by Mike Pingel
The ultimate fan's guide to the hit 70s/80s television series by legendary producer Aaron Spelling. Filled with facts about the show, behind-the-scenes tidbits, rare photos and forewords by Farrah Fawcett and Cheryl Ladd, Angelic Heaven will have you rushing out to buy the DVDs!
$19.75

WHO'S WHO OF STAGE & SCREEN
by C. Elizabeth Lalla
Who's Who of Stage and Screen will make a beautiful addition to any Hollywood lover's collection! Filled with photos, profiles, resumes and contact information for the artists included. Nearly 600 pages, 8x10 size!
$35.00

THE FILMS OF THE DIONNE QUINTUPLETS
by Paul Talbot
An emphasis on their interesting film career of the famous five. Packed with photos and priceless information, every film fan will marvel at their story. Ships in August.
ISBN: 1-59393-097-6. $19.95.

ADD $3.00 POSTAGE FOR EACH BOOK

ORDER THESE BOOKS AND MORE! VISIT WWW.BEARMANORMEDIA.COM

www.ingramcontent.com/pod-product-compliance
Lightning Source LLC
Chambersburg PA
CBHW060556230426
43670CB00011B/1845